The Lore of ARMS

The Lore of
ARMS

A Concise History of Weaponry

WILLIAM REID

ARROW
ARROW BOOKS

Arrow Books Limited
17-21 Conway Street, London W1P 6JD
An imprint of the Hutchinson Publishing Group
London Melbourne Sydney Auckland Johannesburg
and agencies throughout the world

First published in Great Britain by Arrow 1984

Typeset by Text Processing, Clonmel, Ireland

Printed in Spain 1984 by Novograph, Madrid, Spain

ISBN 0 09 936850 1

Contents

Chapter 1

It is quite certain that a hundred centuries ago man's insight had already given him several inventions that were to separate him from the beasts. He had long been able to harden a sharpened wooden point in a fire, and with the most primitive of tools he could shape an efficient bow, with a bowstring of twisted fiber, that would kill at a distance. Bows and arrows remained unrivaled as projectile weapons until long after the gun was invented.

What appear to be the remnants of more than a hundred arrowshafts were found at Stellmoor in Schleswig-Holstein, dating from *c.* 8800–8300 BC. The ends of some are intact, with the tangs of flint arrowheads still set into the tips. A complete tanged point embedded in the breast of a reindeer retains fragments of its shaft, suggesting that a bow was used to shoot the arrow. All the available evidence now points to the development of the bow as a projectile weapon in southern Europe and northern Africa around 15,000 BC, and that it reached the north of Europe during the ninth millennium BC to become the most important weapon for fighting and hunting until the second millennium. It is probably not unduly pessimistic to say that the precise date when early man first hit upon the idea of using the resilience of a wooden stave to propel darts will never be known.

The bow of prehistoric Europe was normally made from a billet split from a yew tree (*Taxus baccata L.*). In climates too cold for the yew, elm (*Ulmus*) seems to have been the commonest alternative, but one bow of pine (*Pinus*) has come to light in Sweden. Surviving bows from *c.* 6000 BC are man-sized, from *c.* 61 to *c.* 71 inches (154 to *c.* 180 cm) in length, usually of D-section, tapering from a stout center, sometimes carved in a well-defined grip, towards nocks shaped to receive the string. Elsewhere, for instance among the Serovo hunters of the Lena Valley, Siberia, a composite bow was in use in the third millennium BC that reveals a sophisticated technique for stiffening the bow with splinters of antler, and creating additional resilience by backing it with sinew. The Lena Valley bows required great skill in the use of the most primitive tools of stone, bone or shell to shape them, an understanding of the reinforcing effect of the leather webs that were bound to some, and of the process of making a bowstring of sufficient strength in a world that knew no silk, flax or hemp.

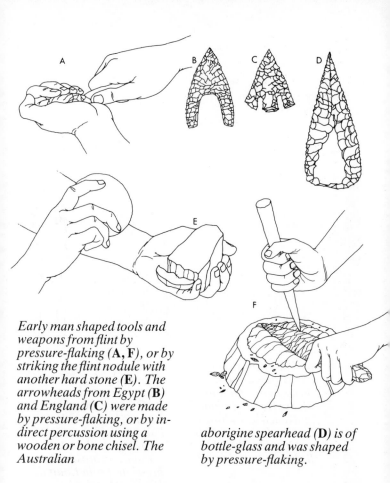

*Early man shaped tools and weapons from flint by pressure-flaking (**A, F**), or by striking the flint nodule with another hard stone (**E**). The arrowheads from Egypt (**B**) and England (**C**) were made by pressure-flaking, or by indirect percussion using a wooden or bone chisel. The Australian aborigine spearhead (**D**) is of bottle-glass and was shaped by pressure-flaking.*

Several types of arrowhead were made during the 7,000 years of the bow's first period of use in northern Europe. The Mesolithic peoples used small sharpened stones set in oblique slots at the tip, in grooves near the tip, or both, to give increased cutting power. In Denmark at the end of the Stone Age a chisel-shaped blade was used, to be followed by arrowheads with barbs and tangs which are found in later burials alongside the earliest metal weapons. It has been suggested that the tanged and barbed head was inspired by bronze prototypes, but finds from the Early Bronze Age site at Bleiche-Arbon, Switzerland, point to the reverse being the case. At that time bronze was rarely used for heads in Europe, no doubt because

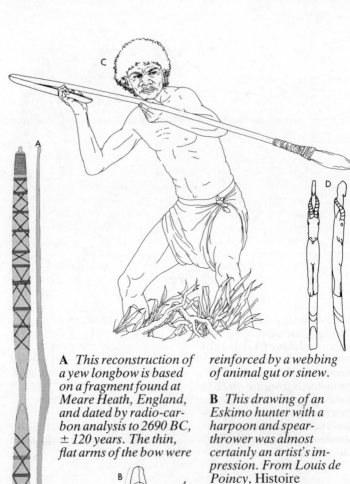

A *This reconstruction of a yew longbow is based on a fragment found at Meare Heath, England, and dated by radio-carbon analysis to 2690 BC, ± 120 years. The thin, flat arms of the bow were reinforced by a webbing of animal gut or sinew.*

B *This drawing of an Eskimo hunter with a harpoon and spear-thrower was almost certainly an artist's impression. From Louis de Poincy,* Histoire Naturelle et Morale, *1658.*

C *An Australian aborigine uses a spear-thrower* (woomera).

D *Two carved spear-throwers from an Upper Paleolithic site, near St. Germain-en-Laye, France.*

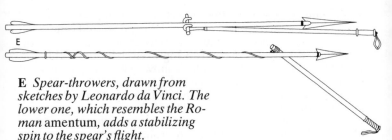

E *Spear-throwers, drawn from sketches by Leonardo da Vinci. The lower one, which resembles the Ro-man* amentum, *adds a stabilizing spin to the spear's flight.*

of its cost of production and the satisfactorily high penetrating efficiency of flint heads, although countless bronze heads have been excavated in Luristan (western Iran) in recent years. Arrow shafts of pine, guelder-role (*Viburnum opulus L.*), ash (*Fraxinus excelsior L.*), yew and alder (*Alnus*) were used in prehistoric Europe.

More likely than not, Neolithic man straightened and smoothed arrows much as primitive men do in modern times. Arrow-makers among the Cheyenne Indians passed selected shafts through a hole drilled in a piece of bone or antler and bent them against this fulcrum until they were straight. The straight shaft was then placed in a semi-circular groove in a piece of sandstone and another similar piece fitted over it. The stones were gripped with the left hand and the shaft drawn through with the right. When it was reduced to approximately the correct size, the shaft was drawn through another piece of bone in which a hole of exactly the correct size was drilled to give its final reduction to a standard diameter. This was essential, for a bow shoots most accurately when used with arrows of consistent weight and spine, or stiffness. As a general rule, the fletcher of Neolithic or Early Bronze Age arrows left the tipe of their shafts rather thick to allow a cleft to be cut into them to receive the head cemented in with resin or birch-pitch, but some were finely tapered. The end of the cleft was bound with sinew. They were probably long arrows; one Danish example from Vinkelmose measures *c.* 40 inches (102 cm). Most peoples have used feathers near the tail to steady the arrow s flight and although none has survived in northwest Europe from this period with its fletchings intact, split feathers about 6.3 inches (16 cm) long were certainly used.

With these weapons, the Neolithic archer used a bracer, or wrist-guard, and a quiver to carry his arrows. It would seem that the first bracers of stone or wood were carried across Europe by the Bell Beaker people, whose practice of burying arrowheads with their male dead is evidence of their appreciation of archery as a means of mastering their poorly equipped neighbors, and of simplifying the physical effort of killing deer and other wild beasts for food and such raw materials as bone, antler, sinew and hides. A quiver is seen on an engraved slab from Göhlitsch, near Merseberg, Germany, which shows a bow and a quiver of six arrows hanging in the eaves of a house.

Bows and arrows were also used both for fighting and hunting in Mesolithic times (*c.* 10,000–6000 BC). Some rock paintings of eastern Spain show deer being driven into a line of bowmen. Others show the line of bowmen "rolling up" to encircle the animals. At the other end of Europe, an engraved stone from Bohuslän in Sweden shows an archer with dogs running down a wild pig. Scenes of bodies of archers facing each other in combat are also found in Spain, and several discoveries of bone or stone arrowheads embedded in skeletons confirm that these little battles were no figment of an artist's imagination.

A pre-Magdalenian painting in the Lascaux pit, executed before *c.* 15,000 BC, shows a mechanical device, the spear-thrower, made and used at the same time as the Paleolithic bow. While less efficient than the bow for casting a light projectile with a fast, flat trajectory, the spear-thrower could lengthen the arc traveled by the arm in the act of throwing and hurl a much heavier weapon than the arrow faster than was possible by hand. The earliest surviving spear-throwers, which were in effect rigid slings, date from *c.* 12,000 BC, but they seem to have become more common before finally dying out *c.* 10,000 BC in the southwest of France. Others found at Kesslerloch, Switzerland, are so close in form to those found at La Madaleine that they tempted Dr. D.A.E. Garrod "to suppose that the founding fathers of the Bodensee colony actually set out from La Madaleine itself."

Several types of thrower are known, made of wood, reindeer antler or mammoth ivory. The main distinction is between the simple unweighted throwers and the slightly more efficient developments where the hook was weighted for a better balanced cast. The tail ends of the weighted throwers were carved in shapes that form the finest surviving Paleolithic sculpture in the round, representations of ibex, horse, or other animal forms. Studies of the weapon have further divided them into "male," with the distal end of the thrower ending in a hook to engage the spear butt, "female," where the butt rests in a hollow, and "androgynous," where it rests in a groove in the thrower. Female and androgynous forms need an almost straight beam of wood or antler, which may account for their relative rarity compared with the hooked "male" type in which straightness is less important.

The spear-thrower had an extremely wide geographical distribution. It was a weapon of the Eskimos and has turned up in remains in Tlingit, Alaska, and in Basketmaker sites in Arizona. It was a votive object among the Aztecs. The Australian aboriginal word for a spear-thrower lent its name, *woomera*, to the Commonwealth rocket range.

Throwing spears used in the Roman army were cast to greater ranges with the help of the *amentum*, a leather thong attached to the javelin behind the point at which it was gripped, its free end held in the thrower's hand. As the javelin was thrown, the thong acted like a flexible spear-thrower. This technique, which interested Leonardo da Vinci, reached its zenith among miners in Yorkshire's West Riding, where nineteenth-century arrow-throwing competitions attracted thousands to watch the champions and bet on the results of throws as long as 372 yards (*c.* 340 m). A piece of stiff string was hitched round the light, 31-inch (*c.* 79 cm) hazel arrow about 16 inches (*c.* 40 cm) from the head, the other end being wrapped round the thrower's forefinger. The arrow was held very loosely, the power for the throw coming entirely from the forefinger pulling against the tightly stretched string as the thrower jerked the arrow forward. Matches were decided by the aggregate distance of an agreed number of throws by each man, twenty or thirty being usual.

Man's first step towards mass production probably came with the development of a forced-draft furnace to fire his pots or bake bread in batches. The same furnace could smelt the available Bronze Age ores, lead, gold, silver and the more practical tin and copper. Once smelted, these could be cast as alloys or in a relatively pure state into a variety of forms which the most skilled flint-knapper could never hope to emulate. Copper and bronze are softer than flint or basalt, but men of widely varying ability and experience could cooperate to cast axes, sickles, spearheads with integral sockets and thong-loops, and slender swords whose tangs were already shaped to receive an applied grip. Once beyond the simplest stone-axe shape, a weapon of bronze is much quicker to make than a comparable one of stone. And whereas a broken stone axe was useless, a fractured sword could be returned to the crucible and recast with little loss.

This reuse of old metal has been frequently confirmed by discoveries like that made by farmers deep-plowing a field in Cambridgeshire, England. They found a 185-lb (*c.* 84 kg) hoard of Late Bronze Age tools that included weapons and decorated mounts that can be dated between *c.* 650 and *c.* 600 BC. With

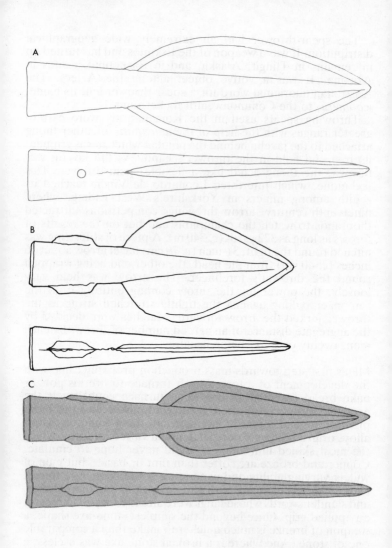

A *A spearhead from East Anglia, c. 1000 BC*

B *and* C *Spearheads from East Anglia, c. 1500 BC.*

them were lumps of bronze that look as though they were poured onto a flat surface after melting and then broken for storage or recasting. Complete and broken palstaves were mixed with socketed axes, hammers, spearheads, swords, knives, sickles, and casting jets from the tops of molds. One of the palstaves fitted exactly into part of a mold that lay among the bronze. Of the fragments of fourteen leaf swords which might have been broken in use in one or at most two places, hammer marks show that they were deliberately smashed into 4- or 5-inch (10 or 13 cm) lengths. The longest of these graceful weapons measures 29.5 inches (74.9 cm), and has finely cut linear decoration from the point to just below the hilt.

The softness of unworked pure copper makes it less than satisfactory for the manufacture of weapons and tools. Throughout the Copper Age, from about 1850 to 1650 BC, smiths hardened copper tools and weapons by hammering, with some additional hardening coming from the presence of about 2.5 percent of arsenic in the metal. From the Early Bronze Age tin was added, and towards the end of the Middle Bronze Age lead was used as a second deliberate additive. There is evidence that, by the time the Celtic smiths had brought ironworking to the north of Europe, bronze founders used different hardening additives in alloys for finished castings and for producing bronze that was to be worked after it left the mold or the crucible.

During the earlier periods, the molds in which flat axes were cast were made from blocks of smooth stone in which several cavities were cut. Once the more complex shapes of the Middle Bronze Age were introduced, two-piece molds of easily worked soapstone (steatite) were common. In the technically most interesting molds, each of the four faces is carved to cast a different tool or weapon.

The economy in weight of these four-tool sets must have been invaluable to the wandering smith. Late Bronze Age molds seem to have been made mostly of clay, although some of mica schist are known. On balance, it was quicker to make a series of clay molds than stone molds which might break on their first charging, for great care is needed to cast in a stone mold if it is not to be destroyed by thermal shock.

Sometimes, when a bronze weapon with a high tin content was being cast, the lighter-colored metal was exuded to form a surface coating. Axes and spearheads excavated in the Soviet Union, Scotland and elsewhere appear to have been accidentally coated in this way, but by Roman times bronze artifacts seem to have been deliberately tinned. Tinning was a deliberate process again in the Middle Ages when iron and bronze spurs were decorated or protected from the corrosive effect of equine sweat and blood by a coating applied by rubbing rods of tin on hot iron or bronze coated with resin to reduce oxidation. Oddly, there are very few cases of tinning on accoutrements other than spurs. Even objects as closely related as stirrups and bits were hardly ever tinned.

The earliest European center of bronze production was Greece, where the bow does not seem to have been used except for hunting after the beginning of the Mycenaean Age. As culture developed within Mycenae's massive walls, slashing swords and defensive armor of bronze, including helmets, cuirasses and greaves (to protect the lower legs) began to be used in Greece, with the thrusting spear continuing throughout the entire period from *c.* 1700 to *c.* 1100 BC when Greek life was dominated by Mycenaean ideas and customs. In Proto-Geometric and Geometric times a pair of throwing spears became common. The end of the Geometric period saw the bow's revival as a weapon of consequence in Greek warfare when the Cimmerians, shooting from the saddle, brought the graceful and efficient composite form to the West.

War as we know it could not be waged until human society advanced beyond the tribal stage, and the development of the city state itself depended on the force of arms to impose unity. When the Greeks established their battle tactics based on the phalanx, the infantry enjoyed an esteem which has never since been equaled. A free man became a *hoplite*, fighting in the bronze armor which was made possible by improved methods of smelting, with an elliptical shield on his left arm, a nine-foot (2.7 m) spear in his right hand. Behind him menial tasks were done by slaves and others who were not free.

By the beginning of the fifth century BC, Greek tactics had evolved beyond man-to-man combat. The phalanx was a relatively mobile force of spearmen when 10,000 Athenian hoplites supported by 1,000 Plataeans stemmed the Persian invasion at Marathon in 490 BC. The lightly armed Persian archers found that the hoplites' armor and discipline enabled them to march through a shower of arrows. Once the hoplites reached their positions at Marathon, and eleven years later at Plataea (479 BC), the Persians learned that an unarmored man with a dagger was no match for a spearman in helmet and greaves, cuirass and shield.

Fifty years later, during the siege of their city, the Plataeans used fire arrows against the siege engines harrying their defences. The earliest Greek leader to use full siege equipment in his army was probably Dionysius of Syracuse. At Motye in

398 BC his towers, rams and catapults were served by artisans from many countries. The peak of Greek military technology was reached sometime before 300 BC with the torsion catapult using twisted skeins, usually of animal sinew and human hair. Vast quantities were involved. Sinope received about three-quarters of a ton of human hair from Rhodes in 250 BC, and several tons were sent to Rhodes as a gift from Seleucus in 225 BC. When Alexander roamed across Asia, his army carried with it the tools and materials with which to make field artillery from native timber.

Long-range attacks could be mounted on engines and architectural structures of wood with fire-arrows shot from bows, crossbows and other artillery. The arrows were normal projectiles wrapped with inflammable material that was ignited immediately before shooting. A development of these was the fire-arrow shot from a gun, immediately anticipating the naval use of red-hot shot and baskets of incendiary material which scattered on impact. As late as 1639, General Robert Ward gave a recipe for "the wild-fire Ball; To be shot out of a Morter-piece or Canon," or thrown by hand. Greek fire grenades, fire-arrows and fire-pots all served the same functions as the thermite bombs of the Second World War and the later napalm and its derivatives. They burned and they terrified.

The invention of torsion artillery has been credited to followers of Dionysius the Elder, but like most inventions it was little more than an advance on earlier techniques, in this case the torsion spring-traps of prehistory. But as science and mathematics developed there were marked improvements in artillery design. The third or second century BC saw the discovery by Alexandrian mathematicians of a formula relating the proportions of the various parts of a torsion catapult to the diameter of the so-called "straining hole" through which passed the bundles of hair or sinew.

Modern experiments have shown that the best arrow-shooting catapults are accurate enough to hit a single man at 100 yards (c. 91 m), a group of men at 200 (183 m) and carry well enough to be dangerous at 500 yards (457 m). The 50 or 60 lb (c. 23 or 27 kg) stones thrown by the engines would crush an improvised wall but were of little value against proper defences. These weapons were used in huge numbers. When Demetrius Poliorcetes initiated his abortive siege of Rhodes in 305 BC, he was astonished that her peaceable merchants could oppose him with so many engines. He put the island's ancient fortifications to a severe test with stone-throwing *petrariæ* and massive 150-foot (c. 46 m) rams said to be swung by a thousand men. Even with such power he could not breach the city walls, built on a plan developed about 400 BC. The inner side of the wall was in the form of a tall arcade, vaulted to within a few feet of the wall-walk. Its full thickness was 15 feet (4.6 m) with the 10.5-foot (3.2 m) recesses spaced at 15-foot (4.6 m) intervals to leave the wall at the back of the recesses about 4.5 feet (1.4 m) thick. When the walls were breached the damage was usually limited to a small length. The recesses served to accommodate defenders and the method of building permitted great savings in materials.

The fragments that survive from a treatise on military architecture and mechanics, written by Philo of Byzantium, confirm that it was a comprehensive account of the principles of fortification as practiced in the second century BC. Philo knew that every fortress had to be built according to the ground, which determined the plan of the 15-foot (4.6 m) thick walls and the salients and curves which would be protected from parapets 30 feet (9.1 m) high. When a wall was thrown up around a town, the engineer was advised to leave 90 feet (27.4 m) or so between the houses and the wall, so that engines and carts could be drawn around easily from one defensive point to another. The safest wall-walks were movable so that when an enemy scaled the wall he then had to draw up his own ladders before he could proceed further. Already by this early date, consideration was given to attacks aimed at destroying the walls by rams, mining or projectiles. The bases of the walls should be bastioned, and areas which might be attacked with siege engines had to be faced with hard stone. The best-preserved defences from Philo's period are at Pompeii, unaltered since lava overwhelmed them in 79 AD. Between c. 400 and c. 100 BC, walls 20 feet (6.1 m) thick and some 32 feet (9.8 m) high, buttressed with piers set at 10-foot (3 m) intervals were built around the city. Rectangular towers project inwards and outwards from the wall at intervals, with openings leading onto the wall-walk on each side. From the Levant to Tarragona, Mediterranean fortress builders had reached a stage of development that Europe's northern cities were not to achieve for some generations.

Slingers who appear on reliefs from the Assyrian city of Nimrud show how their weapons were used in the tenth century BC. Their slings were probably made like one of c. 800 BC from Lahun, now preserved in the Department of Egyptology, University College, London. Its linen strings are plaited by a complicated "square sennate" knot into a strong cord about 44 inches (c. 112 cm) long with a pouch woven into its center and a finger loop at one end. The slinger pushed his finger through the

A four-wheeled battering ram in use against the city of Parga; from the bronze doors in the palace of Shalmaneser III (858-824 BC).

loop and held the loose end in the palm of his right hand. The stone was placed in the pouch and the cord drawn taut with the left hand. The Nimrud slinger then raised his hands above his head and whirled the sling, releasing the loose end of the cord when he judged the shot to be aimed at its target. Representations of slingers in manuscripts of the thirteenth century AD show slings being whirled vertically. Using a crude modern sling in this way the author, flabby and unskilled, has thrown an eight-ounce (227 gr) stone ball to a distance of sixty yards (*c.* 55 m), and balls of three and four ounces (85 and 113 gr) carried over one hundred yards (*c.* 91 m). Even after the gun had begun to drive the bow and the crossbow from the battlefield the sling survived. Many slingshot were found in the *covas de lobo* used by slingers at the battle of Aljubarrota where Portugal ensured her independence by routing the Spanish army in 1385. As late as 1572, the Huguenot slings that thrummed at the siege of Sancerre were nicknamed *arquebuses de Sancerre*.

Perhaps the finest slingers of all time were the Balearic islanders, 700 of whom served Athens during her Syracusan expedition. At the siege of Olynthus, Philip II (382-336 BC) used slingers who threw markedly heavy stones, whereas his son, Alexander the Great (356-323 BC), deployed his as skirmishers only. Strabo describes the Balearic slinger as carrying three slings wrapped round his head. The long-limbed one was for long shots, the short-limbed for close targets and the middling one for medium ranges. Skill with the sling was of such overweening importance that boys went unfed if they could not hit a mark. When Metellus sailed against their islands he had to stretch hides over the decks of his ships to protect the crew from the slingshot.

A development of the ancient sling was the staff-sling, itself the ancestor of the great trebuchet of the eleventh to the sixteenth centuries. As in the flail and the spear-thrower, man's puny strength was given extra impetus. A modified cord-sling was tied to a long staff and the stone thrown with the same action as a modern angler uses to cast with a stiff rod. The staff-sling was especially recommended for naval actions. Most slingers seem to have been of lowly origin, but the author of the fourteenth-century *Speculum Regale* suggests that even for the nobility it is "not less pleasant than useful to throw stones accurately to a great distance with a sling. whether held in the hand or fixed on a staff."

Clashes between Celtic families or tribes were preceded by the obligatory ostentatious display and pretentious bragging of a warrior aristocracy. They probably formed the main market for craftsmen in wood, leather, iron and bronze, who lavished their skill on arms, armor and chariots for these nobles. Unlike the chariot-borne warriors of many other societies, when the Celt was drawn into battle by two ponies, neither he nor his reinsman carried bows and arrows. Although frequently mentioned in the writings of the classical historians, the chariot had gone out of use in Gaul by 55 BC, when Caesar and his armies first saw it used by the Celts in Kent. It was still an important element of the armies the Romans campaigned against in Caledonia in the beginning of the third century AD. To judge by surviving snaffle-bits of iron or bronze they were drawn by ponies which averaged about eleven hands.

As they moved through Europe towards Britain, Caesar's armies came on Gallic towns surrounded by stone and earth walls strengthened with timber ties. The walls were resistant to fire and to the assaults of Roman rams. In the north of the British Isles a number of forts survive from the period. These *brochs* are circular in plan with narrow tunnel-like doors passing through walls 12 to 16 feet (3.7 to 4.9 m) thick into a courtyard about 25 feet (7.6 m) in diameter. The finest are virtually round towers formed by two high concentric shells tied with long stones. Between the shells are little rooms, and staircases leading to galleries around the central chamber lit by daylight. In the broch at Mousa, Shetland, the 45-foot (13.7 m) high outer wall is broken only by the entrance tunnel.

Brochs were never required to resist the onslaught of Roman siege engines, but throughout Caesar's wars in Gaul, and in earlier campaigns, rams, bores and siege towers were used regularly. The ram was almost as old as fortification itself. Assyrian bas-reliefs of the fourth century BC show metal-shod rams set up in a framework of timber covered with hides that protected the engine from fire and its operators from projectiles. The ram was wheeled against the wall or gate, swung back in its chain or rope cradle and crashed against the point chosen for the attack. In an organized defense, the men on the walls tried to hook the ram upwards with loops of chain and rained down stones, javelins and fire. In his treatise on engines, Vitruvius describes a drill designed to bore its way into the stone of fortress walls.

To reduce the advantages that height gave to the defense in greater arrow range and increased projectile velocity, great siege towers were made, some incorporating a ram to give a combined attack. About 750 BC, when Lakish was attacked by the army of Tiglath-pileser III, wheeled engines carried archers within range of the walls. One man of the engine's crew was detailed to splash it with water to prevent its being set alight by the defenders' firebrands.

When the Roman army attacked Heracleum in 169 BC, three picked maniples of 200 infantrymen were trained to form a *tortoise* as they approached the wall. Each man held his shield above his head and closed with those around him so that the shields overlapped like roof-tiles. When Caesar brought his armies north a century later the tortoise was still an effective tactic. Miners also approached under the protection of portable covered passages. Caesar used one to connect his siege tower with the Marseilles city wall. It was 20 yards (18.3 m) long with a thick, sloping fireproof roof. Once at the face of the wall the miners undermined it, supporting the roof of the cavity with wooden props that were eventually burned away, leaving the unsupported masonry to collapse. The soldiers then forced their way over the rubble into the city. This method of breaching a wall was practiced until the nineteenth century.

Siege engines and sapping techniques were by no means essential for the capture of a city, even one defended by strong walls and ditches. When Alaric and his army of something less than 100,000 Goths moved south through Italy in the summer of 409 AD, intent on the capture of Rome, they had no engines with which to breach the great walls built by Aurelian (270-75 AD). These were perhaps the finest architectural defenses in the West and among the greatest works of the later empire. The walls averaged 12 feet (3.7 m) in thickness for their 12-mile (19.3 km) length, with 380 bastions which, like the walls, were repaired by Stilicho shortly before his execution in 408 AD. After a summer of thirst and famine, the Romans had little will to resist, were badly led and divided among themselves. On August 24, as the sentries sheltered from torrential rain, the Goths stormed the Salerian Gate and the adjacent walls. Four days later, when even the Goths were sated with killing, rapine, looting and burning, Alaric led his booty-laden men back to the north leaving Rome to shrink to a coastal strip ruled from Byzantium.

*A Celtic shield boss from
Stratford-on-Avon,
England, c. 400 BC.*

The Trebuchet

The trebuchet (below) was a medieval engine which used the force of gravity to throw heavy projectiles. It came from the East, and first appeared in European manuscripts of the twelfth century. It was used during the siege of Lisbon in 1147.

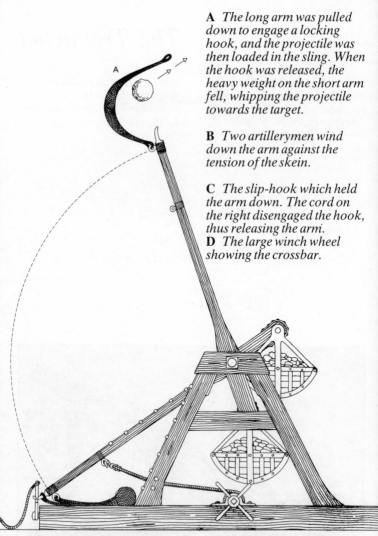

A *The long arm was pulled down to engage a locking hook, and the projectile was then loaded in the sling. When the hook was released, the heavy weight on the short arm fell, whipping the projectile towards the target.*

B *Two artillerymen wind down the arm against the tension of the skein.*

C *The slip-hook which held the arm down. The cord on the right disengaged the hook, thus releasing the arm.*
D *The large winch wheel showing the crossbar.*

E *The winch used to tension the skein, side and plan views. On the right, one end of the skein can be seen in position on the crossbar of the large winch wheel.*
After Sir Ralph Payne Gallwey, The Crossbow *(London, 1903).*

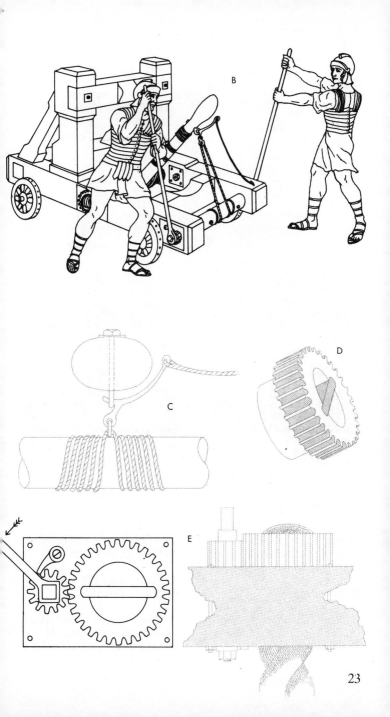

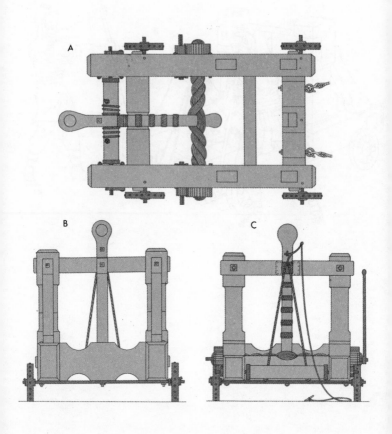

A *Plan view of the trebuchet showing the twisted skein and the arm fully wound down.*

B *Front view.*

C *Rear view showing one of the long levers used for winding down the skein.*

D *Plan view of a wheeled ballista for field use.*

E *Rear view of **D** shown without its stock.*

F *The windlass claws, seen hooked over the cord (**1**), prior to being pulled back by*

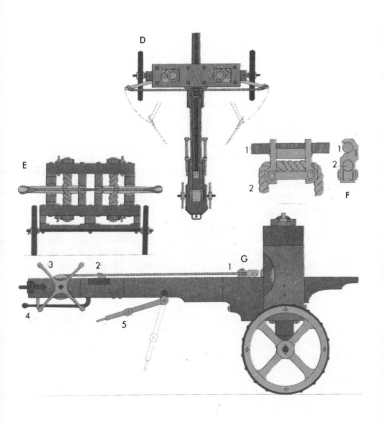

the rope of the windlass (2).

G *Side view of* **D**, *showing the windlass claws (1), the nut (2), the windlass (3), the trigger (4), and the hinged support (5) for elevating the stock. The ballista was used to throw heavy arrows or stones.*

*It resembled a very large crossbow, but it had two separate arms, each powered by its own skein. The skeins were tightened by a windlass (***G, 3***). After Payne-Gallwey,* The Crossbow.

Chapter 2

Gregory the Great revealed a certain pontifical naivety in a letter to the patriarch at Constantinople in 595 AD. "It is the last hour. Pestilence and sword are raging in the world. Nation is rising against nation, the entire fabric of things is being shaken." There had always been disease, and war was a continuing condition. Whichever of Clausewitz's definitions of war one accepts, an act of violence pushed to its utmost bounds, or nothing but a duel on an extensive scale, it had existed for far longer than Gregory's religion.

Evidence of its continuity can be found in the way that the weapons and armor used in northern Europe at the close of the Roman occupation formed the basis of the military equipment of the northern peoples during the Migration Period. Warriors of *c*. 400 AD went into action carrying a shield, a two-edged sword, one or two throwing spears and a thrusting spear.

When modern man looks at a late medieval illustration of a cannon or a tube projecting Greek fire, or reads a contemporary description of either in use, he will at once appreciate how the resemblance between the two can cloud the tracing of their development during the period when they were used side by side. But in the remoter periods, for instance during the sieges of Constantinople in the seventh and eighth centuries, references are specifically to Greek fire poured down on the enemies of the empire by Byzantium's defenders. No exact recipe for Greek fire survives from the period, but its major ingredients were sulfur, pitch, dissolved niter and petroleum, boiled together with less important substances. It was a terrifying weapon, whether used on land or at sea. In 671 AD, according to Theophanes, the ships of the Arab fleet were attacked by fireships fitted with siphons through which Greek fire was pumped, and in his *Tactics*, Konstantinos VII instructed his readers that artificial fire from siphons, hand siphons and *manjaniqs* (Ballistas) should be used against any siege tower brought close enough to the defensive walls.

In the fourteenth and fifteenth centuries, the manuscripts ascribed to Mark the Greek and his copyists recorded that to make "fire for burning enemies wherever they are" the soldier should "take petroleum, black petroleum, liquid pitch and oil of sulfur. Put all these in a pottery jar buried in horse dung for fifteen days. Take it out and smear it on crows which can be flown against the tents of the enemy. When the sun rises, and before the heat has melted it, the mixture will inflame." With a final puff for his recipe, Mark the Greek warned his readers that it was a dangerous mixture to use before sunset or after dawn. In less fanciful use, Greek fire was thrown at men or their engines in grenades of glass and pottery.

Before the beginning of the Christian era, the handbow was modified to serve as an animal trap in which the bow was left bent with an arrow nocked over a game trail. When the victim released the catch that held back the thong, either by pressing a cord or a rod, the arrow was released. Well into the eighteenth century, this form of bow-trap was used in Scandinavia with a sickle-shaped arrowhead. Even when it failed to kill, its slashing wound left a clear blood spoor.

The form of the earliest bow-traps is not known, but a number of dated mechanisms from Chinese crossbows (*Nou*) confirm that the weapon had reached a high degree of development by the Han Dynasty (206 BC-220 AD). The Han crossbow lock consists of a deep, flat, rectangular box of cast bronze into which are fitted a rotating "nut" to hold the cord to the rear when the bow is bent, and a catch to prevent the nut rotating until the trigger, which is made in one with the catch, is released. Crossbows fitted with such locks were almost certainly seen by a hundred or so Romans who were captured at Sogdiana in Central Asia in 36 BC. Perhaps by some such route, or through trade, the concept of the crossbow passed from the East to the West, where it was used, if rather infrequently, by the Romans. At Le Puy, Haute Loire, in France, there are two surviving representations of the hand-held crossbow from the first or second century AD. One interpretation of an ambiguous Anglo-Saxon riddle suggests that crossbows were used in northern Europe in the early Middle Ages, but no firm evidence has yet come to light from earlier than the middle of the tenth century, when the French chronicler Richerus records that *arcobalistæ* were used at the siege of Senlis in 947 AD and at Verdun in 985 AD. These could have been large siege weapons, but a manuscript of between 936 and 954 AD shows crossbows, and they are known to have played a part in the battle of Hjörungsvåg in Norway in 986. The most primitive surviving European crossbows, excavated at Lillöhus, Kristianstad, Sweden, have been ascribed to the late Middle Ages by Josef Alm, who pointed out that the type continued in use among Scandinavian peasants for centuries. The whaling crossbow (*valbåge*), which was still used in the late nineteenth century around Bergen, Norway, is of the same construction. The *arcobalistæ* used at Senlis may well have been of this design with a bow of wood fastened with leather thongs to the front of a primitive stock, or tiller. The stock was split, the upper limb having a slot to take the tensioned cord. A peg passed through the slot, pressure on the hinged lower limb bore on the peg, pushing the cord from the slot to allow it to fly forward. The most complete surviving example, in the Schweizerisches Museum, Zurich, was probably made in the thirteenth century, to shoot the short stiff arrow with thin wooden fletchings and the quadrangular head which gave it the name *quarrel*. Like the other European forms, it was bent by hand, the crossbowman holding the bow down by putting his foot through a stirrup while he pulled the cord to the slot with his hands, or with an iron hook fastened to a waist-belt. The crossbows used in Europe had not developed far beyond this simple type by 1139, when Pope Innocent II (1130-43) and the second Lateran Council decreed in their twenty-ninth canon that the crossbow was a barbarous weapon unfit for war between Christian armies. Its use was interdicted under penalty of an anathema, but this prevented neither the continued arming of Genoese troops with the crossbow, nor Richard I's indulgence in crossbow-shooting later in the century.

No complete Viking spear has been discovered, but many spearheads have come to light in Scandinavia and the lands where Viking influence was most strongly felt. All are of a slender form with a pronounced medial ridge and a hollow conical socket that fitted over the end of the haft. In Scandinavian spears this socket is almost always welded into a closed tube. Some, of the Carolingian type with short lugs or "wings" at the socket, seem to have been made in large quantities in the region of the middle Rhine and carried as far west as Chartres and as far south as Lake Geneva and Austria. A spearhead of this type in the Schatzkammer, Vienna, formed part of the regalia of Conrad I of Franconia (911-18 AD).

The makers of many Viking swords and spears used a technique that has not survived the production of high grade steels from which a modern cutler may select the quality that best suits his purpose. Their blades were pattern-welded from strips and rods of steel and iron twisted and folded together to produce many layers which served at the same time to strengthen the completed blade and to give a subtly decorative surface when it had been polished, lightly etched and re-polished, the steel and the iron reacting differently to the treatment. The technique was used in Europe from the second to the tenth century AD, and Scandinavian and English heroic

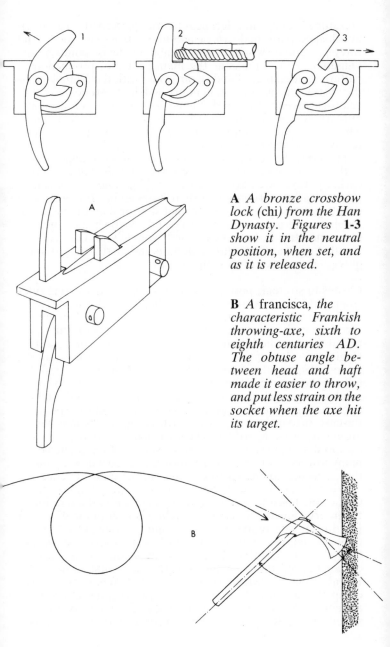

A *A bronze crossbow lock (chi) from the Han Dynasty. Figures* **1-3** *show it in the neutral position, when set, and as it is released.*

B *A* francisca, *the characteristic Frankish throwing-axe, sixth to eighth centuries AD. The obtuse angle between head and haft made it easier to throw, and put less strain on the socket when the axe hit its target.*

literature abounds in references to gray-patterned (*grægmæl*), interlocked-patterned (*brogdenmæl*), twig-patterned and wavy-patterned swords. The available evidence points to the kingdom of the Franks as the main center of production of pattern-welded blades and spearheads, with the Rhineland as the vortex of a vast trade that flourished despite repeated edicts against arms exports. Charlemagne banned all sales of arms and military equipment and swords in 803 AD. Two years later, when the interdiction was renewed, the Avars and Slavs received specific mention.

The bow played a quite major part in many Viking battles. Although arrows and bows have survived in Scandinavia from earlier periods, we have none from Viking times, but it can be said with some certainty that their bows and arrows were of a simple pattern, probably somewhat shorter than the medieval longbow and arrows used in England. Arrowheads found in some quantity in both men's and women's graves are very stoutly forged and were fitted to shafts and carried in cylindrical quivers in bundles of as many as forty.

Castles in strategic positions were invaluable to a strong ruler when held by loyal servants, but they could be a source of trouble if they were in the control of disaffected elements. A few were built in the reign of Edward the Confessor, but it was not until after the Norman Conquest that they spread across England. A description of these forts, which are shown on the Bayeux Tapestry, was written by Jean de Colmieu *c.* 1130. He tells of the practice followed by the nobles of the plain to the southwest of Calais, but his description would undoubtedly apply to the motte and bailey castles elsewhere in Europe: "It is the custom to make a mound of earth as high as possible and dig around it a wide deep ditch. The area on the top of the mound is enclosed by a palisade of the strongest logs, strengthened by as many towers as the nobles can afford. A citadel or keep inside the enclosure commands the entire ring of outer defences."

Where conditions were favorable keeps were built of stone. One of the finest to survive, although not without alteration in the intervening centuries, is the White Tower of the Tower of London. It rises in four stories, a vaulted basement with three upper floors, to a parapet 90 feet (27.4 m) above the ground. One of the turrets that project high above the parapet at each corner housed the observatory of Britain's first Astronomer Royal, John Flamsteed (1646-1719). The White Tower was completed about 1097 on the bank of the Thames, eastward of the city of London and within the angle of the old city wall first raised by the Romans. Its garrison protected and controlled

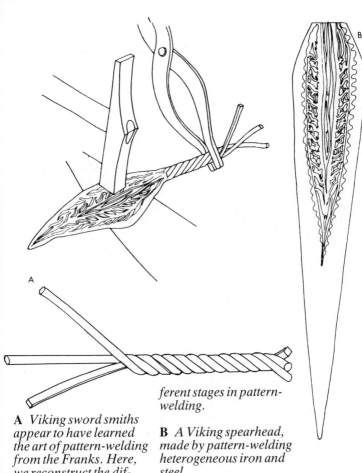

A *Viking sword smiths appear to have learned the art of pattern-welding from the Franks. Here, we reconstruct the different stages in pattern-welding.*

B *A Viking spearhead, made by pattern-welding heterogeneous iron and steel.*

London, for the Tower commanded the approach by river and was threateningly close to the city.

Late in the twelfth century, the castle was enlarged to a great concentric fortress, and today it spreads over 18 acres (7.3 hm). Like many major castles of its period which also served as royal palaces, many trades gathered within its walls and it has housed the royal regalia, a cannon foundry, armories, gunsmiths' and sword cutlers' workshops, a mint where the coin of the realm was struck, and the nation's records extending over the greater part of a thousand years. There has also been a zoo which would have pleased Albrecht Dürer, who suggested a small menagerie as a possible use for the spare space within the defenses of a castle almost three centuries after the great Norman keep echoed to the trumpeting of an elephant sent to Henry III by Louis IX of France. Today, the Tower is the home of one of Europe's outstanding collections of armor and weapons; it is Britain's oldest museum, where each year two million visitors walk in the shadow of a monument to the skill of the Norman military architects who came to England with William I, the Conqueror.

Along with this new knowledge of castle-building, William brought to England a skilled army and a military understanding much wider than anything that opposed him. On the morning of Thursday, September 28, 1066, his invading army landed on the Sussex coast a balanced modern force consisting of cavalry, spearmen and bowmen. When Harold's army arrived, William was faced by a single long phalanx of infantry armed with spears and axes and protected by limewood shields. Against them he arrayed his archers with spearmen behind. In the third rank, his horse waited their chance to smash into the English foot once the arrows had broken their formations and caused the first enemy withdrawals.

After the first Norman volley, much of which was received on the English shield-wall, the cavalry failed to break through, and retired. The second flight of arrows had much more effect, shot as they were high into the air "that their cloud might spread darkness over the enemy's ranks." As shields were raised for protection against the falling shafts, their bearers could no longer swing their great axes freely. William's cavalry burst through. The battle and the kingdom were won and lost. This was one of the first Western battles in which cavalry and shot were successfully combined, although for five centuries the combined tactics had been practiced in the East.

Chapter 3

The catapult, a projectile-throwing engine using the power of recovery of twisted fiber (often human hair), was used in pre-Christian times. In the dry climate of the Mediterranean it worked reasonably satisfactorily in summer campaigns, but when the fibers were wet they lost their resilience and the catapult became almost useless. In the rains of northern Europe the device was impractical, but as late as 1327 Walter de Milemete's lesson-book still illustrated torsion artillery.

More than three centuries earlier a new kind of projectile-throwing engine of war was known in China. It seems to have

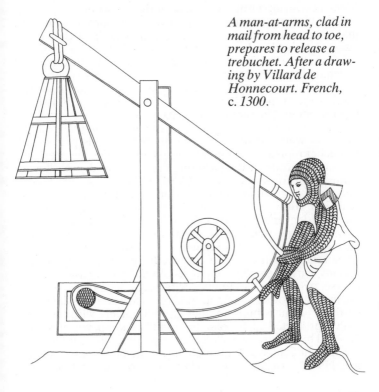

A man-at-arms, clad in mail from head to toe, prepares to release a trebuchet. After a drawing by Villard de Honnecourt. French, c. 1300.

developed from the counterbalanced well sweep (*swape*) in use by the sixteenth century BC in Egypt, where it was called *shaduf*. An unequal lever had a heavy weight fixed to the shorter arm. The longer arm was attached to a rope bearing a bucket that carried the load. This might be water from a well, ore from a mine or soldiers to be hoisted to a fortified wall. The swape is most effective for lifts of between 5 and 15 feet (1.5 and 4.6 m). With a disproportionately heavy counterweight on the shorter end, a fast fall can be achieved, whipping the bucket into the air more quickly, and casting its contents like a staff-sling. This was the Chinese *huo-pa'o*, which made its first appearance in Europe in a Mozarabic manuscript of the early twelfth century, and was used during the northern crusaders' assault on Lisbon in 1147. A manuscript written before 1235 calls such a weapon a *trebuchet* and states that it was used at Cremona in 1199. Trebuckets spread rapidly throughout Europe and wuickly displaced the torsion engines. Yet this new and more powerful artillery did not become dominant in the Mameluke army until the middle of the thirteenth century. It was the first important mechanical use of the force of gravity to make a potent weapon. Modern reproductions of the largest sizes of trebuchet have shown that one built with a 50-foot (15.2 m) arm and a ten-ton counterweight can throw a ball weighing between 200 and 300 lb (*c.* 90 and 136 kg) about 300 yards (274 m). One type of catapult, among the most powerful used by the armies of Rome, threw a stone of about 50 lb (22.7 kg) for about 450 yards (*c.* 411 m).

Since projectile weight was more important than range at the sieges at which artillery was mostly used at this period, the trebuchet represented a great improvement. For the projectile was an extension of the battering ram, built to demolish walls from a safe distance. In *Bellifortis* (1405), Konrad, Kyeser illustrates a splendid trebuchet loaded with a stone ball, and Kölderer's drawings, completed between 1507 and 1512 for the illustrated inventory of the arsenals of the emperor Maximilian I, include one ready to throw the corpse of a horse into a besieged town. The science of fortification advanced considerably at the end of the twelfth century as a result of lessons learned on the campaigns of the Third Crusade, in the course of which the Franks witnessed the power of siege engines, and of sapping and mining. Whenever possible, new castles were now built on high ground, ideally with the inner bailey protected at its rear by a cliff. The approaches were covered by the strongest defenses, sometimes three lines deep.

Château Gaillard, built high above the Seine between 1195 and 1198 by Richard I of England, was among the first of this new type to incorporate these features. Its great donjon points like a ship's bow towards an attacking enemy, to deflect the projectiles from his engines, and a deep, battered plinth and stone machicolations at the battlements served as extra defenses against sapping. Sidney Toy has suggested that this may be the earliest example in western Europe of this latter form of protection.

In 1203-04, soon after they were built, Château Gaillard's defenses were severely tried by Philip II of France. Philip took the town which Richard had built on the Seine below the castle, dug a series of trenches and set up towers from which he could keep watch on the garrison while he starved it out. Most of the inhabitants of Les Petits Andeleys had joined Roger de Lacy's soldiers within the walls of Richar's "Saucy Castle" when their town was attacked, and a thousand people were sent back through the French lines as the siege went on. When supplies ran short, de Lacy kept only those he felt would help in the defense and expelled four hundred more, men, women and children, who were met by a hail of missiles from the French army before being allowed to settle down to die during a winter whose horrors included cold, disease and cannibalism. When spring came, Philip attacked in earnest. Siege engines were mounted on the high ground to the southeast, and another high tower was built from which his crossbowmen could shoot into the castle. The men who filled in the ditches were protected as they worked by a long penthouse which took them up to the walls, where the sappers began to tunnel. The tunnel roof was first propped with timber which was then burned, causing the unsupported wall to collapse. One French soldier of commendable initiative crawled through a latrine from which he reached a chapel. From its windows he lowered a rope by which his comrades entered. After a brief spell of fire, confusion and further mining, the French entered and the garrison was killed.

This execution of everyone within a besieged town or castle, and Philip's barbarity towards the civilians sent out from it, were completely in tune with current military philosophy. If a garrison and its followers surrendered without any show of resistance, they were often treated with courtesy. The least attempt to withstand attack met with the utmost brutality. The men were usually slaughtered, the women and girls raped and everything of value found within the walls taken as booty.

The experience of King Edward I and his barons at sieges in Britain and abroad taught them the weaknesses of forts built with only one postern and one gateway. When Gilbert de Clare, Earl of Hertford and Gloucester, built Caerphilly Castle about

A Swiss war flail: an iron ball, bound with two spiked steel straps, and attached to a haft, 45.3 inches (115 cm) long. Late sixteenth or early seventeenth century.

1266-67 it was of a new form, on an artificial lake-island with extensive outworks and water defenses whose levels could be controlled by sluices. The towers at its outer corners projected so that the entire wall between each pair could be swept by projectiles from arrow-slits and from the battlements. Main gateways pierced the walls on the east and west; the inner bailey had three posterns, the outer bailey two, and each doorway was protected by a portcullis. The drawbridges that served the gateways moved on pivots near their centers. When they were raised, the inner section dropped into a pit that served as an additional defense. The longer outer section rose to close the gateway. The castle was among the most effective fortresses that had been built anywhere up to its time. In 1315, the Welsh overran its water defenses, which themselves saved the walls from attacks by mining, and burned the outer bailey, but they were unable to break into the inner defenses. The method of garrisoning Caerphilly seems to have been fairly typical of its period. In peacetime a few watchmen were left to guard it and the less perishable stores that were always kept in readiness for a siege. When attack seemed likely, up to two hundred men-at-arms and archers might be drafted. The stores in the castle armory in 1300 included 64 aketons, 16 hauberks, 49 bascinets, 15 "chapels," three of which were made in Pamplona, 35 crossbows, 5 bows, 1,000 arrowheads and 3 large composite crossbows.

In 1647, the House of Commons decided that fortresses and town walls would be demolished. At about this time, during the second Civil War, the walls of Caerphilly Castle were severely damaged, its lakes drained and the towers blown apart with gunpowder charges.

The Crossbow

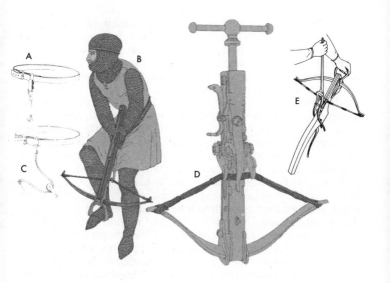

A The simplest spanning-belt consisted of a steel hook attached to a strong girdle.

B With one foot in the crossbow's stirrup, the crossbow-man stooped, engaged the hook on the cord and straightened, thus drawing the cord to the nut.

C A stronger bow could be drawn by using a spanning-belt with the hook on a pulley, which moved on a rope. The free end of the rope would be attached to a peg on the tiller, when the bow was being drawn.

D This very rare spanning mechanism has an integral hook and screw bar. The cord is drawn back to the nut by screwing the threaded handle on the bar.

E The gaffle was commonly used to span light crossbows in the sixteenth century. A version is still used by European crossbowmen. (See also pages 40–41 and 44.)

Chapter 4

By 1300 AD the smelters along the Rhine used water power for large bellows and so could build up the temperatures in their blast furnaces to the point at which iron could be made to flow from the bottom of the furnace into the molds. Also on the Rhine around the same time water powered trip-hammers, first designed to mechanize the fulling of woolen cloth, were modified to forge wrought iron and steel. At the same time the making of steel itself had become more sophisticated.

In the Roman province of Noricum, Celtic smiths had accidentally produced steel during the Iron Age, probably with the discovery of manganese-bearing ores free of sulfur, arsenic and phosphorus. The resilient steel which they made from it as early as 500 BC was traded to Italy. Other Iron Age peoples held wrought iron in the heat of a charcoal forge until it became white hot and then quenched it to make steel, but it was not of the quality of the Celtic product, and neither could compare with the so-called Damascus steel. This was produced by the smiths of Hyderabad as early as the sixth or fifth century BC and taken to Damascus whence it was distributed in the West. Black magnetite ore, bamboo charcoal and the leaves of certain plants were sealed in a clay crucible; the combination was melted with a forced draft into a mass of metal which was alternately melted and cooled four or five times before finally being fused into cakes 5 inches (12.7 cm) in diameter by .5 inches (1.27 cm) thick and weighing around two lb (.9 kg). In Roman times, these cakes were brought from the East by merchants who supplied Rome at Ardules, a seaport on the Eritrean coast of Africa. Later, when the Arabs conquered parts of India, they carried these cakes to Damascus where this extremely valuable material was forged into weapons and armor. Indian iron, or *wootz*, also accompanied the Arabs on their colonization of spain and was perhaps responsible in some measure for Toledo becoming the greatest arms manufacturing center in the peninsula. With *wootz* the Arabs also brought the knowledge of how it was made, knowledge which eventually spread north and east across Europe.

Two battles which were fought within four years of each other around the end of the thirteenth century demonstrated the interdependence of archers and cavalry when faced by determined pikemen.

Two miles south of Falkirk in Scotland on July 22, 1298, English cavalry drove the handful of archers and cavalry in the Scottish army from the field. They then faced Wallace's solid schiltron of 12-foot (3.7 m) pikes wielded by unarmored Scots, which they were unable to break until, after several hours, Edward I ordered his horse to withdraw to allow his archers a clear shot at the Scots infantry. It was not long before the English shafts began to tear gaps in the Scottish ranks through which the English cavalry then charged, to cut down the schiltrons whose main defense disappeared as the solidity of their "hedgehog" was shattered. Some five thousand Scots perished in a battle that was politically inconclusive but which demonstrated all too clearly the vulnerability of unsupported pike phalanxes, however resolute, against a combination of cavalry and skilled bowmen.

The corollary was proved during the Flemish revolt against Philip IV of France. The French heavy cavalry which charged the Flemish pikes outside Courtrai on July 11, 1302, were supported by Italian mercenaries and Gascon javelin men, but there were not enough crossbowmen among them to make a decisive contribution to the crossbow exchanges across the Groeninghebeke. A combination of poor communication, which brought the French horse into action through their own infantry, and the heavy going in the marshy ground beside the stream, threw Robert of Artois' cavalry attack into confusion. Three successive attempts to break the Flemish lines were met with advancing phalanxes of leveled pikes which first broke, then scattered the French army. As at Falkirk, the victors won little political gain but their arms showed, for the first time since Adrianople ten centuries before, that infantry could defeat a mounted force if they did not also have to face the long-range attacks of accurate, well-coordinated archers.

At Crécy in 1346, King Edward III's tactical use of the swift and accurate longbow raised England to the position of one of the world's great military powers. Faced by the Genoese crossbowmen of Philip VI's army and the poorly led attacks of his cavalry, a formation of English archers was able to pour arrows into any assault on its center where dismounted men-at-arms waited as the rock on which any remaining wave would break. Many reasons have been advanced for the failure of the crossbows to support their cavalry adequately: damp cords shortening their range, unsteady footing on wet ground making it difficult for them to draw the cord to the nut, the supposed latent inequality of range compared with that of the handbow, and so on. There are two more likely reasons. The longbowmen could shoot many times faster than their more

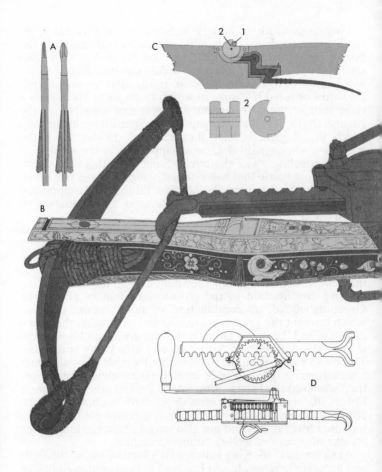

A The commonest medieval type of crossbow arrow, here seen from the side and from above, was of yew or ash and had a quadrangular head. The three fletchings would be of stiff feathers, wood or metal.

B A German sporting crossbow and cranequin, seventeenth century.

C The crossbow trigger, seen in position in the stock. When the trigger is pressed upward, its point drops down out of the notch in the nut (**1**), thus releasing the cord (**2**).

D A cranequin for spanning a powerful crossbow. The loop of cord is slipped over the tiller until it stops against two pegs. When the handle is

turned, the small cogwheel (**1**) turns the large cogwheel (**2**), which engages the triple-toothed cogwheel in the middle. This then draws the ratchet bar, to which the claws are attached, down until the cord is held by the nut.

E Swedish crossbowmen rain arrows on cavalry advancing over ground strewn with caltrops. From Olaus Magnus, Historia de gentibus septentrionalibus (Rome, 1555).

F An Italian crossbowman of c. 1475 spans his weapon with a cranequin. From a painting of the martyrdom of St. Sebastian, in the Church of St. Petronius, Bologna.

mechanically equipped opponents, who were probably able to outrange them. And they were not mercenaries but foreign invaders fighting for their king in the certain knowledge that defeat would mean death.

About the time of the battle of Courtrai, the metalworkers of Europe learned how to make steel of relatively high resilience. Its first obvious use in arms manufacture was by the crossbow-makers. By *c.* 1313, some had substituted a steel bow for wood or for their marvelously ingenious composite bows of tendon, yew, whalebone and horn which made the medieval crossbow such a deadly weapon against men or wild animals. An inventory of the countess Mahaut d'Artois, compiled in that year or 1316, lists eight crossbows *a un pie*, thirty of horn (i.e. composite) *a 2 piez* and one of gilded steel. Modern experiments with steel flight bows tend to emphasize the skill of the fourteenth-century smiths who could make a bow of steel that was resilient enough to give a fast cast on release yet did not jar the stock unbearably. The result of this imbalance between bow strength and stock weight was well known in the seventeenth century when Spanish crossbowmen talked of their less satisfactory bows as "having teeth" (*tener dientes*).

Another Artois document, an account of the work done in the count's castles in 1304, records the purchase from Henri *le serrurier* of bending gear for crossbows which had become too heavy to bend by muscle power alone.

Around the time that the steel crossbow is mentioned in the Artois inventory a French document records an important occurrence in the advance of technology. At Douai in 1313, a watermill was established which had some unspecified connection with the making of edged tools, in which category it seems safe to assume weapons were included, as they were the implements which were of the greatest interest to the majority of great men in any region. The mill's probable use was to turn the stones used in grinding, polishing and sharpening, although there is a possibility that it powered one of the several forms of trip-hammers which have been associated with the metalworking crafts for centuries.

Hitherto, the main requirements of the metalworkers were an ample supply of ores, plate or ingots, charcoal to burn in their furnaces and convenient trade routes to good markets. With the increased use of water power, the last two of these became relatively less important and small workshops were established in more remote areas where there were fastflowing streams. Sometimes these were in small villages where almost every man was engaged in the same trade. In the hills to the north of Lucca in Italy lies Villa Basilica, one of many *Urbes Minores* built of the somber local *pietra serena* that seem to have undergone little change since the late Middle Ages. In 1341, guns were made there by Iohanni Nacchi and Matheo de Villabasilica. In the next century swords, daggers and the distinctive Italian bill were made for customers ranging in rank from town guards to Lorenzo the Magnificent. Five swords were delivered to Lorenzo in 1466 by the agent of the cutler Biscotto, whose name is perpetuated in the *Casa dei Biscotti*. On the wall of the house is a *stemma* still considered to be the coat of arms of the Biscotto family, whose name is engraved on a number of weapons in European collections, sometimes in conjunction with a punched mark. In the Tower Armouries, London, are an Italian bill and a sword, both of the late fifteenth century, stamped with this mark and bearing the inscription BISCOTTO ME FECIT.

A simple device for slowing down an attack by horsemen or by ill-shod infantry was the caltrop. In its earliest form, used in Roman times, a wooden ball bas armed with spikes so that whichever way it was thrown on the ground one or more spikes pointed upwards. By the Middle Ages the smiths made a geometrically ingenious caltrop of two pieces of iron twisted and hammer-welded together so that whichever way it was thrown or dropped in front of a defensive position three of the needle-sharp points served as a tripod for the fourth. Some of Leonardo's engines were designed to throw baskets of caltrops, although even then, at the close of the fifteenth century, they were considered old-fashioned. N·vertheless settlers in Jamestown, Virginia, found them a useful defense against Algonquin Indians in the seventeenth century, they were used by the Swedish army a hundred years later, and they saw service in the Korean War.

By the middle of the thirteenth century, if not earlier, gunpowder had reached western Europe. The formula had been in use in China for pyrotechnic weapons by the eleventh century and may have been first brought to Europe by Arab travelers. By the first quarter of the fourteenth century, the propellant power of gunpowder exploding in a closed tube had been discovered somewhere in Europe, and there is definite evidence of the existence of guns recorded in a Florentine document of 1326 and in *De Nobilitatibus, Sapientiis, et Prudentiis Regum*, an English manuscript by Walter de Milemete preserved in Christ Church College Library, Oxford. The Milemete manuscript, dated 1326-27, includes a miniature

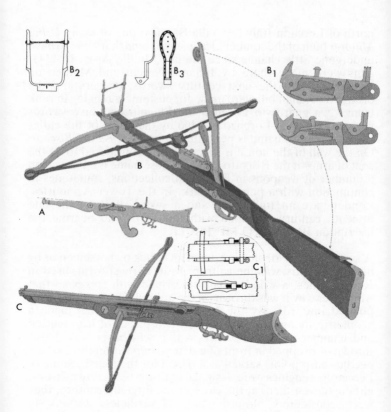

A A target crossbow as used today by some Belgian shooting clubs.

B Bullet-shooting crossbows were made in large numbers in the northwest of England in the first half of the nineteenth century. An integral bending-lever and efficient lock mechanism (**1**) made them quick and simple to shoot. The foresight (**2**) was a metal U carrying a cotton skein threaded with a bead. The hinged rear sight (**3**) had several peepholes, each for a different range.

C For shooting vertically upward at a popinjay set on a high pole or tower, some crossbowmen shoot round bullets from a crossbow with a barrel. The bow is fastened to the stock with a steel bridle, which can be tightened with a tommy-bar (**1**).

showing a man in the armor of the day shooting an arrow from a cannon resting on a trestle. The cannon is in the form of a vase with a bulbous swelling at the chamber to which the soldier is applying a hot match or tinder by means of a long rod. The manuscript shows the fletched arrow in the act of leaving the barrel. In another version in the British Museum the gunner has an audience dressed like himself, and the arrow is still in the bore of the gun. The Florentine decree of 1326 appointed two men to make iron arrows, presumably like those shown by Milemete, iron bullets and *canones de metallo* for the defense of the republic. Five years later, *vasa* and *sclopi* were used in an attack on Cividale, and in 1338 the arsenal at Rouen was issuing "an iron pot to throw fire arrows," the arrows being of fletched iron. Other cannon arrows were fletched with "feathers" of brass and their butts wrapped with leather strips to form a wad that kept the fletchings from rubbing on the bore. It also reduced the windage, that is, the space between the bore and the projectile. Regular velocities, on which reasonably accurate shooting depends, can only be achieved when the loss of gas is constant. The ideal gun has a perfectly shaped projectile which fits its bore exactly, conditions which were not fulfilled even approximately until modern times.

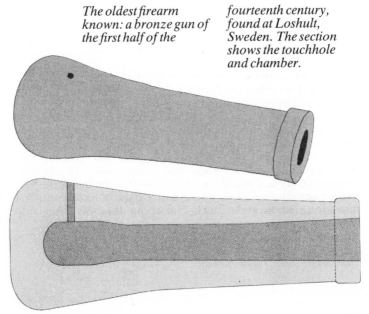

The oldest firearm known: a bronze gun of the first half of the fourteenth century, found at Loshult, Sweden. The section shows the touchhole and chamber.

A little bronze gun was found at Loshult in Swedish Scania in 1861, unfortunately on a site which cannot be dated by other evidence. It is so close to the form of the guns in the Milemete sketches, although much smaller, that most students consider it to be from approximately the same period. It is almost certainly the eArliest firearm known. It is roughly vase-shaped with a bore of 1.4 inches (36 mm) at the muzzle, tapering to 1.2 inches (30 mm) before opening out again to a powder chamber of 1.4 inches (36 mm) into which the vent or touchhole is drilled at a right angle. As the gun has no fastenings, one must assume that it was strapped to a wooden stock with bands of iron or some other material more perishable than its own bronze. Since no fourteenth-century illustration of a hand-held firearm is known, one can only guess at the form of the attachment. Like the guns in the Milemete sketches it was fired with an iron rod heated in a brazier or by a piece of smoldering tinder held in the firer's hand.

The gunpowder used in these early guns varied from country to country, perhaps even from city to city, and by 1546 different proportions were used for large and medium guns and for mortars. The proportions of saltpeter to sulfur and charcoal recommended by fourteenth-century writers varied from 6:1:2 (Marcus Graecus, *c.* 1300) to 22:4:5 (Montauban, *c.* 1400). Even the least effective gave a massive expansion of gas on ignition. A pound (.45 kg) of black powder produces about forty cubic feet (1.1 m23) of gas on combustion, hence the need for the thick-walled chambers even at an early date.

Within fifteen years or so of the first illustrations of firearms, and before they made any great impact on war, some guns were made in two sections; one part was the chamber for the powder charge and the other the barrel, a directional tube that took the projectile. The chamber was wedged into the rear of the barrel when firing. In 1342, the leather-wadded arrow mentioned above was fired from a gun made this way in the Artois castle of Rihoult. The lighter guns of this early period were of cast bronze or wrought iron with stocks of one of four basic types so that they could be fired when held in the hands. The earliest were probably tied to a wooden stock with metal bands. Others had socketed breeches, a third group had the breech beaten out into a long handle and a fourth had a point that was driven into the stock.

Chapter 5

Throughout the history of war, it has been an almost invariable custom for the weapons and armor of the fallen to form part of the loot of the victors. The Bayeux Tapestry shows the stripping of mail shirts from the dead and similar scenes can be found in other medieval sources. However there were exceptions to this rule, and excavations at Visby on the island of Gotland in Sweden have produced tangible evidence of one such occurrence. There, in July 1361, the peasants were defeated in three battles by the soldiers of the Danish king Waldemar Atterdag (1320-75). Five graves where the dead were buried outside Visby's city walls have been excavated, and among the skeletons of almost twelve hundred people buried in three out of the five was found an extraordinary hoard of armor. The shields, helmets and weapons that were used by the dead were carried off by the Danes, but summer heat seems to have discouraged any serious attempt to take the body armor. Most of the armor from the graves was mail, some two hundred coifs and the remains of many hauberks rusted into virtually inextricable masses.

When the Visby graves were opened, the excavators seized upon a unique opportunity to assess and analyze the causes of the victims' deaths. Their results illuminate the method of fighting of the period and give an invaluable guide to the killing power of the weapons used. The situation and nature of the wounds which were found on the skeletons show that they were inflicted with axes, crossbow arrows, swords, maces, spears and lances. Wounds to flesh alone, from whatever weapon, obviously could not show in this analysis, but as more than ten percent of the deaths were due to arrow wounds in the cranium we can assume that a much higher percentage than this figure shows died from arrow wounds elsewhere on the body. At reasonable ranges, say up to fifty or sixty yards (46 or 55 m), the heavy projectiles thrown by the composite crossbows then in use throughout Europe would smash through mail or lamellar armor, although they would probably be stopped by the sort of coats of plates recovered at Visby.

In the year that the Gotlanders fought and died beside Visby's square-towered walls, three Tuscan merchants formed a partnership in Avignon. Toro di Berto, Niccoló di Bernardo and Francesco di Marco Datini traded primarily in arms, for which there was a buoyant market in the city owing to the presence of soldiers of the papal court as well as the Breton and English merceneries who had infested southern France in the four years since the Truce of Bordeaux.

For the greater part, their stocks came from Italy. The shop in Avignon was probably fairly typical of the sort of place where the manufactures of the huge workshops of north Italy were handled. In one respect it seems to have been slightly behind the times, as no firearms appear on the stock lists although, in the forty years since the Milemete manuscripts and the Florentine decree of 1326, references to guns became more and more frequent. By 1364, the Commune of Perugia was ordering bombards small enough to be easily carried, and the very early gun from Loshult in Sweden is small enough to be fired while held in the hands. From the date of the Perugia order until the end of the fourteenth century, hand firearms are mentioned in numerous records in England, France, Germany, Italy and elsewhere. Sometimes they are described by a vernacular word such as the High German *Donnerbückse*, but more often they are called by some version of the onomatopoeic Italian word *bombarda*.

Despite the frequency of these accounts, only two hand-held guns other than the Loshult gun have survived from before 1400. One, now in the Germanisches Nationalmuseum, Nuremberg, was found in the ruins of the Hessian castle of Tannenberg which was destroyed by artillery fire in 1399. The second – known as the Mörkö gun after the island of that name – was a random find fished up from the bed of the Baltic near Nynäs in Södermanland and now preserved in Statens Historiska Museum, Stockholm. Both are of bronze, their polygonal barrels especially thick at the chamber where the touchhole is drilled through the barrels from a recessed pan which held the priming powder. An integral socket is cast into the butt end of each to receive a wooden stock or tiller. An English account of 1373-75 gives the cost of fitting helves to guns and hatchets in the same way as pike hafts were attached: *x, pro heluyng viij gunnorum...ad modum pycoys....xiij s.* ("Item 10, for stocking eight guns in the style of pikes, thirteen shillings.") Of the two, the Mórkó gun is the more elaborate. Just behind the pan above the breech is the head of a man modeled in the round, his hair and beard trimmed in the fashion of the last quarter of the fourteenth century. The facets of the hexagonal barrel are engraved with religious inscriptions. A fluke below the barrel is designed to be hooked over a parapet, or some other support such as a tripod, to take the force of the

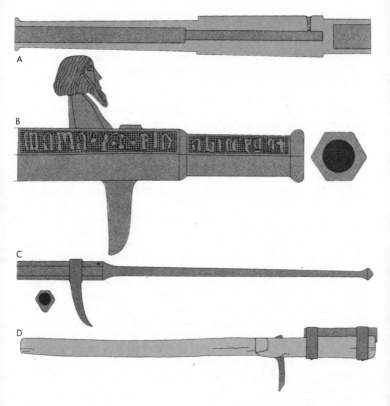

A *A cast bronze hand-cannon, discovered during excavations on the site of the Castle of Tannenberg, Hesse, Germany. The gun must have been made before the castle was destroyed in 1399, and is, therefore, the oldest which can be dated with certainty. The section shows the reduced bore of the powder chamber.*

B *Another cast bronze gun from the late fourteenth century. This was found in the sea near Mörkö, Sweden, and*

is engraved with religious inscriptions. The bearded head may represent Jesus Christ.

C *An iron hand-cannon, from the ruins of the Castle of Vedelspang, South Schleswig, Germany, destroyed in 1426.*

D *A Swiss iron hand-cannon, still bound to its original stock by iron straps. Late fourteenth or early fifteenth century.*

recoil. Throughout the following century lugs of this type became common, and guns fitted with them were given the German name *Hackenbúchse* that became the French *arquebuse* and the English *Hackbut* and *Harquebus*.

Guns from the early years of the fifteenth century, but made with iron stocks of a variety of shapes, are similar in many respects to those from Mórkó and Tannenberg. There are examples at Berne, Brussels and Nuremberg, but the most surely dateable is in the Tøjhusmuseum in Copenhagen. It was found in 1859 at the site of the castle built at Vedelspang in South Schleswig in 1416 and destroyed ten years later. The iron barrel, which burst in service, tapers from 1.05 inches (27 mm) at the muzzle to .62 inches (16 mm) at the breech to which a long rod terminating in a knob is forged. It probably represents the standard handgun–if in fact there was such a thing–for both infantry and mounted troops, for a drawing dated 1449, of which there are several copies, shows an armored man shooting a gun of this type from horseback. The gunstock ends in a ring like that on the Brussels example, and a cord passing through the ring and round the shooter's neck supports the butt against his breastplate, while the barrel is supported by a forked rest fitted to the saddle. The rider's right hand holds the lighted match that ignites the charge, his left steadies the barrel and directs it at its target. One manuscript copy in the Bibliothèque Richelieu in Paris shows the mounted gunner and, in another illustration, a mule with three such guns mounted on a packsaddle. The drawing is titled *Asellus portans in sella tres scopitos*. The gun looks like a most impractical appliance. The foot soldier of the day does not seem to have used a rest. He either supported the gun across his shoulder like a modern recoiless rifle or gripped it, lancelike, against his chest with his upper arm, steadied it with one hand and, with a smoldering match, fired it with the other.

By the end of the century that first saw cannon used in war, the gunmakers had already developed this new arm into a much more formidable weapon than that shown in the Milemete manuscripts. Their first step towards the production of a repeating gun was taken when the movable chamber appeared some time before 1372. In that year a gun was described as equipped with three chambers. Each could be kept ready charged, to increase the cannon's rate of fire over one which was loaded with powder, wad and ball from the muzzle. The chambers, or "pots" – shaped rather like modern beer mugs – were fitted to the rear of the open-ended barrel and locked in position with a transverse wedge. The most obvious weakness of these early breechloaders was the loss of gas on ignition around the ill-fitting chamber. Even when a wad was used between the powder and the ball, the considerable gas loss, despite dozens of designs intended to prevent it, remained an unsolved problem until Pauly's invention of the self-obturating cartridge, patented in 1812. Another way in which the gunmakers attempted to speed up firing from a strongpoint is shown in manuscripts of the early fifteenth century. The most likely attempt to have had some possible measure of success is shown in the *Codex Germanicus 600* in the Staatsbibliothek, Munich. The gunner stands behind a horizontal circular turntable with four short guns radiating from the center. Each could be pointed – aimed is too precise a verb for such an imprecise action – and fired at the target in turn until all were discharged. An arc at the base suggests that the turntable could also be tilted to give some elevation. The design survives in later manuscripts and printed books, including most published editions of Vegetius and Valturius.

Throughout this early period in the history of firearms, cannons and handguns had to be fired by a red-hot iron or coal, or a smoldering cord (match) held in the gunner's hand. When a handgun charge was ignited by these means the gunner had one hand only to support, steady and point the gun while he applied the fire. The invention of the matchlock, more important at this stage in history than any breechloading mechanism, was the first major improvement in firearms design. The matchlock was invented before 1411, when it appears in *Codex MS 3069* in the Österreichische Nationalbibliothek, Vienna, as a pivoted, Z-shaped lever which placed the match, attached to one end, precisely into the priming powder when the free end was squeezed towards the stock. The shooter was now able to take a much better grip on the weapon than was possible when one hand was devoted entirely to the process of firing. This new aid was the precursor of a long line of variations of the same basic design lasting into the middle of the nineteenth century. Its developed form, the snap matchlock, continued to be made in Japan almost until the end of the nineteenth century.

While some of the individual trades involved in the manufacture of arms for war and the chase could be covered by a single craft guild such as the mailmakers, the lorimers or the fletchers, the rise of gunpowder artillery brought forth a further set of workers. The making and serving of the new cannons needed several crafts: iron and bronze had to be cast and forged, massive carriages for the larger guns and the stocks of the smaller had to be shaped and joined, gunpowder and gunstones all had to be prepared by specialists.

The combination of all these skills produced a new breed of men, the master gunners, who appeared in most Western countries by or soon after the end of the fourteenth century. They were usually in the direct employ of cities or princes who prized the skills recounted in a document which describes the gunsmith Merckel Gast of Frankfurt in the last decade of the fourteenth century. Gast could make gunpowder that would last sixty years, using saltpeter which he himself could separate and refine. He could restore spoiled powder so that it could be used. He was also a gunner in the sense that he knew how to shoot with the weapons, handguns and larger arms, which he could cast in iron. Even these skills were not enough in themselves, as a German Firework Book of *c.* 1420 tells us that the master smith should be a thoughtful employer, and should be able to make all the chemical products appropriate to his craft, as well as firedarts, fireballs and other pyrotechnic devices that could be used to deter or kill an enemy. The gunner's subject was already sufficiently large for it to be considered essential for the master smith to be able to read and write. Too much had already been written for one man to remember–understandable when one recalls that the gunner was also frequently called on to advise on attack and defense, to lead troops or to direct the construction of fortifications. The temporal instruction was paramount, but the firework books give more than lip service to the spiritual. Anyone working with such devilish instruments of destruction as guns and gunpowder should never forget his Christian responsibilities. The vision of God should be always before the gunner's eyes – even when he squinted along the wrought iron or the cast bronze of one of his own dire creations.

The development of autonomous cities and territorial states, each with its own army, which increased throughout the fourteenth century, led to a wide and general diffusion of knowledge about all military affairs. Teachers like the anonymous authors of the firework books wrote of tactics, strategy, inventions and developments and this led to a series of manuals from German and Italian cultural circles. Outstanding among the authors of these textbooks of military technology is the German military engineer Konrad Kyeser of Eichstätt in Franconia. In an influential illustrated manuscript dedicated to Rupert, Count Palatine, his brother princes and the Estates of Christendom in 1405, Kyeser discussed guns and gunpowder, war carts, rams, cranes, pumps, pontoons, life belts and many other appliances for use in war. His *Bellifortis* is the work of a great patriot in a now unfashionable tradition, for he saw his native Germany as "justly famed for her determined, strong

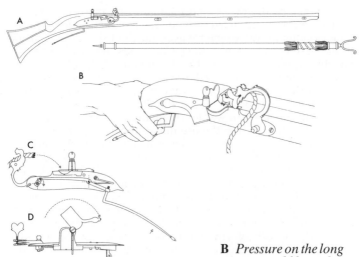

The invention of the matchlock, sometime before 1411, was the first major improvement in firearms design. It enabled the gunner to fire while steadying the gun with both hands.

A *A matchlock military musket and rest. The gun was so heavy that a rest was necessary for aiming accurately. Probably German, late sixteenth century.*

B *Pressure on the long trigger would lever the serpentine, which held the glowing match, into the priming pan, thus firing the charge.*

C *Side section view of the matchlock, showing the spring-and-tumbler system which activated the serpentine.*

D *Top view of the matchlock showing how the pancover is opened before firing.*

and courageous soldiery...her free crafts...mechanical knowledge and...many industries." Chauvinistic as this boast might seem, it was not made by an ignorant, untraveled man, for in his own epitaph, Kyeser wrote that he was well known as "Bellifortis, the conqueror of whole armies," from Norway to Sicily and from Spain to the Ukraine.

Warriors had ridden into battle in chariots since the third millennium BC, and the fourth century AD saw the Goths using their carts as a form of mobile fort, but it was not until the appearance of the developed handgun that man, vehicle and projectile arm were fused into an effective tactical unit. In the long Bohemian war which ravaged much of southeast Europe from 1420 to 1434, Jan Žižka's Czech peasant army, raw and poorly-armed, but fanatical and brilliantly led, relied on the tactics of the *Wagenburg* in their violent struggle against the full might of the imperial armies. Like the combination of archers with dismounted heavy cavalry, the *Wagenburg* was essentially a defensive device, but was less maneuverable than the English unit. It developed from the use in battle of carts carrying from sixteen to twenty infantry, drawn by teams of up to four horses, the drivers wearing helmets and protected by large shields. The infantry were armed with crossbows and handguns, flails, and "hooks" which were probably some form of bill or halberd.

Towards the end of the Hussite movement the proportions of horse to foot to wagons was fairly consistently laid down as 700 cavalrymen to 7,000 infantry and 350 wagons. When under attack the Czechs formed laagers by chaining the wagons together, and the cavalry of the empire charged repeatedly without ever penetrating them successfully. When time allowed, the carts were not only chained but entrenched, with the excavated soil piled around the wheels. To allow the defenders to sally, openings left at diametrically opposed points were closed only by chains, posts and spikes. When, as was at first almost inevitable, the onslaught of the German cavalry was repulsed by crossbowmen and handgunners, the chains were removed and a squadron of Hussite cavalry charged out to cut down the disorganized enemy.

The Germans seemed never to learn from their defeats at the hands of the bulwarked Czechs, and when their enemy added artillery mounted on special wagons, the imperial cavalry refused to face the *Wagenburg* at all. The Czechs were free to loot and burn their way through Meissen, Bavaria and Thuringia almost unhindered. The end of the Hussite Wars came only after Czech troops of the moderate Calixtine Party lured Prokop's Taborite cavalry from the shelter of their laager at Lipan, massacred them in the open field, and then turned on the undermanned wagons to complete the victory. Indecisive generalship and attacking flair combined to sweep the Hussite form of the *Wagenburg* from Europe's battlefields for ever, but it left behind the roots from which firearms proliferated across the continent. The cartdrivers' shields developed into the distinctively Bohemian *pavese*.

Chapter 6

The sultan Mahomet II (1432-81) has been called the first great gunner in history, a title he earned at the siege of Constantinople in 1453, when he led a vast army against Christendom's last Eastern fortress. The previous autumn he had severed the city's routes to the north and quartered at Adrianople (modern Edirne) an army of 50,000, including 15,000 Janissaries who fought in mail with bow, sword and mace. They were the firstline troops, supported by a near-rabble of *bashi-bazouks*, and local peasants who had been forced into the sultan's service. When they besieged Constantinople's triple walls they dragged with them fifty-six small guns in fourteen batteries, and thirteen heavy cannon which opened fire on April 5, 1453.

The siege guns were the work of Urban, a founder from Walachia or Hungary, who cast them at Adrianople. They needed sixty oxen to drag them on the march, with two hundred men to guard them and keep them on the road, which had to be leveled for their passage by two hundred more. If we accept one contemporary account each massive stone shot weighed about half a ton and was 30 inches (*c.* 76 cm) in diameter, capable of crushing the thousand-year-old wall built by Theodosius. But almost as quickly as the wall was breached the defenders repaired it, for each ball took two hours to load. Nevertheless, the guns undoubtedly played a major part in the conquest of the city. Eventually, on May 29, after Turkish failures to mine the walls, the defense yielded to repeated and enervating day and night assaults by *bashibazouks*, levies and Janissaries in the face of projectiles and Greek fire.

Great guns of the type used by Mahomet's armies guarded the entrance to the Sea of Marmara for another three hundred and fifty years. One bought from Turkey in 1868 by Britain's Board of Ordnance may have been among the guns which damaged six of Sir John Duckworth's ships in 1807, when he passed through the Dardanelles and attempted to invest Constantinople. The shots came from the forts of Kilid-Bahr on the north of the Dardanelles, and Chanak on the south. The gun was brought to the Tower of London, where it now stands in the grounds, flanked by stone shot weighing about 650 lb (294.8 kg), which a 300-lb (136 kg) powder charge could throw for a mile (1.6 km) across the Dardanelles Strait. The Tower gun was cast in 1464 by Munir Ali, a Turk whose name is modeled on its muzzle. It weighs 18 tons and required the mining, transport and refining of many times that weight of ores for its making. It was cast in two pieces so that men with levers could unscrew the breech from the chase when it had to be moved. Three years after it was cast, Kritoboulos described the technique which Munir Ali must have used. A mass of the purest clay was made plastic by kneading for several days. Then linen and hempen strips were added to strengthen the substance before it was molded to a long core or mandril the size and shape of the bore, with the chamber tapered to one-third the diameter of the muzzle. The mandril was set up like a pillar and a cylinder molded around it leaving a space of about 9.5 inches (24.1 cm) to receive the molten metal. The cylinder was also of clay buttressed with iron and timber and with an outer mound of earth to support the mold when the bronze was poured in. Two furnaces built adjacent to the prepared mold took three days and nights to melt the copper and tin to a consistency at which it could be poured in through pipes till the mold was filled and the mandril covered to an extra depth of thirty inches or so (*c*. .8 m). When the bronze had cooled and contracted the molds were broken, the metal polished and the inscriptions and decoration cleaned up with handtools.

When firing, the gun was mounted in an openwork cage of heavy oak timbers with the breech abutting a solid wall to reduce the recoil which Kritoboulos and his contemporaries believed, wrongly, would disturb the already inaccurate aim. On top of the powder charge the gunners rammed home wooden plugs so tight that they could only be removed by firing. The shot was rolled in, the gun elevated by wedges to the angle that experience had shown to be more or less correct and the powder in the touchhole ignited. A single shot from *Elipolos*, the City-taker, could bring down a fortress tower, but great guns such as this could also burst with disastrous consequences. On August 3, 1437, James II of Scotland was killed at the siege of Roxburgh by *ane piece of ane misformed gune that brake in the shuting*. And one of Henry V's bombards, *The King's Daughter*, burst at the siege of Harlech.

Iron guns were also subject to bursting. The biggest survivor is *Mons Meg*, a gun constructed of welded parallel rods of iron, laid like staves of a barrel, around which iron rings were shrunk on when white hot to bind them into an almost permanent fascine. Like the Tower Dardanelles gun, *Mons Meg* has rectangular slots at the front and the rear of the chamber to receive the capstan bars which were used to unscrew the two parts. The serious corrosion which has affected every surviving

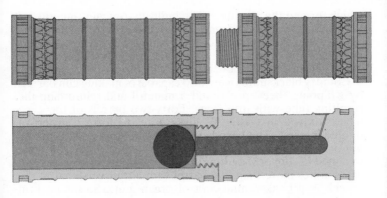

A bronze gun made by the Turk Munir Ali in 1464. Weighing 18 tons (18,288.7 kg), it was cast in two sections which could be screwed apart when it had to be transported. A 300-lb (136 kg) powder charge would throw its 650-lb (294.8 kg) gunstone for a mile (1.6 km). The gun was mounted in an openwork cage of heavy oak timbers.

early iron gun has made it unwise to attempt this separation. The gun, now lodged on the ramparts of Edinburgh Castle, shows a rent near the breech where, after two hundred years of use, it gave way in 1680 when firing a salute in honor of the Duke of York.

Scientists and artillerymen showed an interest in guns of this built-up construction more than a century ago, when a number were examined and described. One at Mont St. Michel, Normandy, was described as being made of longitudinal bars, 2.75 by 1 inches (7 by 2.5 cm), bound by 2.75-inch (7 cm) hoops. Another in the Rotunda, Woolwich, has fourteen longitudinal bars arranged in a circle, two deep, with molten lead poured into the interstices of the imperfect welds. Thirty-five rings which were driven over the tube had their edges tapped down when hot to give a neat external join. The soldiers who examined this gun reported that the quality of the iron was almost as high as that of the best wrought iron used by William Armstrong in gunmaking. A bronze sleeve lined the section which formed the chamber. The built-up iron guns mentioned here all seem to date from around the end of the fifteenth century, but they continued in use alongside cast bronze guns until well into the sixteenth century, perhaps because their manufacture was not beyond the skills of provincial smiths.

Country blacksmiths were also capable of making gun barrels by wrapping sheet iron round a mandril and reinforcing the resulting tube with iron rings. Forty-two barrels of this type have survived in Castle Wemyss, Fife, to form a group of unique interest. The barrels vary in caliber and length, but all are of the same construction. Below the barrels an iron yoke wrapped in copper sheathing serves as trunnions and in several cases unites more than one barrel with a transverse bar at the breech in a bank reminiscent of organ guns. So far no firm conclusion has been reached as to when or where they were made, but the barrels appear to date from the sixteenth century. Perhaps they were forged locally to arm the castle, or salvaged from some ship that foundered off the Fife coast. Exposure to the local atmosphere has left them encrusted with coal dust from the mines that have surrounded Castle Wemyss for many centuries, mines that provided the fuel for the founders who cast carronades in Napoleonic times.

In Mahomet II's day the city of Adrianople was also famous for its bowyers, with Usta Sinan, the craft's most highly respected member, teaching his skills to the children of princes. His bows were much sought after and widely exported: "If in all Arabia or Persia a bow from Adrianople is bent, it is one of Usta Sinan's." It seems probable that the introduction of the composite crossbow into Europe about the time of the last Crusade (1270-91) was the result of contact with the bowmakers of the East, where several types of crossbow were in use during Saladin's reign. The construction of surviving bows from Asia Minor is so close to that of the composite crossbow as to make it very likely that the latter derived from the former. Peter the Saracen is among the earliest of the crossbowmakers whose names are recorded in England.

Composite or, as they are sometimes known, "horn" crossbows were used alongside wooden crossbows by the Huns, by the Moslems in Spain and Sicily, and in Byzantium. They were made with several minor variations, but basically the bow consisted of a lath of wood to which were glued strips of horn, leather and sinew, often covered in birchbark and varnished or painted to keep out the damp. By the twelfth century, if not much earlier, a more efficient means of holding the cord in the tensed position was in use. The nut, a short thick cylinder of horn, antler or bronze, rotated in a recess in the top of the stock or tiller. A quadrant notch was cut in the nut to receive the drawn cord, and diametrically opposite, a second, smaller notch engaged the trigger sear when the larger notch was uppermost. Pressure on the free end of a simple Z-shaped trigger allowed the nut to rotate to release the cord, so projecting the arrow which lay in a shallow groove on the fore-end. To make the arrow lie more securely in its groove, the upper notch of the nut was slotted to receive the butt of the arrow, and by the fifteenth century a curved spring of horn bore down on the arrow shaft just in front of the nut.

When this form of crossbow mechanism was first introduced, the crossbowman bent his bow by placing his foot in a "stirrup" attached to the front end of the stock and pulling the cord to the nut with two hands. The same basic lock and release mechanism survived, though the makers of more powerful crossbows developed more efficient ways of drawing the cord. A simple iron hook attached to a waist-belt gave way in some countries to a hook fitted with a pulley through which passed a stout cord, one end being attached to the waist belt and the other to a peg on the upper side of the stock. When the crossbowman had the cord in position and straightened his back, the pulley gave him a mechanical advantage of 2:1. The *gaffle*, basically a simple system of hooks and levers, was made either to pull *or* push the cord to the nut. These devices were all quite strong enough for relatively weak hunting crossbows, but for the very powerful crossbows used in war, whether by foot soldiers in the field or from prepared positions, the windlass – first illustrated in Europe by Kyeser *c.* 1405 – was the most popular accessory in the richer parts of Europe. Mechanics working in Cambodia had shown the cranked windlass to be a practical method of spanning a crossbow in the thirteenth century. The legend that it was introduced to the Khmer kingdom in 1172 AD by a shipwrecked army officer from China, where the crank had been known for a thousand years, underlines the international nature of arms development and the fortuitous means by which ideas were disseminated.

Within a generation of Kyeser's illustrating the windlass for bending crossbows, the cranequin was invented, probably in Germany, as it is first recorded in German manuscripts of the first half of the fifteenth century. It was a rack and pinion device, stronger than the gaffle and so much more manageable than the windlass that a strong crossbow could be spanned while on horseback. In its earlier form, the wheelcase that housed the cogs was small, the mechanical advantage achieved was relatively slight and the loop which fastened the cranequin to

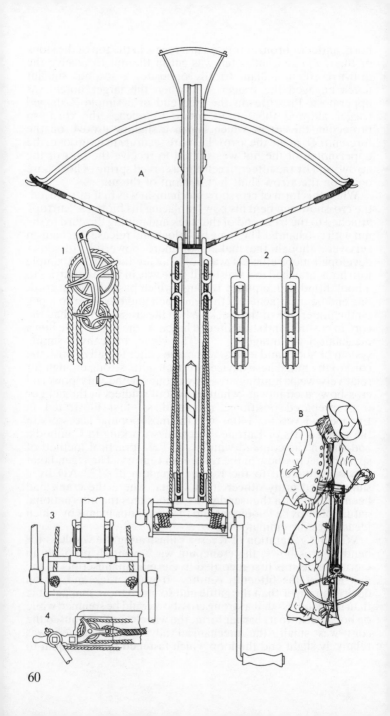

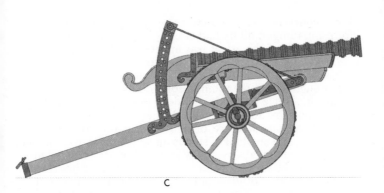

C

A *The cord of this heavy seventeenth century crossbow was drawn to the nut by a powerful windlass, seen here in place.* (**1**) *Side view of the front pulleys, fixed to the double hook which bears on the cord.* (**2**) *Plan view, showing the position of the double hook.* (**3**) *Plan view of the rear pulleys, spindle and handles.* (**4**) *Side view showing how the rear pulleys are mounted on a socket which fits over the butt of the tiller.*

B *A crossbowman winding a windlass.*

C *A wrought-iron field gun, captured during the Burgundian Wars of 1474-77. Length of barrel 62.2 inches (158 cm); caliber 3 inches (7.5 cm); and total length 11 foot 10 inches (360 cm). One of seventeen surviving guns believed to have been taken from the Burgundians, it is preserved in the museum at La Neuveville.*

the stock was sometimes of metal. From the end of the fifteenth century the stock-loop was almost invariably of cord, and the wheelcase was usually large enough to take cogs and gears of a size to give considerable multiplication of the power applied to the handle. Wheelcases and the ratchet bar are more often than not etched with scenes of the chase. Some are decorated with applied gilt brass plates engraved and fretted with the signs of the zodiac. As so many were the toys of the rich, their decoration received the same attention as did guns, pistols, swords and other personal arms of the period.

Italian printers published editions of the military works of Valtuius in 1472, of Pliny in 1476 and Frontinus in 1480. All were read by Leonardo da Vinci, and when he was called to the

Sforza court at Milan in 1482 as a sculptor and founder, his interest in things military had already been aroused. His claims to knowledge of the art of war are recorded in a letter in the *Codex Atlanticus* which is attributed to the master, but which is very similar in tone and content to memoranda written by earlier engineers. Like them, Leonardo knew how to help the soldiers in a siege by making ladders, penthouses and portable bridges and by draining wet ditches. His founder's skills included the manufacture of light and heavy ordnance, and mortars to shower a hail of stones on an enemy. He could plan deep mines, and make assault wagons to carry men and guns to the heart of the stoutest enemy formation. Among his assorted "endless means of offense and defense" were the engines of the ancients, catapults and mangonels, and the trebuchets which Leonardo refers to as no longer in common use, but which Mahomet II had sent against the defenders of Rhodes in 1480.

While in the duke's service, Leonardo gave Ludovico's armorer, Gentil dei Borri, drawings of his suggested designs for armor for horse and foot. Like many other artists, he designed halberds, swords and the conceits that were beginning to appear as ornament on almost every cast cannon, but these made little contribution to the science of war.

In 1499, when the French entered Milan, Leonardo took service with the Comte de Ligny who ordered a report on the state of Tuscany's defenses. The task was interrupted by the sudden return of the Sforza regime and Leonardo moved on to Venice where he was again employed as a military engineer. Three years later he was inspecting fortifications for Cesare Borgia, drawing plans and recommending improvements but adding nothing to the progress of military architecture. From Milan in 1509 he was driven south to Rome where the San Gallo brothers were introducing the final phase in the development of Italian fortification, and here Leonardo carried out limited commissions for Giuliano de' Medici. After Marignano, when Italian castle builders were employed to ring France with a chain of fortresses, Leonardo took his place at the court of Francis I, employed for the first time as an artist. When he died at Amboise in 1519 he had spent most of his life as an engineer, surveying, modifying and designing castles. He left a mass of sketches which have given him the reputation of a great original thinker in the field of armor and arms, despite Bertholet's protestations, made as early as 1902, at this disproportionate adulation of his mechanical skills. His war machines were largely distilled from the works of the ancients, adaptations of engines which were already on the verge of an obsolescence as complete as that of chivalry itself. The trebuchet was still in

Maximilian's arsenal in 1510, but the gun, the god of sieges for almost two centuries past, had relegated it to the task of flinging such nauseous loads as rotting carcasses into besieged towns.

The multi-barreled organs and the assault wagons had been drawn by Kyeser more than a century earlier, and Leonardo's sketches of naval armament were borrowed from Francesco di Giorgio who was also the source of his most up-to-date ideas on fortifications – low-walled, with powerful bastions to bear the weight of the defensive cannon which the new fashion caused to be mounted on the walls.

When Leonardo referred to long-hafted Danish axes, he was probably describing a weapon which had been in use in Viking times, and from which the Scottish fighting axe of the sixteenth century and the berdish were probably derived. A number of Scots documents of that period refer to the "Dens (i.e. Danish) Ax," and it may even be that the Lochaber axe originated from the war axes which the Norsemen brought across the North Sea on their voyages of pillage and colonization. But there is a possibility that the Danish axe mentioned in Leonardo's notebooks was the small-headed axe carried by Norwegian farmers until recent times, a type also found in Poland where the *ciupaga* is used as a combined tool and walking stick.

In Leonardo's lifetime, Charles VIII brought the employment of artillery to another of its great peaks. In 1494-95, Charles took Italy as he had planned. Machiavelli used the phrase "chalk in hand," as whatever objective Charles marked on his maps was soon won for him by his gunners. But Commines records that even the most efficient artillery in the world, the terror of the French king's enemies, only disabled a dozen men at Fornova in 1495. The emergence of cannon as the dominant arm on the battlefield, envisaged by Europe's military leaders, was not affirmed until Marignano, twenty years later.

For all his reputation, the chivalry of Pierre du Terrail, Chevalier de Bayard (1475-1524) did not extend to his treatment of the handgunners who opposed him. He fought alongside Francis I at Marignano and earlier earned glory even in defeat at Guinegate in 1513, but the new warfare was not really to his taste. Between his first great battle at Fornova in 1495 and his death by musket shot beside the Sesia River in 1524, he had seen the proportions of cavalry to infantry in the armies of France decline from two to one to about one to ten. Perhaps in an attempt to slow, if not reverse the trend, he ordered the execution by shooting of all captured hackbutmen.

This act was probably only marginally less cruel and contemptuous than the practice of the condottiere Gian Paolo Vitelli, to whom men who used handguns were fit only to be blinded and have their hands struck off before being turned out into a fatally illiberal world.

Vitelli died in 1499, the year of the first recorded use of the word *moschetto* to describe a firearm. Firearms, whether hand-held or heavy artillery, were often named after real or mythical birds or animals, and in this case the word indicates, as does the English equivalent *musket*, the male sparrow hawk. Hand-held firearms had been made as early as *c.* 1408 with a wooden shoulder stock to make them easier to fire from the shoulder. Although they had been used in battle for many years they were not yet accepted as suitable weapons for men on horseback, who retained a contempt for the foot that was to last until the machine gun finally drove cavalry from the battlefields of Europe and America.

Chivalry as Bayard and Vitelli knew it is unimaginable without the horse, and it could not have been easy to be chivalrous to an enemy who could knock a knight from his mount while still out of range of the lance. The centaur of antiquity became the knight of the Middle Ages, master of Europe. It is not difficult to understand his grimness in the face of the challenge from the gunmakers, who were on the verge of relegating him to the realm of fables.

Chapter 7

By *c.* 1500, the crude multi-barreled guns used in the fourteenth and fifteenth centuries to defend bridges and gateways from fixed positions were being mounted on wheeled carriages as light field artillery. They were normally of quite small caliber, about musket bore (.75 inches or 1.9 cm), and consisted of a number of barrels mounted in tiers in a wooden frame. They were made to fire simultaneously and could lay down a devastating weight of shot in a confined area either in attack or defense. The resemblance of the grouped barrels to the pipes of a musical organ is said to have given these new weapons the name *organ*, which appears in a number of English documents, and the German name *Orgel* and *Orgelgeschütz*, but the derivation is by no means certain. Elsewhere on the Continent, the names *ribaudequin* and *ribaude* were in use from *c.* 1340 to describe defensive engines which varied from a simple cart armed with spears to an armored chariot carrying one small cannon (1431) or organs with as many as nine (1476).

After sporadic attempts to perfect the organ gun in many parts of Europe, including a Scottish patent granted to William Drummond in 1626, it saw a brief success in Denmark in the middle of the nineteenth century. There the court gunmaker

A wheeled gun-shield, from a manuscript book of military instruction by R. Meyer, dated 1609; formerly in the Prince of Liechtenstein's library. The hand-gunners walk behind a metal screen which also serves to protect the driver and horse, which pushes the cart.

Nicolaj Johan Løbnitz created an *orgelespingol* with two banks of ten obsolete musket barrels each loaded with fifteen charges which fired in turn. The Danish espingol, combining the characteristics of the organ with the "Roman-candle" effect to deliver 300 shots per minute, saw service against the Prussians at Dybbøl in 1864. One known to have been captured in the assault is preserved in the Museum für deutsche Geschichte, Berlin.

The development of military equipment in the fifteenth and sixteenth centuries was at the same time conservative and international–two traits which have only rarely slipped from the military scene. Almost exactly a century after Žižka's Hussite *Wagenburg*, with its missile-bearing infantry conveyed by and sheltered in war carts, had set such serious problems to the German generals, a spy's report of a similar weapon in the Scottish army facing England was discounted as untrue. Sir William Bulmer wrote that he did not believe the tales he had heard from his spies that among the artillery inspected by James V at Lawdor were carts drawn by barded (i.e. armored) horses and fitted with swords. The next day, on October 20, 1523, he admitted that there might be some truth in the story that the Scottish army had six carts covered with steel and brass, each carrying eight men and "certain guns." Barded horses pushed these carts and were thus protected by them. In Henry's own army there were "prawns" in which a light gun and its crew were protected by a reinforced cone which could be wheeled towards an enemy with the gun protruding from the apex.

The principle of firing a number of shots in a volley from a series of barrels placed together on one stock survived until well after the development of fixed ammunition. In its smallest form, the so-called duck's foot pistol, a number of barrels splay outwards from a single gunstock and action. A late eighteenth-century English example of this form, preserved in the important collection of firearms in Istanbul's Askeri Muzei, has five short barrels fitted to a sporting gun stock and lock. Weapons of this unselective type commended themselves to prison officers, ships' captains facing mutinous crews, and others who might have to quell a number of men singlehanded.

Innsbruck was the home of Maximilian I's main cannon foundry, although he still ruled the southern provinces of the Low Countries where many bronze guns were cast by the master founders Hans Poppenruyter and Remy de Hallut. The painter and architect to Maximilian's court at Innsbruck was Jörg Kölderer, in whose studio part of an illustrated inventory of the contents of Maximilian's arsenals was prepared between

1504 and 1508, the remainder being cataloged from 1515 to 1519 by Wolfgang Reisacher, also a painter in Innsbruck. Between 1507 and 1512, Kölderer produced an illustrated record of some of the imperial artillery on the march. Bronze guns forming the field, fortress and siege trains are drawn by horses harnessed in teams of eight for the massive bombards (*Hauptstücke*) down to a single animal for the little falconet. Carts are loaded with pikes, halberds and less warlike tools. A four-wheeled carriage bears a stamping mill for "mealing" gunpowder.

About the date of the Kölderer drawings, if not slightly earlier, gunners first fired their charges with a piece of smoldering slow match held in a linstock. This allowed them to stand clear of the recoiling gun and the flash from the touchhole. The majority of surviving examples consist of a short haft with a bifurcated head, and a clip of some form at the end of each limb. Many are fitted with a spiked foot which could be stuck into the ground, and some have a vertical spear blade to form a weapon if needed. More ornate linstocks bear the arms of the state or the nobleman who employed the gunner. Others have concealed blades like a brandistock's. They continued in service with very little variation in form as reserves for quicker and more efficient ways of lighting the cannon's charge which came into use at the end of the eighteenth century.

Artillery made very little progress in the reign of Maximilian I, but hand firearms became very much more efficient with the introduction of the wheellock, in which the friction of a moving steel disk struck fire from a piece of pyrites held against its edge. The accidental shooting of a Constance courtesan by a young man from Augsburg suggests that by the first few days of 1515 the new mechanism was already in use. On January 6, Laux Pfister was toying with a loaded gun when it went off, shooting the poor woman through the chin and neck. Pfister's expensive accident – it cost him over a hundred florins at the time and twenty florins a year for the rest of his victim's life – may have been caused by a snaphance lock, but at such an early date a wheellock seems more likely.

Within three years, these self-striking guns were sufficiently common in Styria to cause Maximilian I to address a letter patent to the inhabitants of the archduchy banning their manufacture and use. The embargo, dated November 3, 1517, was primarily aimed at those who might carry concealed arms, as the lighted tow of a matchlock could hardly be hidden under a robber's cloak whereas a primed and coked wheellock could.

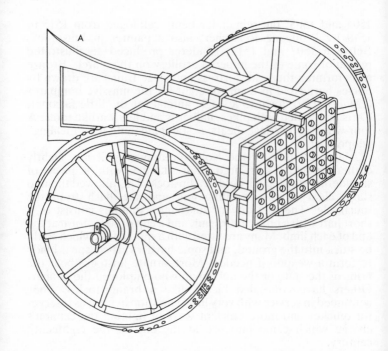

In addition to a fear that wheellock and snaphance guns could form a public danger, Maximilian, "the last of the knights," may have dreamed of stemming the polluting spread of the powder reek that had already begun to sully the brilliant colors of chivalry, which had fewer champions in each successive generation. None of these early wheellock mechanisms survives to confirm the reasoned assumption that they resembled a sketch in Leonardo da Vinci's *Codex Atlanticus*. The drawing probably dates from *c.* 1500 but could be from any time between then and the artist's death in 1519. As is so often the case with the work of Renaissance engineers, it is difficult to say whether the sketch is of a new invention or of something seen by the artist. A lock made to Leonardo's drawing suggests that it was an original design.

One of two sketches of tinder-lighters in a manuscript of 1505, once owned by Martin Löffelholz, a Nuremberg aristocrat, may indicate that Leonardo's design was its original or that the *Codex Atlanticus* and Löffelholz drawings come from the same unidentified source. The opinion that the

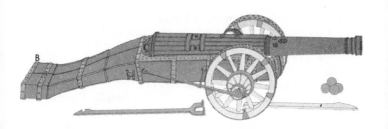

A *An* Orgelgeschütz *(organ-gun) with forty musket-calibre barrels set in five rows of eight, and bound together with iron bands which also form a pivot on the axle. From* Codex 10816 *in the Nationalbibliothek, Austria, first quarter of the sixteenth century.*

B *A field gun, from the inventory of Maximilian I's arsenal at Innsbruck, drawn by Jörg Kölderer, c, 1507.*

original was probably Italian is supported by three crossbows incorporating short wheellock guns in the Palazzo Ducale, Venice. They appear to date from the second decade of the sixteenth century and may therefore be the earliest surviving wheellocks, although the earliest which can be dated at all firmly is a combined wheellock gun and crossbow in the Bayerisches Nationalmuseum, Munich. It was made between 1521 and 1526 for the archduke Ferdinand, later Ferdinand I (1503-64), whose arms it bears, and is probably the work of a Nuremberg master. The earliest dated wheellock was made in Augsburg for Ferdinand's brother, the emperor Charles V, in whose great *Inventario Iluminado* it is illustrated. It is a saddle carbine (*arcabuzillo do arzón*), with Bartholme Marquart's sickle mark on its barrel and the date 1530 on the upper facet of its breech. Like so much of Charles V's arms and armor, it is today in the Real Armería of Madrid's Palacio del Oriente.

The wheellock was supplanted by the flintlock throughout most of the Western world, beyond which it never flourished, by the middle of the seventeenth century, although in Germany and those states which were still under her influence it lingered on for another hundred years, accepted as a weapon for target and game shooting. The majority of these later locks are entirely recessed into the stock with only the squared end of the spindle protruding through the flat lockplate. A freakish survival of the mechanism occurred in France, where so much was done to render it obsolete, in 1829, when Le Page of Paris made a pair of wheellock pistols long after he was deeply involved in the development of magazine percussion arms.

Wheellock arms with rotating chambers are rare, as the fact that they had to be spanned between shots meant that they could never achieve a rate of fire sufficient to justify their weight. Even as it became obsolete, the matchlock was a more efficient method of firing a revolving gun. Before the end of the sixteenth century, the snaphance was fitted to revolving muskets and carbines. The earliest is dated 1597. Most northern European countries seem to have weapons of this type, and examples have survived from Russia, France, Germany and England. The majority of their cylinders had to be rotated by hand, but a pistol in the Tower of London has an advanced mechanism which rotates the cylinder when the action is cocked. However, with the exception of Puckle's guns, all the early designers of revolving guns, and to a lesser extent of pistols, found that the escape of gas between the chambers and the breech was too difficult to tame, and to fire the gun with the lock close to the eye was especially risky. The revolving gun with a single barrel was virtually shelved for two centuries.

A *A wheellock mechanism, ready to fire the inner side, with the mainspring (1) compressed and the pyrites (2) resting on the serrated wheel (3).*

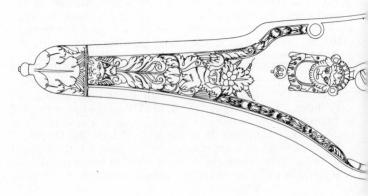

B *A wheellock pistol of a very early form, found in a bog at Komárno, Czechoslovakia, near the Hungarian border. The 11.5-inch (29.2 cm) barrel is engraved with a formalized vine pattern. The short, wooden butt fits into a* *socket formed by an extension of the breech plug. Probably Italian, c. 1530.*

C *A wheellock of very high quality. Franco-German, possibly Lorraine, c. 1620.*

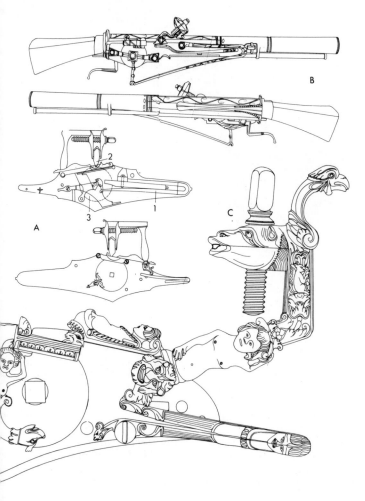

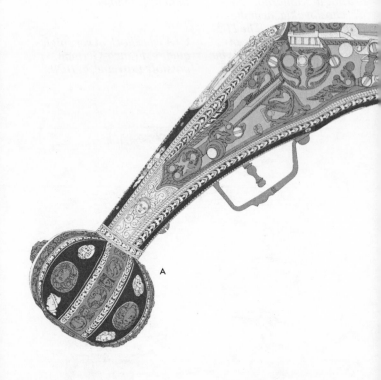

A

A A German wheellock pistol, c. 1580. The stock is veneered with ebony and inlaid with strips of engraved stag antler and mother-of-pearl. The butt is inset with copper gilt strips decorated with birds and masks. The spaces between the strips are decorated with female heads, also copper gilt, and inlaid with masks of mother-of-pearl. Stamped on the lock plate are the marks of the maker Wolf Stopler and the city of Nuremberg.

B A carbine, dated 1533 and inscribed on the stock "HOTTHP" for Herzog Ottheinrich Pfalzgraf, the owner, who was Count

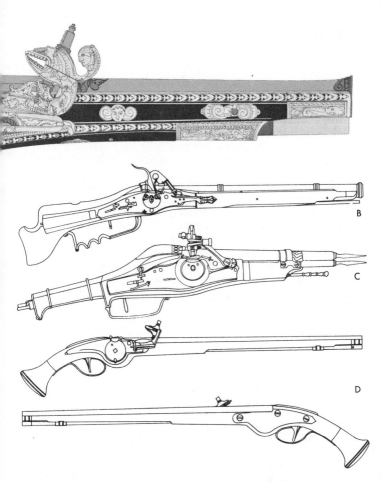

*Palatine of the Rhine
(1502-59).*

*the crowned Pillars of
Hercules. South German,
(Nuremberg?), c. 1540.*

C *A revolving pistol for
shooting darts. The three barrels can be brought in turn
into alignment with the lock.
The wheel cover bears
Charles V's motto* Plus Ultra,
the imperial eagle and device,

D *A pair of pistols with walnut stocks and ivory pom-
mels. The Italian barrels are
signed* LARZARINO
COMINAZZO. *Dutch, mid-
seventeenth century.*

Chapter 8

France began 1515 with a new king. Louis XII, "Father of the People," died on the first day of the new year, leaving his plans for the reconquest of Milan to be completed and executed by his cousin - german, Francis I. Nine months after his succession, on September 10, 1515, Francis led an army of 20,000 pikemen, 10,000 harquebusiers, 2,500 lancers and 70 guns across the Ticino towards Marignano. His intention was to prevent the Swiss under Arnold von Winkelried from joining their allies of the Hispano-papal army at Piacenza, while allowing francis to maintain contact with his own support, 9,000 Venetian foot and horse under Bartolomeo d'Alviano.

On the afternoon of the 11th, 22,000 Swiss infantry with a few horsemen and a handful of guns reached San Donato where they deployed three massive squares in echelon. The first square met skirmishers of Francis's army on the right at about 4 p.m., and soon had these harquebusiers in disorder, failing only by a hair's-breadth to capture the allied artillery before their impetus took them past the first square of German halberds. By the time the Swiss came to the second square of German landsknecht mercenaries their own second square was on their left, and only a charge by Francis and his cavalry checked their advance before darkness forced the armies to disengage. The third Swiss formation had not been in action and remained fresh for the main task on the following day.

A ditch and a hundred paces of open ground separated the two armies during the night truce which allowed Francis to regroup. When the Swiss renewed their onslaught at dawn they moved against a convex crescent. Their main assault, from the intact third square, fell on Francis' left where his artillery was deployed. It carried all before it until 8 a.m., when the mercurial d'Alviano led his Venetian cavalry into the Swiss rear, allowing the allied army time to regroup once more and counterattack with such ferocity that the encircled Swiss square was destroyed. The remains of the two surviving formations retired, to ponder, perhaps, their betrayal by overconfidence and obsolete tactical beliefs, the main factors contributing to their defeat after three centuries of dominance, in "this battle not of men but of giants." The well disciplined men of the Confederation and their leaders had learned, by a costly lesson, the new significance of light cavalry supported by hand firearms and artillery. The myth of Swiss invincibility died with 12,000 pikemen at Marignano. Francis left 6,000 of his own army and 100 of d'Alviano's invaluable cavalry dead by the river.

At Bicocca in 1522, the Marquis di Pescara demonstrated the value of firearms in defense. Sword-and-buckler men could beat down pikes, but they proved inadequate in the face of firearms and cavalry, and it was left to the generals of the first part of the sixteenth century to explore the best tactics against pikes and firearms, for at Marignano the harquebus had offered conclusive proof of its supremacy over the pike alone. Six years later, at Parma, the Spaniards seem to have used the musket for the first time in war. Six feet (1.8 m) long and weighing 15 lb (6.8 kg), it was fired from a fork-shaped rest and threw its ball about 240 yards (*c*. 220 m) with greater killing power than the older lighter harquebuses.

A sunken road traversed the field at Bicocca, and behind it the imperial army was drawn up with the musketeers in four ranks, the pikemen massed in the rear. As the Swiss mercenaries of the French army came within range each rank fired in turn, and the Swiss were decimated and forced to retire. Two years later at Sesia, Pescara's musketeers maneuvered independently in the open, the pikes being relegated to an auxiliary role. At Pavia in 1525, Pescara's musketeers won for the imperial army the most decisive battle of the generation by steady shooting and maneuvering. If he had not already earned the title of "the father of modern infantry," Pescara would most certainly have won it at that battle, for there he initiated modern infantry tactics of fire and movement.

At Pavia, artillery was of little value to either side. However, fire from their musketeers is said to have been decisive not only in delaying the Swiss and thinning the ranks of the French foot, but most of all in the way it disabled the squadrons of men-at-arms once they had split up following their first charge. From the shelter of trees and hedges the musketeers kept up a fire which brought down many horses and men, yet they could not be reached by their opponents' lances and no corresponding force of French light infantry seems to have been launched against them. The main conclusion that can be drawn from this battle is that the importance of firearms was still very much on the increase. It is perhaps worth noting, in the light of what happened at Pavia, that French military opinion had formed a league table of the value they placed on each type of soldier fighting in the armies. First came the Swiss infantry, then the German landsknechts, third the French and Spaniards together and fourth and last the Italians.

At Pavia, the Spanish army was led by the emperor Charles V, an exceptionally able cavalry leader, whose splendid personal armory, perhaps the best ever assembled by one man for his own use, is described in one of the most informative of all armor documents. The watercolor drawings in the *Inventario Iluminado* show the military and tournament arms and armor, clothing and banners kept in the emperor's *cámaras de armas* at Valladolid. Two copies, each of eighty-eight numbered folios, were made about 1548 to identify the arms and armor which had been garnered from many parts of Charles' vast empire. One copy was held by a senior equerry, the other by the armorer responsible for the maintenance of the equipment. But even by the date of the inventory, parts of some of the fifteen garnitures ascribed to the emperor had been mixed with elements of others.

The page of crossbows in the *Inventario* shows that the windlass, far from being rendered obsolete by the handier, more modern cranequin, was still preserved in Charles' armory. Lighter crossbows for arrows or for bullets were bent with the simple, effective lever that Englishmen knew as a "gaffle" from the Spanish *gafa*, a hook. No leather covers for crossbows, which are also shown, have survived from the sixteenth century although they are known from many inventories. Many of the pistols and guns are shown with their cases and the little pouches which held their accessories.

One among the many sporting crossbows which survive from the first years of the sixteenth century was made to shoot round bullets instead of arrows. It is ascribed to Maximilian's daughter, Margaret (1480-1530), and it is painted with the arms of Austria and Burgundy against a red and gold ground. It still uses the turning nut to hold the cord when the bow is spanned, but its integral spanning mechanism represents a transition from the medieval crossbow, bent by hand or with one of the detachable mechanisms of gaffle, windlass or cranequin, to more sophisticated weapons.

Obviously the path of the bullet or the arrow along the central line of the stock makes a simple peg from sight impracticable on crossbows. On those used to shoot arrows the upper angle of the quadrangular head, or a small peg set on the arrow, is enough for a front sight, but when a round ball is shot from a pouch at the center of a double cord, the front sight was formed of two vertical pegs. A wire rod stretched between the pegs carried a bead which could be moved horizontally to adjust the point of aim. The rear sight of most bullet crossbows is a vertical plate pierced with a series of peepholes. A notable exception is the Franco-Italian form which has a high metal

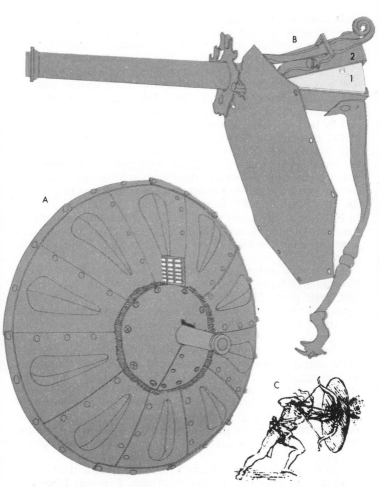

A *A shield with a breechloading matchlock pistol, from the arsenal of Henry VIII, probably made in the workshop of Giovanbattista of Ravenna, c. 1544-47.*

B *The barrel, breech and handle from a gun-shield. A separate chamber is loaded into the breech at (**1**) and held in position by the hinged and spring-loaded bracket (**2**) until fired by a matchlock.*

C *An archer shoots a bow fitted with a protective shield. After a study by Leonardo da Vinci.*

arch, notched at its apex, set above the action. There is an interesting parallel between the very simple mechanism used in these deep-bellied stocks and the detailed sketches that accompany Leonardo's drawing of a giant crossbow.

In sixteenth-century Germany, the bullet crossbow (*Schnepper*) was especially popular in a steel-stocked version with an angular wooden cheek-butt. Two late examples signed by Christian Trincks, a Dresden maker who moved to Strasbourg shortly before 1710 and was listed in the *protocoles corporatifs* of the gunmakers' company between 1714 and 1732, have a detachable slide between the foresight pillars so that arrows can be shot as an alternative to bullets. Although the evidence of a direct connection is lacking, the German *Schnepper* seems to have inspired the bullet crossbow made in northwest England in the eighteenth and nineteenth centuries.

In England an inventory taken in 1547, within a few months of the death of King Henry VIII, lists vast quantities of armor and arms owned by the king for his personal use and for issue to his army and navy.

Among the ordnance stores in the Tower of London were thousands of bows, bowstrings and sheaves of arrows, cannon with their projectiles, richly gilt hafted arms and many other types of weapons. At Westminster were swords with scabbards of leather and velvet, horse harness, breechloading handguns, gilt spurs and others of silver, and longbows with pouches on their strings for shooting bullets instead of arrows. The richness of the accumulation can be imagined from such brief references as *Targetts of Stele fringed w2t Redde silke and golde and lyned w2t vellet-vj*, and *one horne for Gonnepowder garnished with silver and guilte*. Even among such splendor, pride of place must surely have gone to the magnificent armor for horse and man referred to in the previous chapter, which was made for Henry by Italians who had been brought to England to work for the king.

At Greenwich, where Henry VIII had established an armor workshop in 1515, the master workman, Erasmus Kirchner, continued to care for several armors made for his late king together with a mass of other fine arms and armor. Of the many sporting guns listed at Greenwich and Henry's other storehouses, two have been preserved in the Armouries, with four of the king's personal armors, including the Vreland suit, and a series of the shields incorporating matchlock guns, which were probably made by Giovanbattista and his company at Ravenna *c.* 1544-47. These *Targetts steilde w2t gonnes* are the logical, if hardly practical, development from the longbows with shields that Leonardo drew in his sketchbooks, and the

A landsknecht loads his matchlock musket. A bandolier of powder charges and a powder flask are slung across his chest. After a woodcut by Niclas Meldeman, which wrongly shows the lock on the left of the stock. German, Nuremberg, c. 1530.

composite bows with shields that are described in some medieval Arabic manuscripts.

The 1547 inventory lists military stores kept at the Tower, including some taken at Flodden Field in 1513, when the chronicler Hall says that the Scots lost *5 great curtalls, 2 great culverynges, 4 sacres and 5 serpentynes, as fayre ordnance as hathe bene, beside other smal peces.* The iron guns listed formed only a tiny part of the total in the kingdom, for many guns were cast abroad, and throughout Henry's reign English gunfounders and the men brought to the kingdom from the Continent were amassing artillery *matériel* in the forts and bulwarks around the coast. Just as he founded armor workshops at Southwark and Greenwich and staffed them with foreign armorers, the king brought Peter Baude from France, Arcanus de Arcanis from Cesena in Italy, the Piedmontese Bernadin de Valois, and others who not only cast the guns but are believed to have taught the native craftsmen their skills. Many of these guns have been preserved in the Tower of London since Henry's death, though others were destroyed in a fire in 1841.

Artillery, using the word in the strictly modern sense of cannon and mortars, used by the armies of England, came from many towns on the continent of Europe, among them Tournai, Nuremberg and Malines, the home of Hans Poppenruyter.

Other towns, which cannot now be found even in minor gazetteers, also produced bronze guns for Henry VIII. A culverin cast at Fuenterrabia in the spring of 1518 has doubtless long since returned to the crucible, but an account of the costs incurred when it was cast under the eye of a Bristol merchant, Thomas Badcock, shows the part played by unskilled female labor. Women were employed to dig the pit in which the mold was cast, to carry the wood to melt the bronze (the remains of an earlier gun which had failed its proof firing), to dig out the cooled gun and to drag it to the nearby castle where it was proved. For this they were paid and fed on cherries, bread, cider and wine. The major charges were of course for the wages of the specialists. The barrel was cast around a core built onto an iron rod made by the smith Savadyng de Varte. When the core was withdrawn it left a hollow gun barrel which required only to be straightened and polished inside with borers which de Varte also made from 16 lb (7.3 kg) of iron supplied by Badcock. The mold was prepared by "The king's fondidor," known only as Jacobo, who also modeled the royal arms "and other conceits" in wax as part of a process which was almost exactly as Diderot described two centuries later.

An account of Henry VIII's artillery train, by no means the biggest in Europe, was taken in September 1523 by its keeper Geoffrey Hughes. There were seventy-four cannon in the Tower of London. The gunners responsible for seven massive bronze bombards, each drawn by twenty-four horses, down to those in charge of little falconets were paid according to the importance of their pieces: two shillings a day for the bombards, from which 80 lb (36.3 kg) of powder shot a 250 lb (113.4 kg) ball, down to eight pence a day for the falconets.

The destruction wrought by the heavier guns in siege warfare was immense when one remembers that they shot stone or iron balls, not high-explosive shells. Against the walls of Bray in October 1523, during Henry's adventures in France, his gunners took only two hours, from 4 till 6 a.m., to breach "a gap as broad as a cart." A week later at Montdidier, the great ordnance was laid a mere 40 feet (c. 12 m) from the walls. Four volleys brought down a length of wall "hard by the myghtie strong bulwerke, the strongest that evyr I saw."

The smaller caliber cannon, for use against men and horses, were extremely effective when fired into bodies of infantry, which were still massed shoulder to shoulder as the Spartans and the Thespians who died at Thermopylae. In proportion to the few handguns in the list prepared by Hughes, thirty only, other weapons seem still to have dominated Henry's military thinking, or else the supply had not yet been able to meet the demand. Seventeen thousand bows and bowstaves, fourteen thousand bills and bill heads, which were later to be fitted to ash helves at one penny each, and eight thousand morrispikes were the most numerous weapons in the Tower in 1523, making a list of arms that seem antiquated when compared to those of Francis I's nine thousand harquebusiers, routed at Pavia a couple of years later.

Henry VIII's divorce from Catherine of Aragon led to his excommunication by Pope Paul III, who then preached a crusade which he hoped would bring England back into the papal fold, after invasion by the combined forces of Charles V and Francis I. Among Henry's countermeasures was a program of fortification unequaled in England from the departure of Rome's legions until 1939. Much of the revenue from the recently dissolved monasteries and even some of their actual stones went towards the costs of these new forts, which were built to take account of cannon. These were not the first English fortifications designed to resist gunpowder (the first were at Dartmouth), but they were among the earliest anywhere to escape from the architectural conventions of the medieval military engineer.

Chapter 9

In 1598, when Paul Hentzner visited the Tower of London, he remarked on the ordnance, among them some very large guns from Henry's reign. Like ships and forts, these monsters made heavier calls on capital for tools and materials than did the old-style handicraft worker. The development of heavy cannon in the fifteenth and sixteenth centuries and the consequent consumption of iron, wood, coal and human skills, brought new demands on the mines, the forests and the workshops of Europe. With these came a need for finance, which forced even emperors and kings to resort to the moneylenders. They in turn took over royal mines as security for the loans without which wars of defense or expansion could not be fought. Power was forged out of the interdependence of war, finance and mining, now mechanized beyond any previous needs. But mining had become the key industry whose uncertainty, like that of warfare itself, increased the possibility of speculative gain. Not only iron, copper, zinc and tin came from the earth, but also saltpeter and sulfur for gunpowder. The forester's axe gave not only the wood for gun carriages and ramrods, but also the charcoal to heat the blacksmith's forge and the founder's furnace.

The products were self-consuming, since the mining and metalworking operations themselves needed raw materials for their development. In the sixteenth century, Bauer described the convenience of water power in pumping out mine shafts. Underground it could replace the power of horses or man's own puny efforts. The fifteenth century had seen the introduction of watermills to crush ore. They also worked the huge bellows that were needed to increase the quantities of ore to be reduced to workable iron. A century earlier, waterwheels powered the hammers in an ironworks near Dobrilugk, Lausitz, in Germany; they lightened the work of the sawyers in at least one Augsburg mill, and turned grindstones in many cities. About 1350, Nuremberg metalworkers saw Rudolph's wiredrawing machine operated by the same power. These were all important, but the use of water power in the mines and the forges made perhaps the most immediate impact on the development of weapons that occurred during the later Middle Ages.

The most famous European treatise on archery, *Toxophilus*,

was published in London in 1545, too late to have much effect on war or hunting although it is still almost required reading for serious archers. Its author, Roger Ascham (1515-68), was Queen Elizabeth's tutor. He wrote first of archery as a recreation and then as an instrument of war. In the second part of his book he told how a man could become expert with this difficult weapon.

In his discussion of equipment he began with the bracer and the shooting glove. The bracer protected the left wrist from the string's smack, saved the wearer's sleeve from wear, and ensured that the string had a smooth passage over the last few inches of its travel. Ascham suggested no specific material for the bracer–examples are known made of different sorts of stone, ivory, horn, bone, wood, leather, gold and other metals–but stressed that buckles and straps should be fitted so that they could not catch the string. He was more definite about the materials for the shooting glove, which should be of leather, lined with the rich fabric called *scarlet*. Strings should be of good hemp, flax or silk, the materials not being important so long as they were well made and of the correct thickness and length for the bow.

The use of the gunner's quadrant. The muzzle of the gun was raised until the plumb line showed the correct elevation for the range required. For maximum elevation, the gun-carriage trail was lowered into a hole. From Niccoló Tartaglia, Three bookes of Colloquies. ... *(London, 1588).*

Good classicist that he was, Ascham knew the bows of antiquity and their materials, but to him only yew was suitable. The satisfactory bowstave was slender, long, heavy, strong and straight without knot, gall or windshake. It was the same color throughout and straight-grained. Although a generation earlier the law of England required all bowyers to make two bows of elm or some other inexpensive wood for every one of yew–a statute ordering subjects between seven and sixty years to practice with the bow created an immense demand–these "mean" bows were beneath Ascham's notice. He did not presume to teach the bowyers their craft, beyond suggesting that they should see that staves were seasoned before they began the process of manufacture. When carefully wax polished a good bow was fit to be kept in a cover of best wool within a leather or wooden case.

The width of his knowledge adds point to Ascham's account of the woods used for arrows in the sixteenth century. He names fifteen as suitable for the steles, or shafts, ranging from the exotic red brazilwood to the humble, if more effective, ash. But as the bow's efficiency and quality were governed by the craft of the bowyer, so the arrow depended on the fletcher, whose skill in selecting and combining wood, feathers and steel head was paramount. To Ascham, goose feathers were best; stiff, from an old bird, for the heavy arrow and more pliable, from a younger bird, for the swift flight arrow.

In Ascham's day, arrowheads were made in five types: the broadhead, the forkhead, the bodkin, the birdbolt and the simple, relatively blunt, target head. He discarded the first two as less effective in war than the bodkin, which, with its stiff straight point, was lighter and so flew straighter with a lower trajectory, and had no unsettling aerodynamic effects. Against mail, brigandines or even plate armor it achieved better penetration than any other type. A fact which probably did not escape Ascham is the psychological difference between shooting an arrow into a man and into a beast. The sight of an arrow sticking deeply into his body is enough to incapacitate most men, but only loss of blood, some severe damage to its body or death will stop an animal. Against big game or an unarmored enemy this effect is best achieved by the barbed broadhead, whose wide cutting edges produce the greatest slashes. For smaller game the forkhead and its close relative, the crescent, with forward curved wings, were popular. The blunt bird-bolt with a heavy stunning head was used for centuries against small birds and ground game, whose flesh could be too badly damaged by the slash of an edged arrow. Blunts are still used today for shooting at the popinjay.

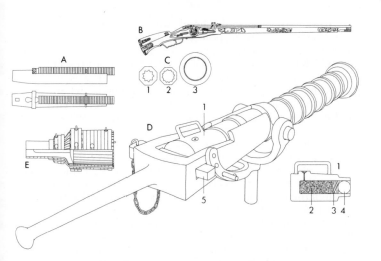

A *A gun composed of wrought-iron hoops and staves welded together. It was fastened to a heavy oak bed. Recovered in 1836 from Henry VIII's ship* Mary Rose, *which sank near Spithead in 1545 when maneuvering against the French fleet.*

B *A wheellock rifle carried by the bodyguard of Christian II of Saxony, the barrel dated 1598. The wood of the stock has been stained dark brown and inlaid with engraved bone.*

C *Styles of rifling found in seventeenth- and eighteenth-century barrels. (1) "Star" rifling in a so-called "Holstein" gun which has the mark ascribed to Balthasar Dressler and dated 1609. (2) "Twelve-groove" rifling in a* weapon dated 1634. (3) *"Microgroove" rifling in a heavy Polish rifle, c. 1740.*

D *A wrought-iron breech-loading cannon, for use from the parapet of a fortification or from the gunwale of a ship. The gun could be reloaded quickly by using separate, pre-charged chambers which would be locked in alignment with the barrel by a transverse iron peg. (1) Chamber. (2) Powder. (3) Thick wad. (4) Ball. (5) Peg.*

E *A medieval bombard (Steinbüchse), known as* Der grosse Pumbart von Steyr. *It was constructed of rings and staves of wrought iron. The gun, which weighs about 9.9 tons, could throw a stone ball of 34.6 inches (88 cm). Probably Austrian, c. 1425.*

Arrows with very similar heads were used by crossbowmen. If their crossbows were powerful, the heads were often very much bigger and heavier than a longbowman could use. One type which the latter never shot was the very large crescent head used to sever ships' rigging. By contrast, it was also the projectile shot from spring traps in Scandinavia, where some with horns spanning more than eleven inches (*c.* 30 cm) were used in the seventeenth century. The typical crossbow arrow used in war was fitted with a head formed by a short socket with heavy quadrangular tip. The name quarrel for this type seems to derive through the medieval Latin *quadrellus* (diminutive of *quadrus*, a square). The crossbow arrow of the Middle Ages and the Renaissance was always short and stiff, without a nock, although the butt end was sometimes strengthened with a bone or horn plaque. As its fletchings were necessarily much stiffer than those of a longbow arrow, feathers were rarely used. Slivers of wood, leather and even brass were set on at a slight angle to give the rotation in flight which, at a very early stage in the development of projectile-throwing weapons, had been found to make the flight of an arrow or spear much truer.

The theory of rotational stabilization to make projectiles more accurate was known to the makers of arrows for many centuries before it was first introduced to firearms. There are several traditional accounts of the time and place where a gunsmith first made a rifled gunbarrel, that is, cut a series of spiral grooves (refling) into the bore of a gun to make the bullet spin in flight. All that can be said with any certainty about the first rifled gun is that it was probably made around the close of the fifteenth century. A number survive from the second half of the sixteenth century, most for civilian use against animals.

Among the European rulers who experimented with early issues of rifles to their armies were the Landgrave of Hesse and Louis XIII, himself an avid gun collector, but none seems to have seen sufficient advantage in the rifle's accuracy to encourage its general military use. This had to wait until the nineteenth century. However, sporting rifles were often used before then for sniping, just as in the world wars most armies issued especially accurate rifles to frontline troops trained in the sniper's craft. It was certainly many years after the discovery of rifling that it presented any challenge in warfare to the clumsy, inaccurate, smoothbore musket, or the fast-shooting accurate bow in the hands of a skilled archer.

In 1545, the year when Ascham presented a copy of his book to Henry VIII at Greenwich Palace, the king's ship *Mary Rose* sank near Spithead. This unfortunate event has, however,

Niccoló Tartaglia (c. 1506-59), from the title page of his Quesiti et Inventioni Diverse *(1546). Born at Brescia, Italy, he was a lecturer at Verona before becoming professor of mathematics at Venice.*

provided evidence of the size and strength of the war bow of the day, for among the ship's armament were a number of bowstaves, recovered from the wreck by divers in 1836. The bowstaves' age precludes a test of their draw weight, but they would appear to need about 100 lb (45.4 kg) to pull them to full draw. In 1574, thousands of bowstaves from the yews that grew in and around the bishopric of Salzburg reached northern Europe by way of the Rhine and the Main. They were sold in London's Stillyard by Nuremberg merchants for %15 to %16 the hundred. Cheaper bowstaves came from Switzerland, Poland and Italy. These were thought by some to be "the principall finest and steadfastest woods by reason of the heate of the sun, which dried up the humiditie and moisture of the sappe." Some bows made for Henry VIII's army were marked with a rose and crown. Elsewhere, the cities where they were produced sometimes insisted on their bows being marked. At Cambrai for example, they were stamped with an eagle, at Lille painted with the town arms.

In addition to the individual weapons of her crew, the main

armament carried by the *Mary Rose* consisted of built-up iron breechloading guns mounted on timber beds. One in the Tower which retains its chamber still has a stone shot of approximately 5.5 inches (14 cm) lodged in the bore near the breech. Two lifting eyes are forged on one of its hoops. A group of guns of this type in the Tøjhusmuseum was salvaged from a wreck, thought to be of *c.* 1400, found near the island of Anholt in the Kattegat. They vary in length from 61 to 95 inches (154.9 to 241.3 cm) and fired balls of 2.3 to 7 inches (5.8 to 17.8 cm). The guns are strapped to wooden baulks. Their chambers were locked in position by a transverse iron bar during firing. Smaller guns, port-pieces or bases, were used from the fifteenth century for close-quarter fighting, shooting a charge of bullets or pieces of metal which spread like a modern shotgun charge. They often had trunnions on one of the barrel hoops. These swiveled in the loops of a spigoted pivot which pegged into a vertical hole in a ship's bulwarks or the walls of a fort.

One writer of the highest significance was Niccoló Tartaglia, who had claims to fame as the first important Italian writer on fortification, and as one of the first to enquire into the movement of projectiles. He was probably the inventor of the gunner's quadrant used to set the angle of elevation and thus the range. Perhaps more important than any of these was his attitude to science in relation to war, for Tartaglia, whose surname was derived from his childhood speech impediment (*tartagliare* = to stammer), was possibly the first scientist with a conscience. About 1531 he was asked what elevation a gun should be given for maximum range, a question that was the seed from which grew a whole crop of discoveries and hypotheses. However, as Tartaglia felt that there was something inherently evil in the furthering of a craft whose end was the destruction of human life, he scrapped the results of his calculations and researchers. But a threat to religious faith or homeland has often amended a scientist's moral view. For Tartaglia, the self-taught son of a Brescian letter-carrier, the rumor of the impending attack on Christendom by Suleiman I was catalyst enough. His findings were hurriedly redrafted and appeared in print in 1537 under the title of *Nuova Scientia*.

His "New Science" brought further enquiries from military leaders of the day, inspiring in turn his *Quesiti el Inventioni Diverse*, published in 1546 with a dedication to Henry VIII of England. Six of the nine sections which made up these "question and inventions" dealt with military matters and remained of sufficient interest to earn publication in English in the year when England was threatened by the Spanish Armada.

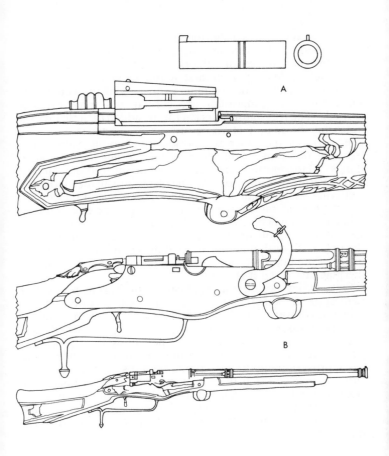

A The breech, shown with a reconstructed chamber, of a breechloading wheellock gun (the lock is missing), described in a seventeenth-century inventory as "King Henry Eights fowling piece." The gun was more probably used by the king for target-shooting.

B The breech of another of Henry VIII's breechloading firearms, a fowling piece, with a matchlock fitted at a later date. The lock has been removed in the illustration under, which shows the 26-inch (66 cm) long barrel, marked with the royal initials HR and the date 1537.

This 1588 edition was a shortened version containing only the "Three bookes of Colloquies concerning the arte of shooting in great and small peeces of artillerie, variable randges, measure, and waight of leaden, yron, and marble stone pellets, mineral saltepeeter, gunpowder of diuers sortes, and the cause why some sortes of gunpowder are corned and some are not corned." The translator, Cyprian Lucar, added to these his own notes on the manufacture of fireworks, gunpowder, match, gun-carriages and other accessories; on shooting cannon and mortars; on architectural drawing and "other commendable things." He omitted Tartaglia's comments on the tactical maneuvering of armies, on drawing plans, and on the method of fortifying a city. Some of Tartaglia's ideas ranged far beyond the theories of his contemporaries, others may have seemed ridiculous even in his own time. For example he asserts that the second of two shots fired from a cannon will carry further than the first as "it doth find the air not only wholly stirred with the pellet of the first shot, but also much tending or going towards the place to which it is shot."

Sixty years before the publication of Tartaglia's papers Leonardo da Vinci had enunciated some theories on the principles of trajectory, but the calculations seem to have bored him and it was left to Tartaglia to father the science of ballistics. Unfortunately, as Tartaglia was not himself a practicing gunner, he was unable to give his theories the tests which would have proved them to his contemporaries. Until Tartaglia, gunners believed that their projectiles flew in a straight line after they left the barrel, but Tartaglia saw that a "piece of artillery cannot shoot one pace in a straight line" and expounded the truth that the higher the velocity of a projectile the flatter the trajectory.

The first forty years of the sixteenth century, the age of Erasmus and Luther, of Michelangelo, Holbein and Rabelais, saw numerous developments in the technology of killing. Maximilian issued his edict against the wheellock in 1517 and the weapon was banned by the duke of Ferrara in 1522, but these and other similar prohibitions did little to slow arms development. In 1529, a repeating gun shown in a German book of fireworks was loaded with alternate charges of powder and bullets (*Klotzen:* hence *Klotzbüchse* for the type) which were drilled and filled with gunpowder. When the charge nearest the muzzle was ignited, the flame of the discharge also passed backwards through the succeeding ball to fire its charge, and so on till the ball nearest the breech was discharged. This "Roman-candle" effect was a rapidfire development of the form, shown in a manuscript of a century before, in which the projectiles filled the barrel and each charge had its own touchhole. In England, patents continued to be granted for multi-shot, single-barreled, muzzle-loading firearms for another century and more. A revival of the principle was used by the American forces during the war of 1812, when a repeating gun designed by Joseph G. Chambers was ordered for the United States Navy and the Commonwealth of Pennsylvania, Chambers' home state. As well as 850 muskets, rifles and pistols, none of which has survived, a few swivel guns were made. A total of 224 shots could be fired from their seven barrels.

These attempts to increase the rate of fire did not achieve the acceptance that was accorded the breechloading gun, which used a separate chamber. Among the most famous survivors, and perhaps the earliest, are two guns in the Tower Armouries, relics of King Henry VIII's personal gunrooms. Henry's guns, which have lost their locks, are similar in many ways to breechloading guns in Leonardo's *Codex Atlanticus* but their chambers are differently secured. The loader opened a hinged lid above the breech to insert an iron chamber loaded with powder and ball. One gun bears the king's monogram and the

Handgunners shooting at birds. From Tartaglia, Three bookes of Colloquies. ...

date 1537 on its barrel. A mark on its breech may indicate that it was made by William Hunt, Keeper of the King's Handguns and Demi-hawks from 1538, a year when he also worked on Henry's artillery. The butt of the smaller of the two guns was covered with velvet like so many of the weapons listed in the 1547 inventory, where guns of this type are referred to as *chamber peces*.

A new weapon name, pistol, was first used about this time. The first true pistols were made in the previous decade, although some of the little handguns of the fifteenth century could be fired when held in one hand, and in Bohemia the word *pist'ala* (a *pipe* or *whistle*) was used to describe a short, light gun. These early pistols either have a very narrow butt that follows the line of the barrel or else they look like the contemporary sporting guns. Some are indented for the fingers, others have spirally carved butts, both types terminating in a swelling to give a secure grip. All but one of the survivors have wheellock ignition, the exception being a matchlock pistol with three revolving barrels, probably the *schioppo da serpa con tre cane* listed in an inventory of 1548, and now in the Palazzo Ducale, Venice.

A year before the inventory was taken, the first flintlocks are referred to in Florence and in Sweden. The snapping movement when the sear is released to allow the flint to strike the steel gave rise to the name *snapplås (snaplock)* by which the mechanism was known in Sweden, and it is there that the earliest flintlocks are found. A musket with a Nuremberg barrel in the Livrustkammare, Stockholm, is probably the only survivor of thirty-five fitted with snaplocks at Arboga in 1556. Locks of this type continued in use for almost three hundred years in the Scandinavian states and in the western regions of what is now the U.S.S.R. In turn, many of the improvements which were applied to the other varieties of European locks were also used on this northern form, but the basic design retained its long curved cock until the end of the flintlock era.

Almost every improvement in firearms mechanism made around the middle of the sixteenth century was intended to make game shooting more successful, and so more pleasant for the aristocracy and their guests. One device was the set-trigger, which was fitted to a sporting weapon to increase the precision of its discharge. There is considerable tension on the nut of a crossbow or the sear of a wheellock when the weapon is cocked, and a heavy trigger pressure is required to release it unless some mechanical aid is interposed. As the pressure can disturb the aim, an independent mechanism to make it lighter was developed about 1540. In the simplest design, a hammer is

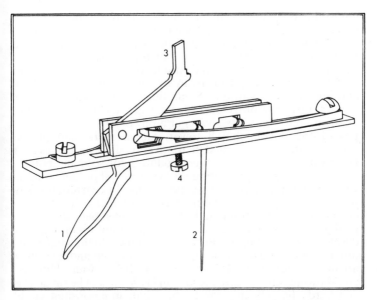

A set-trigger allows the release of the action with the minimum of disturbance. Pressure on the rear trigger (1) compresses the spring of a link between the sear and the slender front trigger (2).

When the front trigger is lightly touched, the sear is knocked free by a vertically operating hammer (3). The release pressure can be adjusted through the screw (4).

pulled back against the action of a strong spring until it is held by a catch which itself moves under the impetus of a second spring. When the catch is withdrawn the hammer is released to strike the gunlock or the crossbow trigger. In a variety of forms, some extremely complex, the set-trigger has continued in use until today for game rifles, and for target shooting in some countries with ancient traditions such as are found in the Swiss and German *Schützenfest*.

The formal *Schützenfest*, using guns, was being shot to strict rules on standard targets by the end of the fifteenth century, and several European cities claim that their shooting clubs are directly descended from medieval companies of citizens assembled to man the city walls. The trophies and insignia of societies with long uninterrupted histories often record the names of their prizewinners and officers, and collars of finest goldsmith work are frequently hung with tiny replicas of the society's weapons, its heraldry and its targets.

The commonest target represented in these collars is the popinjay, a wooden bird set on a high pole. Achilles' archers shot at a white dove tied to the masthead, and a live or modeled bird has made a target for many exacting crossbow, longbow and firearms competitions. Some Belgian crossbow clubs still shoot at tiny brass birds set 164 feet (50 m) high on a perch. One Scottish archery society shoots at a pigeon-sized target at the top of the parish church tower. Saxon marksmen of the seventeenth century earned their prizes by shooting pieces off a large wooden eagle, each piece counting for so many points.

The tradition of presenting the winner of shooting contests with a small replica of the weapon he used occurred in many parts of Europe. At a shoot at Holborn Fields in 1583 the citizens of London competed amid the richest pageantry for a gold gun worth three pounds, "to be given unto him that best deserve it by shooting in a Peece at the Mark." In the same year, other London archers shot for five bows of gold and five silver arrows. After the Restoration, in 1661, four hundred crossbowmen shot before the king in Hyde Park. The range was 480 yards (c. 439 m), far farther than longbowmen could manage. The crossbowmen also released showers of whistling arrows–an exercise, it was said, that charmed three infantry regiments into laying down their arms to watch. Almost every one of these shoots had the same prime purpose, to keep the populace interested in shooting, practiced with their arms and so ready to defend their country, their city or even their village.

Although the small hand-thrown explosive projectiles known as grenades were used in the early sixteenth century, notably at the siege of Arles in 1536, it was not until some sixty years later that they were shot from a hand-held gun. The hand-mortar was introduced to give the grenadier greater range than he could reach by throwing. An example of c. 1590 in the British Museum bears its maker's mark and the city stamp of Nuremberg on its wheellock. The bronze barrel, with a constricted powder chamber, has the characteristically stubby form that continued for centuries. Its stock, like those of most others of the type, is based on the contemporary sporting gunstock, and looks almost too slender to bear the recoil from a charge of powder sufficient to throw the two-inch (c. 5 cm) diameter grenade. Another similar hand-mortar in the Armeria Reale, Turin, has a forked rest to prop the weapon on the ground, on a rampart or even on a horseman's saddle. The short grenade mortar remained a standard arm in some armies until

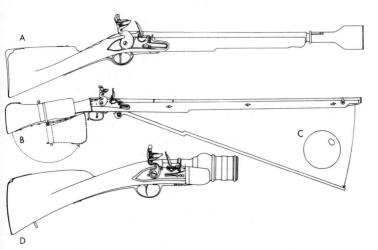

A *An English mortar-carbine, dated 1747.*

B *An English musket and hand-mortar, probably designed and made by John Tinker, in 1681. The butt hinges open at the end of a hollow "barrel" to take the grenade.*

C *A cast-iron grenade to be thrown, or fired from a hand-mortar.*

D *The most typical form of hand-mortar, with a stubby brass barrel, the lock engraved JOURSON. French, mid-eighteenth century.*

E *British infantrymen firing grenades from the discharger-cup of a Short Magazine Lee-Enfield Rifle, Mark I.*

95

the middle of the seventeenth century. Between 1657 and 1660, in their wars against the Danes, Swedish infantry shot small grenades fitted with hollow rods filled with an incendiary compound which served as a fuse. The rod fitted the musket barrel and, in theory, the time taken by the fuse to burn after it was lit corresponded to the grenade's time of flight. It was not at all unusual for the fuse to burn too fast, with disastrous results to the firer.

A little later John Tinker, a fireworker in Britain's Office of the Ordnance, invented a "new way of shooting Handgrana-does out of a small mortar-peece." This was in 1681. Two of fifty, made at a cost of £5.10.0 each in 1685, are probably amont the arms preserved in the Tower Armouries, although they cannot be certainly identified. Their flintlocks are engraved with the royal cipher of King James II (1685-88), and are designed to fire either a musket ball from the barrel or a grenade from a chambered cup that forms the root of the butt. To fire the grenade, the hinged wooden end of the butt is opened to reveal the cup, which is then loaded like any other mortar. When a shutter between the cup and the flash-pan is raised and the action fired, the mortar is discharged. Another form of grenade launcher, illustrated by Surirey de Saint Remy, looks like the infantry mortar of the Second World War, but has a short, cupped barrel set on a tubular spike with a second spike as a prop.

Muskets and carbines using a detachable cup for grenade firing were in use by the third decade of the eighteenth century. The cup was fitted by a screw thread, a spring catch or an L-shaped slot engaging a stud on the barrel such as attached the contemporary bayonet. The British Army used cups of about 2.6 inches (6.6 cm), between 1728 and 1747, a period when designers reverted to the sixteenth-century type in which the mortar-cup is mounted on a short, thick gunstock fitted with a flintlock. The important group in the Bernisches Historisches Museum has the front of each lock tilted downwards to bring the pan in line with the touchhole, but a bronze two-inch (c. 5 cm) diameter mortar by Jourson (of Rennes?) and a steel-cupped three-inch (7.6 cm) example by John Hall of London, both of c. 1740, have their locks set level as in the standard musket.

A French series of *grenadiers* dated 1747 is engraved with the French royal arms and those of the Comte d'Eu (1701-75), Grand Maî d'Artillerie. Their long, banana-shaped butts have a spike at the lower end which was stuck in the ground when the firer had the stock tucked under his right arm. He then gripped a pivoted handle with his left hand, while with his right

A *Reamers, for drilling out and polishing the bores of cannons, had bits which can be likened to the heads of jousting lances. The machine in the upper right of the illustration is manually operated, while that in the foreground is a more sophisticated water-powered version incorporating a sled on which the cast barrel is drawn onto the reamer.*

B *A simple cogwheel allowed two reamers to be driven simultaneously. Both illustrations are from Vannuccio Biringuccio,* Pirotechnia, *1558 edition.*

he fired the grenade which was fitted with a wooden tompion (*ensabotée*).

Most grenade launchers of the sixteenth and seventeenth centuries had a fault in common. Once the fuse of the grenade was lit, a misfire in the musket lock could cause a serious accident. It was presumably this danger that caused the Council of Maryland to comment in 1694 that although the hand-mortars sent out from Britain were "good of the sort," they would prefer some in which the fire from the charge would light the fuse. Perhaps they had heard of the Swedish rodded grenades of 1657-60. Presumably this danger of grenades bursting in their cups was the main cause of their falling from favor about 1750.

The Russo-Japanese War saw the renaissance of the grenade launcher, when the Japanese adopted Marten Hale's grenade. A rodded version was fired from rifle dischargers, and the development of efficient, reliable time fuses and igniters led to a revival of interest in the discharger and to its worldwide use in the early twentieth century.

The grenade fired from a muzzle cup followed the style the Swedish used in the seventeenth century. A steel rod screwed into the base of the grenade was a sliding fit in the bore of the rifle; the grenade was fired by means of a blank cartridge. Various rod lengths were used, those in the British service being from 6 to 7.5 inches (15.2 to 19.1 cm). Rodded grenades had several disadvantages and their use was discontinued by the German army at the beginning of 1917, when special mortar-like devices designed to throw grenades were in full production.

In 1540 a Venetian, Venturino Roffinello, printed the first book to encompass all metallurgy as it was then known: *Pirotechnia*. Its author was a mine manager and metal founder from Sienna, Vannoccio Vincenzio Austino Luca Biringuccio (1480-*c*. 1538). While Biringuccio traveled around Italy learning his craft, a number of relevant books appeared in Germany and other countries. They contained little that would be new to such a practical man, who could claim that he wrote of nothing that he had not seen with his own eyes, often in his own foundries. He experimented to produce, among other things, well-proportioned cannon designed so that no part was too light for safety or too heavy to move easily. In this context his motto was "Weigh everything and trust no man." His book appeared in nine editions, was badly translated into French, Latin and English and was widely plagiarized in Spain and Germany. Of its ten books, numbers VI, VII and X are of special interest to

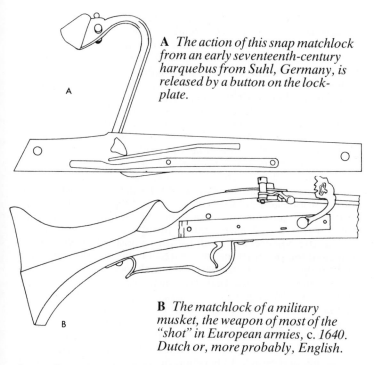

A *The action of this snap matchlock from an early seventeenth-century harquebus from Suhl, Germany, is released by a button on the lock-plate.*

B *The matchlock of a military musket, the weapon of most of the "shot" in European armies, c. 1640. Dutch or, more probably, English.*

the student of arms. They refer only to gunpowder weapons and reflect Italian military attitudes of the day. There were still no standard sizes for guns although founders were beginning to show some consistency in the thickness of the cannons' walls and in the relationship between caliber, i.e. bore diameter, and length, for the barrel had to be long enough to allow all the powder to burn before the ball left the muzzle. Iron balls, which could be more accurately formed, were fast replacing stone, allowing the gunner to shoot with greater power and accuracy. The guns known to Biringuccio as *smerigli* and *moschetti* (merlins and muskets) were achieving some popularity with captains of infantry, as their iron and lead balls of 1 to 2 lb (.45 to .91 kg) were dangerous at long ranges, yet the weapons could be fired quickly by one man.

Harquebuses and pistols shooting a ball of an ounce (28 gr) or so were also coming into common use to usurp the place of mounted and infantry crossbowmen of earlier days. Mortars, on the other hand, were no longer appreciated by Biringuccio and his Italian contemporaries, *gli moderni*, although elsewhere they remained in service from their invention to the present day with only occasional periods of disuse.

His notes on casting show that the craft had changed little since Urban's time, but Biringuccio dealt at length with the finishing of gun barrels once they had been broken out of the molding pit. The clay was first picked out of the ornaments, which were then scrubbed clean with a wet brush, and the plain and decorated surfaces were planished with hammers. The chamber was reamed with a three-pointed scraper like a jousting lance-head (*come un ferro di lancia da giostra a minimo*) before the touchhole was drilled with a bowdrill. As gentlemen expressed a preference for the new bored-out barrels in hand-held firearms, whose accuracy suggested that cannon too should be bored smooth, Biringuccio illustrated his ideas for a treadmill boring machine and its tools. He was less sound on gun-carriage construction, where he wrongly recommended that axles should tip upwards at their ends to spread the wheels, but he did warn against other weaknesses and gave the proportions for a correct balance between weight and strength. Even types of wood and shapes of nails to be used are described at length. In discussing iron projectiles for cannon and muskets he suggested that larger balls should be cast in clay or plaster molds, greased with oil or lard, which could take several at a time. Smaller balls could be similarly cast, or forged from cubes cut from iron rods. The cube was heated, then hammered in a hemispherical hollow in the anvil with a round-headed punch. In Biringuccio's experience, some smiths could work iron well and steel badly, or vice versa, but they all knew that if either metal was to be strong it had to be shaped with the hammer on an anvil and not with the grinding wheel or the file. This applied to all sections of the craft, from the anchor and anvil makers to the gunsmith, sword cutler and armorer.

While some gunmakers worked to improve the wheellock, others were engaged in making a matchlock which would give fire to the priming more surely than the older design with its one-piece serpentine. Towards the end of the fifteenth century, two different types were made in which the cock formed a separate part of the lock mechanism. The works were fitted to the inside of a flat metal plate and recessed into the stock. The principles of these snap matchlocks are much the same. A spring acts on the tail of the cock, which is pivoted towards its center, holding it in the pan. One of several different methods is used to retain the cock above the pan under the pressure of the compressed spring so that the match does not ignite the priming. When the retaining sear is withdrawn by a trigger or some other form of release, the match holder drops under the influence of the spring and the match ignites the powder in the pan. When Portuguese traders traveled to Japan in 1542 their muskets were fitted with snap matchlocks which were to serve as the models for Japanese *Teppō* guns and pistols until the middle of the nineteenth cetury. Only one matchlock pistol is known in the West, unless the gunshields from the armory kept for Henry VIII's personal guards can be included.

Chapter 10

Towards the end of the sixteenth century, a lively discussion sprang up as military books, which had not formerly been common in English, began to come onto the market in some numbers. The hoary old dispute as to whether the bowman or the harquebusier was more efficient in warfare appeared yet again. It was a parochial controversy, argued only by Englishmen. The most important advocate of the longbow was Sir John Smythe, whose armor is illustrated in the Jacobe Album. Smythe, who was as experienced a soldier as any proponent of the musket, had six points of preference for the bow over firearms, the most important being the effective argument that a bowman could let off six shots in a minute to one every two or three minutes from the musketeer when he followed his drill carefully. The musket weight–it is several times heavier than the bow–exhausted soldiers on a long march. Moreover it was a much more complicated arm than the longbow, easily deranged by the piece clogging and fouling with gunpowder dirt. When it broke, as it did easily, it could only be repaired by a trained smith. Rain or mist spoiled the powder, and the match could be blown out by the wind.

The complication of loading made it simple for any but the steadiest of troops to mishandle their arms. One man may forget to insert the wadding between powder and ball, while another may omit the wadding that keeps the ball in the barrel. Smythe told how he had seen bullets rolling from the muzzle of a caliver for the want of wadding. "This is why when musketeers of a raw sort shoot point-blank at whole battalions, sometimes only few are seen to fall." The trained archer, on the other hand, brought up from childhood with the bow as his toy, shot more truly than any harquebusier, whose inaccurate arm limited him to shooting at very close range while a good bowman was dangerous at 150 to 200 yards (c. 137 to 183 m). Archers could fight effectively in ranks six deep, when the rear ranks shot with a high trajectory over the heads of those in front, whereas harquebusiers could stand only two deep. To Smythe, firearms were only useful for accurate shooting from "bulwarks, mounts and ramparts of the fortress," when the soldier could support his musket on a wall or on a rest, or when he was firing from behind cover.

Smythe's leading opponent in the complex controversy was

Humphrey Barwyck, who disagreed with Smythe on almost every point. Archers were no longer the accurate shooters of Smythe's youth, and if bad weather was pernicious to firearms it was no kinder to bows. Wet bowstrings became slack, and after a march in the rain the glue that held arrow feathers to the steles softened and the feathers dropped off. As Smythe charged the musketeer with nervousness in battle, Barwyck recounted that he had seen archers who failed to draw their arrows to the head and shot wildly without aiming, to get off as many shafts as possible as the enemy approached. Barwyck saw little value in archers standing more than two deep, for then the rear ranks could take no real aim but shot only at hazard into the air. Their efficiency declined much more quickly than that of musketeers if they were not properly fed, because so much depended on the strength of back and arms. "If he have not his three meals a day, as is his custom at home, nor lies warm at nights, he presently waxes benumbed and feeble, and cannot draw so as to shoot long shot." The last of Barwyck's points may well be a tilt at Smythe's outdated experience, for with the improvement of firearms and constant drilling, experienced men were then capable of shooting many more times than was possible in Smythe's day. By the end of the century they could shoot forty times in an hour, and Barwyck thought that this rate could be improved.

Barwyck was supported by Sir Roger Williams, one of the toughest men to serve in the wars of the Netherlands, who valued five hundred good musketeers more highly than fifteen hundred bowmen, as he had found that the quality of archers was so mixed that out of five thousand he would be lucky to find fifteen hundred good shots. The verdict went against the bow and in 1595 the modernists had their way when England's Privy Council ruled that archers would no longer be enrolled in the train bands, which now required only harquebusiers, caliver-men and musketeers. However, the official obsolescence of the longbow as a weapon in the armies of Britain did not preclude a company of Scottish archers traveling to the Île de Rhé with the Duke of Buckingham on his abortive expedition of 1627.

Gifts of armor and arms were common from the earliest recorded times. These gifts, passing from one country to another and usually motivated by political expediency, had the effect of blurring the dividing lines between national styles. Even when the donor, the recipient and the date of a gift are known it is not always possible to identify its elements. As a conspicuous example, crossbows and parts of two

An archer in pikeman's armor draws his longbow while holding the pike that will defend him against a cavalry charge; after William Neade, The Double-armed Man *(London, 1625).*

Flint and Steel

A *An Italian pistol, the snaphance lock made c. 1690 by the lockmaker and iron-chiseler Matteo Acqua Fresca* *of Bargi, near Bologna. The barrel is by Giovanni Battista Francino the Younger, of Brescia.*

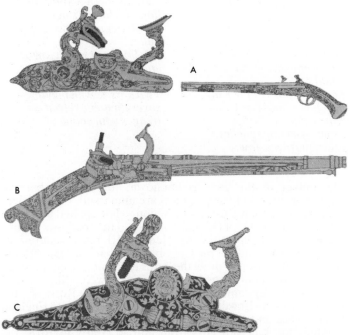

B *A Scottish snaphance pistol with so-called "fish-tail" butt. Apart from the working parts, which are of steel, the pistol is of brass. The lockplate is stamped with the mark attributed to James Low of Dundee. Dated 1626 on the barrel, and 1624 on the fence at the end of the pan.*

C *An English snaphance gun lock, probably part of the "Present of Spain" sent by James I and VI to Philip III in June, 1614. Guns in the gift were described as* two plaine and two with massie *(sic)* gould. *This lock is heavily gilded against a blackened background.*
(See also pp. 108-109 and 112.)

sporting guns in the Real Armería, Madrid, are the remains of two gifts which James VI and I sent to Philip III at Valladolid. The extravagant "Present of Spain," which was sent in 1614, reflects James' love of sport. It included splendid weapons and portraits of the donor and his family, fine horses, hounds and other animals.

Fowre fowling pieces, two plaine and two with massie gould.
Six crossbowes, thre plaine and thre with massive gould.
Six ryding trownks, thre plaine and thre with toppes of gould.
Fowre pictures of the King, the Quene, and Lady Elizabeth and the Prince.
Fowre water Spagnelles, fowre mastives, fowre Irishe grehoundes

and thre tomblers, two cormerants, twelve couple of houndes for the stagge.
Six pied connies, two pied bulles.
Ten horses of which fowre amling.
Fowre amling mares.
Two horses, with theyre covers of grene velvett frenged with gould.

The maker of the guns is unknown, for the two barrels, snaphance lock and trigger guard are unmarked, but he might have been Stephen Russell of London, who supplied a £45 gun sent to Christian IV of Denmark in 1608. The crossbows are of a simple English type used by Henry VIII three generations before. The Yeoman of the Crossbows probably selected them, and the gaffles used to draw the cords to the nut, from the stock of one of the many crossbowmakers who were still active in London, descendants of the Lecriands and Russells, the Billiards and the Bawdesons who brought their craft to England from France and the Low Countries a century earlier.

James too received gifts from abroad. Early in 1618, the Muscovite ambassador brought him presents that included Turkish bows in jeweled bow-cases, scimitars with precious scabbards, four knife-cases powdered with turquoises and other stones, and a dozen gerfalcons and hawks, whose hoods were embroidered with pearls. As the description comes from a Venetian ambassador's report, the "Turkish" bows were perhaps made in the armory in the Kremlin, Moscow. Composite, recurved bows were known in Russia since Athens hired Scythian archers from the steppes in the fifth century BC. The secondary weapon of the Scythian was the long straight sword, but by the twelfth century at the latest, curved swords were wielded in Kievan Rus by horsemen protected by

Arms and armor of a harquebusier, or light horseman, comprising a pott helmet, a cuirass, and bridle-gauntlet worn over a buff coat. His sword and carbine are carried on broad shoulder-belts, and his pistols are in holsters at his saddlebow. English, c. 1640.

kite-shaped shields, conical helmets (*shishák*), quilted doublets and brigandines (*kuyák*), armor which saw Russia through the Time of the Troubles.

Flintlock

The earliest known flintlock with combined steel and pancover is in the Gosudarstvennij Ermitazh, Leningrad. It is signed in full by its French (Lisieux) maker, who made it, according to tradition, for Henry IV, which dates it therefore from before 1610. It fulfils the definition of a true flintlock as laid down by Torsten Lenk in Flintlåset

(Stockholm, 1939), in that it has the steel and pancover made in one piece, and the sear acts vertically in two notches in the tumbler on the inner end of the cock spindle to give full-cock and half-cock positions.

A An Italian flintlock pistol, signed GIO. BOTTI, c. 1700.

B A holster pistol made in London, c. 1650-55. The lock is of the English type with a back-catch or "dog." The plate is signed WILLIAM

WATSON FECIT, and the barrel bears the proof-marks used during the Commonwealth, from 1649 to 1660.

C *Locks of a double-barreled sporting gun, signed JOSEPH MANTON and fitted with the maker's patent "gravitating stop" safety device and waterproof pans, c. 1814.*

D *The earliest known flint-lock gun, probably made about 1605-10 for Henri IV of France. The blued barrel is enriched with gilded panels, and the stock is inlaid with engraved mother-of-pearl. The gilt bronze mounts bear the arms of France and Navarre and the signature of the maker: M. LE. BOVRGEOYS. A. LISIEVL.*

E *Flintlock pistols made in Paris by the Swedish brothers Gustav and Peter Rundberg of Jönköping, and signed LES RUNDBERG, SVEDOIS, À PARIS; c. 1750.*

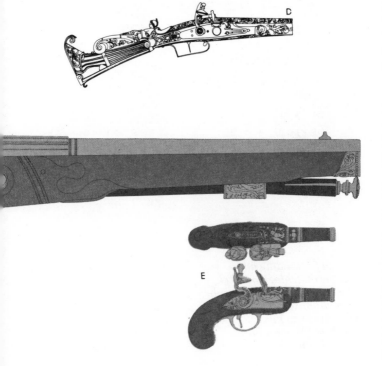

The drill for loading and firing the matchlock musket, as described by Johann Jacob von Wallhausen in his Kriegskunst zu Fuss *(The Art of War on Foot) (Oppenheim, 1615).*

A measure of gunpowder is poured from a charger into the barrel, and is followed by a wad and bullet which are forced home with a ramrod. The musketeer replaces the ramrod in the pipe under the

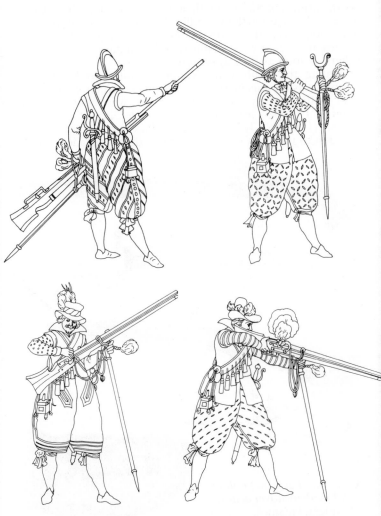

barrel and shoulders his musket, prior to marching off.

When about to engage the enemy, the musketeer halts, rests his musket and spots his target. He then blows on the match, which he has been carrying looped in his hand, to make sure that it is hot enough to ignite the powder. He clips it in the serpentine, aims and fires. The match is removed from the serpentine and the musketeer strides off.

As the armies of the sixteenth and early seventeenth centuries increased in size and their handling became ever more complex, many books were devoted to methods of fighting, and reports of battles and sieges were snapped up by military romantics and others as soon as they appeared.

Among the military innovations credited to Maurice of Orange was the raising of the status of construction engineers who, until the early seventeenth century, were considered the scum of Europe's armies. In his *Five Decades of Epistles of Warre* (London, 1622), Francis Markham applauded the decision to make them carry swords with their spades, for the

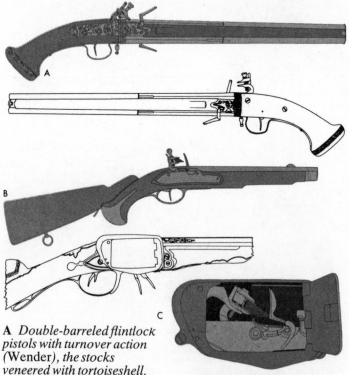

A *Double-barreled flintlock pistols with turnover action* (Wender*), the stocks veneered with tortoiseshell. Probably Dutch, mid-seventeenth century.*

B *Danish flintlock pistol, cavalry model of 1808-15, with detachable stock.*

C *An enclosed flintlock, protected from the weather by a box with a hinged side-plate, from a double-barreled sporting gun signed* BOUILLET A PARIS. *French, c. 1780.*

"poore pioneer...at all approaches, mounts, trenches and underminings" faced as much danger as most other soldiers.

Like many military writers of his day, Markham tested himself – or relieved the boredom of study – with a spell as a volunteer under Pelham, with whom he served at the siege of Sluys. The Prince of Anhalt employed him in the troubles that arose from the disputed succession to the bishopric of Strasbourg before he obtained a captaincy under the Earl of Essex in France and Ireland. He later returned to the Low Countries with Sir Francis Vere. The experiences of his service formed the basis of the *Five Decades*, which ranges from levying, which he knew well from his work as muster-master at Nottingham, to the training of the privileged gentlemen "voluntaries" who armed themselves according to their own fancy and were less disciplined than Markham thought proper: "As well might a man rule a herd of wild Bulles as a Band of such unruly Colts." The shot and the pikes, whose arming he described, did not share the freedom of the dilettante voluntaries. They served under a discipline that was little less barbarous than that which drove Mahomet II's *bashi-bazouks* into Constantinople, and their weapons and armor were already uniform within smaller units, if not yet in armies.

The shot were to carry muskets or bastard muskets, as the harquebus was now quite outranged by these heavy weapons by four hundred paces to about one hundred and twenty. The bigger, stronger men used the musket while the bastard musket was the weapon of the "more weake, little and nimble." The musket had a 4.5-foot (1.4 m) barrel of full musket bore (1.5 oz or 42.5 gr) with a pearwood or walnut stock; to be carried with it were bullets, a mold to cast them, a worm with which to draw the charge, turnscrews and a priming iron. It was fired from a wooden rest fitted with a spiked shoe at the bottom, a half-hoop of iron at the top and two strings, used to sling it on the left arm when it was trailed.

When the word flintlock appeared in the last quarter of the seventeenth century, it seems to have referred to any gunlock which ignited the charge by sparks produced by a piece of flint hitting a pivoted striking plate. The sparks fell into a shallow pan full of priming powder. The flintlock is most precisely defined as a snaphance lock which has its steel and pancover combined and has a vertically operating sear to engage in half-cock and full-cock notches in a tumbler on the end of the cock spindle. In the sixteenth century snaphances were fitted with a tumbler linking the cock and mainspring, and one survives from the second half of the century with a combined steel and pancover. A lock which conforms to the definition given by Dr. Torsten Lenk was in the private firearms collection of Louis XIII of France (1610-43) and was said to have been made for his father Henri IV (1553-1610). It bears the full signature of Marin le Bourgeoys, who has been suggested as the inventor of the mechanism.

This form of lock does not seem to have been made outside France before c. 1640, but the next twenty years saw its diffusion throughout Europe except for Italy, Spain and the peripheral lands of Scandinavia and Scotland which retained their own lock styles for another century or more. In Spain and Italy the snaphance, the miquelet lock and its Italian form were popular. In Spain in particular the flintlock was thought much inferior to the native miquelet. One version, first noted about 1700 and now known as the Madrid lock, bears an external resemblance to the flintlock but is, in fact, a developed version of the miquelet. Two horizontal sears project through the lockplate to engage the breast of the cock at half-cock and its tail at full-cock. The Scottish lock is a close typological relative of the Madrid lock, but appears to be an independent development from the snaphance. In its final Scottish form the breast of the cock is held at half-cock — the safe position — and a sear engages the tumbler at full-cock. In an intermediate form the full-cock sear engages a hook on the tail in close esemblance to the Madrid lock.

Before the native flintlock was developed, both wheellock and matchlock ignition mechanisms were used in Scotland, but none survives which can definitely be said to be of Scottish manufacture or even to have been used there. The earliest surviving Scottish firearms date from the end of the sixteenth century. All are fitted with a distinctively Scottish form of snaphance lock which was in use by the penultimate decade of the sixteenth century. This lock has a separate pancover and steel, the cover being connected to the tumbler by a rod which pushes the pancover forward before the flint strikes fire on the steel. On the end of the pan is a small circular or hexagonal fence or shield, often engraved with the date of the manufacture. However, the dates can be accepted only with reservations as many surviving pieces have detachable pans held in position by one or two screws so that they could be replaced as they were burned through. The early mechanism continued to be fitted to Scottish firearms until about 1685, by which time a more advanced form of snaphance lock was used all over Scotland. This second type, which appears to have been used from about 1647 to just after 1700, used a sear which worked horizontally as in the earlier forms, but which now engaged a notch in the tumbler.

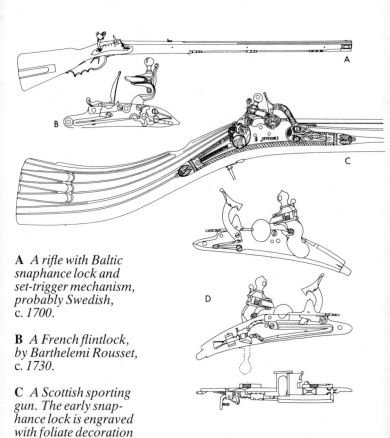

A *A rifle with Baltic snaphance lock and set-trigger mechanism, probably Swedish, c. 1700.*

B *A French flintlock, by Barthelemi Rousset, c. 1730.*

C *A Scottish sporting gun. The early snaphance lock is engraved with foliate decoration and grotesque animals, and inscribed with the maker's monogram $ and the name of his town, JNVERNES. The fence is dated 1684.*

D *A late Scottish snaphance lock, dated 1617, is shown here after it has been fired. It comes from the left-hand pistol of a pair. After Charles E. Whitelaw.*

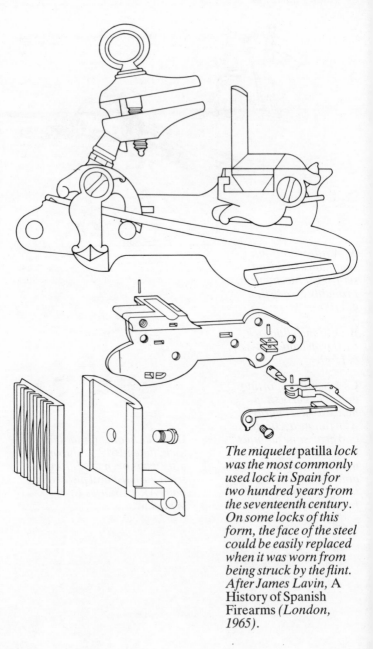

The miquelet patilla *lock was the most commonly used lock in Spain for two hundred years from the seventeenth century. On some locks of this form, the face of the steel could be easily replaced when it was worn from being struck by the flint. After James Lavin, A History of Spanish Firearms (London, 1965).*

Chapter 11

When the great ship *Wasa*, built for Gustavus II Adolphus, was brought to the surface in April 1961, a microcosm of Swedish naval life as it was when she capsized in 1628 was salvaged with her. Among the personal arms which were salvaged with the hull were a number of the light birding-pieces with rifled barrels between .25 and .40 inches (6.4 and 10.2 mm) caliber which get their name, *tschinke*, from Teschen (Cieszyn) in Silesia. Most survivors seem to have been made there between the early seventeenth century and the middle of the eighteenth. The "hind's foot stock" was held against the shooter's cheek while he released the efficient mechanism. The first *tschinkes* had wheellock ignition, but they were also made with flintlocks. The first half of the seventeenth century forms a new period in the history of artillery in Europe. Henri IV of France

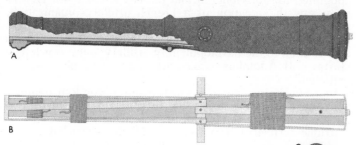

A *A "leather" cannon of c. 1630, preserved at the Tidö armory from before 1657 until it was transferred to the Livrustkammare, Stockholm, Sweden, in 1858. X-ray photographs have revealed a complex structure. The copper-lined iron barrel was reinforced with alloy and splints bound with iron wire and rope. The whole was wrapped in layers of canvas and had three wooden* rings fitted to give it the shape of a cast gun, before the final leather covering was nailed on.

B *A section of the Tidö cannon.*

C *The cannon seen directly from behind.*

A field gun, illustrated by Joseph Furtenbach in Architectura Universalis *(1635).*

(1589-1610) first realized the immensity of its potential, and set about improving it for the benefit of his own kingdom. Maximilian de Béthune, Duc de Sully (1560-1641) was appointed Master-General, and the last ten years of Henri's reign saw the creation of a French artillery organization. Among the four hundred guns cast for the king's use were a number of fieldpieces. Maurice of Nassau also made his contribution to the development of artillery, but it was left to Gustavus II Adolphus to give artillery its true place on the battlefield.

In his German campaigns Gustavus used iron four-pounder guns, each weighing about 600 lb (272 kg), drawn by two horses. With these rapidity of fire was achieved by the use of cartridges instead of the old method of ladling the powder down the barrel into the chamber. Two of these guns were attached to each regiment and were directly under the orders of its colonel. Gustavus may therefore be credited with the idea of the battalion system of guns, which had its advantages in those days of imperfect organization, but which like many other things military was to continue into a period when the system had become quite outmoded. In addition to these technical innovations Gustavus realised the importance of concentration of fire, so he frequently massed his guns in strong batteries at the center and flanks. He saw the need for both light and heavy ordnance, using the lighter guns to protect the heavy artillery in retreat. During the Thirty Years' War, the advantages which artillery could win when properly handled became quite obvious. The imperial artillery was as cumbersome as the Swedes' was mobile. The guns under the command of the German general, Count Johan Tilly, were chiefly 24-pounders, each of which needed twenty transport horses and twelve horses for its accompanying stores wagon; the service of these

118

guns was primitive, and they could be moved only with great difficulty during the course of an action.

Many foreigners gravitated to Sweden in the early seventeenth century, attracted by her growing military ascendancy under Gustavus II Adolphus. Among them was an Austrian colonel, Melchior Wurmbrandt, who demonstrated in 1625 a light leather-covered gun that was probably based on a design he had seen in Zurich three years before. The king was impressed, and Wurmbrandt received an order for three- and six-pounders, the first of which were delivered in time for the siege of Wormditt in October 1627. The guns were never intended for siege work, but their mobility so suited the king's idea of how artillery should go into action that he took eight to the mouth of the Vistula the next summer. His troops carried them over ground that was thought to be impassable to artillery and came unnoticed within range of the Polish fleet, much of which was destroyed. A year later, ten leather guns taken by the Poles at Honigfelde were considered so important that they were immediately sent to Wallenstein for his inspection.

Abroad, much of the credit for Gustavus' victories over the Poles was given to the new weapon. An English broadside of August 7, 1628, claimed that they gave:

as good and better service than his Copper Cannon: for as fast as the souldiers are able to march, the Cannon is convayed along with them, having but one horse to draw the biggest of them, and three or foure men can carry the biggest of them on their shoulders over any straight place, or narrow Bridge whatsoever, so that the *Polls* are not aware ere the Cannon *play* upon them, for it will shoot with as great force as any other: which makes the Polonians say, his Maiestie useth Devilrie: but that is all untrue: for I my selfe have heard those Cannon severall times shott with as great force as any other.

This overstated the value of leather guns, which were soon discarded in favor of bronze cannon in the calibers Gustavus II Adolphus considered most suitable for his new tactics. These also involved the appreciation of the need for alterations in infantry and cavalry. His new army showed radical differences from the Spanish model, which had undergone little development during the previous half-century. Gustavus shortened the long pike by almost a third to 11 feet (3.4 m), gave lighter body armor to the men who wielded it, and drilled them to fight with musketeers in companies of six files deep. Gradually, for it was an expensive business, the shot were armed with increasing numbers of wheellock muskets, made lighter than the old matchlocks so that the musket rest could be discarded.

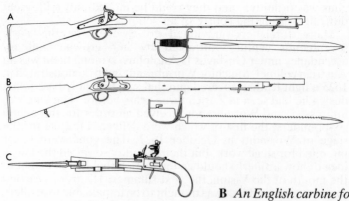

A *This experimental, Brunswick pattern, smooth-bore carbine, the lock plate engraved R1 MANUFACTORY ENFIELD and stamped 1841, was based on the first model of the Brunswick rifle, the pattern of which was sealed in 1837. The large sword-bayonet was attached by means of a stout, rectangular standard welded to the barrel.*

B *An English carbine for sappers and miners, pattern of 1839, dated 1841. The first model saw-back sword-bayonet, shown here, was unsatisfactory and was replaced in January, 1843.*

C *A flintlock pistol by H.W. Mortimer with a bayonet hinged to the side of the brass blunderbuss barrel. English, c. 1780.*

Despite Swedish improvements in tactics and the way they were broadcast, there was little improvement in English artillery at that time, but in the invasion of 1640 leather guns were used with effect against the English at the Scots' passage of the River Tyne. Many Scotsmen who had served with Gustavus had imbibed his new tactics.

When Charles I took the field in 1642, he had a sizeable train of artillery. However it was markedly immobile, and he was obliged to leave his guns behind for a while, though they were with him at Edgehill on October 23, 1642. The next year, at Bradock Down, an instance occurred of the use of field artillery first covered by cavalry. At Roundway, Charles' guns were handled so well that they prepared the way for cavalry, and eventually enabled the king to seize the enemy's batteries and turn them against him. In other battles of the Civil War artillery seems to have been almost useless. The twenty-five guns on the

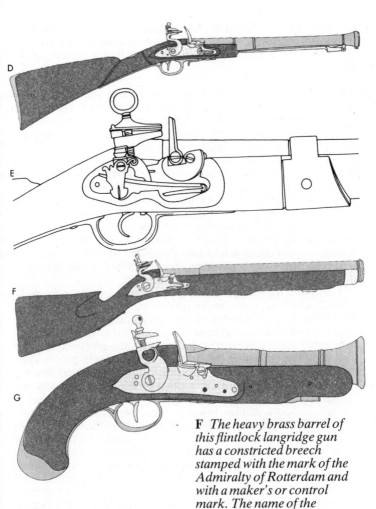

D A brass-barreled blunderbuss with folding bayonet. The lock is signed GRICE, LONDON. English, c. 1780.

E The miquelet lock of a brass-barreled swivelmusketoon. Spanish or Neapolitan, c. 1790.

F The heavy brass barrel of this flintlock langridge gun has a constricted breech stamped with the mark of the Admiralty of Rotterdam and with a maker's or control mark. The name of the maker, Jan Maliman, is engraved on the beveled lock plate. Dutch, c. 1710.

G A French flintlock pistol with brass blunderbuss barrel flaring sharply at the muzzle, and stamped with the control mark of St. Etienne, c. 1790.

royalist side at Marston Moor were soon neutralized by Cromwell's flank attack, and in no engagement of the Civil War did ordnance assume the importance it had attained on the Continent.

At Ypres in 1647, a hundred years before the posthumous publication of Puységur's *Mémoires*, his men stuck daggers into the muzzles of their muskets. It was not necessarily a new idea, as blades may have been made in the sixteenth century for attachment to hunting firearms to give the *coup de grâce* to a wounded beast, but before the end of the seventeenth century this new arm, so simple in conception, altered infantry tactics in several European armies. About 1700, British, French and German military leaders acknowledged the value of the socket bayonet by abolishing the pike. This let them reduce infantry to a single class and made the handling of troops slightly less complicated. Infantry could reload under the cover of their comrades' bayonets, could face cavalry in the open with some hope of survival, and when foul weather made shooting impossible they still had a useful weapon.

The name for knives of this type, *bayonet*, derives from the French word *bayoner*, meaning "to put a spigot in a cask." From the second quarter of the seventeenth century at the latest, it has been used almost universally for knives and swords utilized to make a firearm into a feasible thrusting weapon. The first type was the plug bayonet, usually a single-edged knife with a tapering wooden handle that could be jammed into the muzzle. Most were short, but others with knuckleguards and straight blades like the contemporary hanger served also as swords in some armies towards the end of the seventeenth century. By then a much more satisfactory means of attaching the bayonet to the muzzle so that the gun could still be fired had been invented in France, the credit for this new socket bayonet being generally given to Colonel Martinet–his Christian names are unrecorded – *Inspecteur d'Infanterie* under Louis XIV. A short tube is linked by a curved neck to a blade of slender triangular section. The tube, or socket, slipped over the muzzle to be held in position by a protruding stud which engaged a Z-shaped slot.

As early as *c*. 1650 some guns were made with bayonets permanently fixed to their barrels. For convenience they were usually hinged to fold back along the barrel when not needed. The first maker of a hinged bayonet is unknown, but as late as 1781 a patent was granted to John Waters of Birmingham for his "new invented PISTOLS WITH A BAYONET," which covered virtually every known type of permanently attached retractable bayonet, whatever its design. The spring bayonet was fitted to many weapons intended for use in a confined space, like the little pocket pistols of the late eighteenth and early nineteenth centuries and the blunderbusses used on board ship or from the box of a mailcoach. A few special military units such as Italy's motorized Bersaglieri carried Mannlicher-Carcano carbines with spring bayonets in the Second World War, but the design never achieved general acceptance for military arms.

Most scholars accept that the English word blunderbuss derives from the Dutch *donrebusse* (*donder* thunder + *bus* gun), which is found in documents from north Holland as early as 1353. Brandenbroch "the crossbowman" supplied Deventer with *una pixide dicta donrebusse*. Others bought by the town in 1354 were of two sizes, the larger twice as dear as the smaller.

By the middle of the seventeenth century, the name blunderbuss referred specifically to a gun with a short, large-bore barrel that often flared at the muzzle. The large caliber allowed the shooter to load several balls or fragments of metal at a time, making it a suitable arm for defense against massed enemy. The flared muzzle made loading quicker, and at the same time it was a more threatening sight than a smaller bore weapon. Armies and navies used blunderbusses, some with oval muzzles, in a variety of sizes up to light artillery calibers until the percussion period, and they enjoyed a certain popularity with tollgate-keepers and mailcoach guards. A brass-barreled blunderbuss in the Tower Armouries is signed Rigby and engraved MAIL GUARD NO. 1 and BELFAST & DERRY 1.

Blunderbuss pistols were also made in brass and steel for the occasion when one man had to face a mob. The so-called duck's foot pistol was made for a similar role with a number of barrels splaying out from a single lock mechanism which fired them all at once.

The blunderbuss was used in the same role against men as the shotgun was against animals. A hail of scraps of metal or scattered shot gave the shooter a better chance of hitting a small or elusive target, or one against which only a snap shot was possible. Some law-enforcement agencies have used shotguns for a century or more as less lethal at ranges beyond fifty yards (*c*. 46 m), but until recent times they have been proscribed by international agreement for use in war.

Among the many inventions designed to make shooting with ordinary firearms quicker, more certain and more accurate was the self-spanning wheellock. The cock of one, shaped like a couched stag, on a gun made by Jacob Zimmerman in 1646, is linked to the wheel spindle by a rack and pinion mechanism so that the spring is tensioned when the pyrites is lowered into the firing position. Like most of these exotic lock forms, the Zimmerman self-spanner was obviously made to claim the attraction of some important patron. Another such invention of c. 1650-60, made to simplify the use of wheellock arms, was the rifle with turn-off barrel by Michael Gull, who was admitted to the Vienna gunmakers' guild in 1647.

Gull was also the maker of a wheellock rifle with mounts of enameled gold, a rare style of decoration on arms. The most famous example of such a firearm is the marvelously conceived and executed wheellock rifle made by Daniel Sadeler and David Altenstetter for their patron, the emperor Rudolph II, at his Prague court between 1603 and 1610. A gold-hilted rapier made for the emperor Maximilian II, preserved like the Sadeler-Altenstetter rifle in the Kunsthistorisches Museum, Vienna, is the finest extant sixteenth-century sword decorated with enamel. The medium had a brilliant, brief revival in a group of presentation smallswords made in London and Paris in the last quarter of the eighteenth century and the first of the nineteenth. These were considered suitable tokens of appreciation to military and naval heroes from a grateful government or from a group of private citizens.

Gull was working at an especially productive period for Germany's gunmakers, not only in their own land, but abroad, where they were employed at a number of royal courts. One family, the Kalthoffs, whose members worked as far afield as London, Moscow, Copenhagen, France and the Netherlands, was responsible for the first firearm that would shoot several times from integral but separate magazines of shot and powder.

A *A wheellock repeating rifle made by Peter Kalthoff, court gunmaker to Duke Ferdinand of Denmark, later Ferdinand III. This rifle, inscribed ANNO 1645 and DAS ERSTE (The First), is the earliest known example of a weapon of this type. It was probably made at Flensburg.*

B *A self-spanning wheellock with a totally enclosed action, by Jacob Zimmerman, signed and dated 1646. The movement of the cock, holding the pyrites, compresses the spring which drives the wheel when the trigger is pressed.*

125

A wheellock magazine gun made by Peter Kalthoff in 1645 is inscribed *Das Erste*; a year later he made another with a flintlock mechanism. These two repeating guns, and others by Matthias Kalthoff and the Caspars, father and son, store their shot in a tubular cavity below the barrel and powder in their hollowed out butts. When the shooter turns the pivoted trigger guard, a charge of powder is transported from the butt to the front of the lock, which is connected by a short passage to the box-like breechblock. The block, which has three holes, can be moved by the trigger-guard across the face of the breech; when one hold collects a ball from the magazine and drops it into the breech, the second is filled with powder and serves as the powder chamber, the third primes the pan.

These marvelous new guns could fire up to thirty or forty shots at a time. Although they were considered too complicated for general military use, marksmen of the Royal Danish Foot Guards received an issue of one hundred, and they are thought to have seen service at the siege of Copenhagen in 1658-59 and again twenty years later when Denmark declared war on Sweden.

As early as the first decade of the seventeenth century, a gun was made that used the power of air pumped into a chamber under pressure and stored until the moment of shooting. Marin le Bourgeoys made a gun on this principle to shoot darts which had wooden hafts fitted with iron points and a paper tompion at the rear to make a close fit with the barrel. Only a drawing of it survives, but several examples of early airguns exist from the middle of the century. Almost all have the compressed-air chamber built around the barrel, a system that was used for a century, until the reservoirs were made to serve as the gun's butt, or else a separate spherical reservoir was employed. The earliest, in the Livrustkammare and the Tøjhusmuseum, were made by Hans Köhler about 1644, when Otto von Guericke and his workmen were struggling to perfect a smooth piston and a tightly fitting cylinder which would make the airgun even more efficient. Köhler worked in Kitzingen, a little town fifteen miles (24.1 km) east of Würzburg where Athanasius Kirchner, professor of physics and mathematics, had published a description of a more primitive air-powered gun between 1630 and 1640.

On the lockplate of an airgun made by Johann Kock of Cologne in 1654 is an engraving which shows a gun of this type being pumped up. The shooter holds down the pump handle with his foot as he moves the gun up and down. A year later, some enemies of Oliver Cromwell, the Protector, planned to assassinate him with an airgun bought in Utrecht. The gun, which was credited with a range of 150 yards (*c*. 137 m), had a valve mechanism that enabled ti to shoot seven times with each pumping. Accidents caused by the reservoir bursting during compression led to this design going out of fashion in the forties of the nineteenth century.

When compared with guns which use loose powder, the airgun has the distinct advantage that it can more easily be adapted to a magazine system, as there is no danger of the entire charge in the magazine exploding when the charge is fired. One such accident, which occurred with dangerous frequency in the magazine guns of the eighteenth century, inspired an Italian inventor serving in Austria to design a magazine airgun. Bartolomeo Girandoni (1744-99) designed his gun in 1779, and it was subsequently introduced into the Austrian army for use by some Jäger units as the Model 1780. When the flask which formed the butt was fully charged by some 2,000 strokes of its separate air-pump, the projectile had a muzzle velocity of about 1,000 feet (305 m) per second. Its first ten shots were effective at 150 yards (*c*. 137 m), the next at 120 yards (*c*. 110 m) or so, and the range then fell off rather sharply. So long as there were bullets in the tubular magazine and air pressure in the flask, rounds could be shot at intervals of a few seconds. Only Austria used the air-rifle in a military role, but others similar to Girandoni's design were made in many other countries, including England.

In 1747, Ludwig VIII, Landgrave of Hesse (1691-1768) used an airgun to kill a 22-point stag weighing 480 lb (*c*. 218 kg). The Lewis and Clarke Expedition of 1804-06 carried an airgun. But sportsmen did not agree on their efficiency; in little more than two decades the airgun was not considered powerful enough "for buck or deer shooting...[but] for rook shooting it is very well calculated." The value of reduced noise and the absence of smoke hardly made up for the weapon's lack of power and the immense care that had to go into its making.

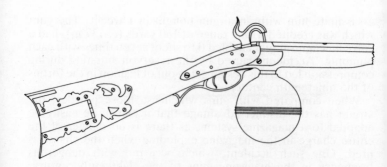

An airgun with a compressed-air globe set below the barrel. The stock is of the style found on Kentucky rifles. Pennsylvanian, c. 1830.

Chapter 12

In the 36th World Championships on Venezuela's Conejo Blanco ranges in November 1954, Russian marksmen won seven individual and eleven team world championships. The weapons they used were not the product of a factory established after the Revolution, but of one which has a tradition stretching back to Czar Boris Godunov (1552-1605). Towards the end of the sixteenth century the czar established a cannon foundry 120 miles (*c.* 193 km) south of Moscow. In 1705, as part of his divine mission to create a modern Russian state to match the industrial and military potential of those he had seen in the West, Peter I Alexeievich founded at Tula a state factory to make small arms for the Russian army and navy. At first weapons were made on a cottage industry basis. The gunmakers worked in their own homes on a quota of military swords and firearms, the best makers also producing a limited quantity of arms for the imperial court. This method of production continued after the construction of the factory buildings and waterpowered machinery in the second decade of the eighteenth century, when the city's craftsmen maintained a remarkable degree of specialization. Tula's considerable output of enriched arms reveals the very strong influence of contemporary western European fashion, which came to Russia with the gunmakers whose immigration was encouraged by Peter the Great and his successors. The names of fifteen German and Scandinavian gunmakers who worked at Tula are recorded, but no French name appears on the lists although Tula's standards of gun

An embossed and gilt powder flask, from a garniture made for the Empress Elizabeth (1709-62) at the Tula factory. Russian, 1752.

decoration were almost those of the gunsmiths of Paris.

Early in the eighteenth century one of a number of French pattern books, Nicolas Guérard's *Diverses Pièces d'Arquebuserie*, was published in Paris, and a pirate edition appeared in Nuremberg soon after. The book, which was soon known to the gunmakers of many countries, contained two designs for gunstock inlay which seem to be the only patterns used by the Tula stockmakers. The metalwork of Tula sporting guns and their accessories tends to be elaborately chiseled and gilt, the barrels characteristically covered with symmetrical interlaced scrollwork. The stocks, locks and mounts reveal a strong German influence, and a Russian style is only found in the native elements introduced into Western patterns and the occasional faulty rendering of Western motifs. The old Russian decorative styles of inlay in stag antler, mother-of-pearl and brass wire, which derive so much from the East, are little in evidence after 1705.

Three years after he established the factories that were the basis of future Russian arms production, Peter the Great was the architect of another success when he smashed Charles XII's Swedish army at Poltava. On the first day of 1708, Charles, replete with victories at Klissow, Cracow, Narva and Grodno, crossed the Vistula with an army of 40,000 men. By July he had forced his veterans through the Russian army at Holowczyn, and Moscow seemed to be his for the taking. His past lessons well learned, Peter knew better than to meet his fanatical adversary in pitched battle. The Russians snapped at the flanks of Charles' army, harried his communications until winter, the worst for a century, and finally broke him. Before midsummer of the following year Peter settled his difficulties with the rebellious Cossacks and had 80,000 men and forty guns near Poltava. They waited behind a quadrilateral of entrenchments protected by redoubts a few hundred yards from the enervated Swedish army whose leaders, in the absence of the recently wounded king, argued themselves into an impossible position from which they had to attack. Of the 17,000 Swedes who first faced Peter I and his generals on June 28, 1709, 4,000 made the final assault on 40,000 Russians who hardly needed the searing hail of grapeshot from their artillery to stop the charge. The Swedish king escaped to Turkey to fight again and to die of a ball through the head at the siege of Fredrikshald, Norway, on December 11, 1718, still only thirty-six years of age. Charles' spectacular career was brilliant, especially in his handling of his armies against formidable opposition and in his detailed attention to the equipment of his armies.

Within a hundred years of the invention of cannon, several founders had attempted to make practical multi-barreled guns, some of which were effective. A fourteenth-century example was described as having one barrel for a large gunstone and ten small barrels for bullets. A three-barreled gun by Peter Baude, who worked at Houndsditch, London, between 1528 and 1546 survives, although damaged, in the Tower of London. A hundred years after Baude's day Antonio Petrini sketched a double-barreled cannon, the barrels of which were joined at an angle of 30°, and which fired two cannon balls joined by a chain. Petrini claimed that his gun would produce "the greatest destruction," but one would imagine that the gunner would be more likely to suffer injury than would his enemy.

The double-barreled, double-shotted cannon was resurrected during the American Civil War. A builder in Athens, Georgia, designed one which was cast at the local foundry in 1862. The barrels, diverging by some three degrees, were loaded with two six-pounder balls linked by an eight-foot (2.4 m) chain. The "inventor," John Gilleland, claimed to have shot it convincingly, but he failed to sell it to the Confederate War Department. Reports of the gun's trial show that the linked balls could not be aimed accurately. They flew like *boleadoras* due to the impossibility of firing the two charges simultaneously, the variations in the effectiveness even of equal loads of powder, and the difference in friction generated between each barrel and its ball. The gun now stands before Athens City Hall, a monument to a ballistic misunderstanding.

Infinitely more sensible than double-shotted cannon, although not quite as good as their makers hoped, was a new form of magazine breechloading mechanism which was being made about the middle of the seventeenth century in Europe. The inventor is unknown, but some writers give the credit to an Italian, Giacomo Berselli, although modern American collectors name the design after Michele Lorenzoni, Matteo Acqua Fresca's leading rival at the Florence court of the Medici. The design incorporates two tubular magazines, for the powder and the bullets, which pass through the butt and are separated from the breech by a cylindrical breechblock. A lever on the left rotates the breechlock so that, when the gun is held muzzle downwards, a charge of powder and a single ball drop into the holes in the block. They are carried round to the barrel where the ball is lodged and the powder container serves as a powder chamber. Simultaneously, powder from a priming magazine drops into the pan and the lock is cocked. Other gunmakers used the system in Europe and America until the middle of the nineteenth century when it formed the basis of

A

B

and holsters. *From Nicolas Guérard,* Diverses Pièces d'Arquebuserie *(Paris, c. 1720).*

A *A Parisian gunsmith's workshop at the end of the seventeenth century. On the left, the young apprentice learns from the master gunmaker. On the right, a journeyman removes a breech plug from a barrel. In the window hang pistols, guns*

B *The silver-inlaid stock of a flintlock sporting gun made in 1749 for the Empress Elizabeth. The motifs are from Guérard's pattern book.*

C *An Italian flintlock magazine rifle, .55-inch (14 mm) caliber, with the "Lorenzoni"*

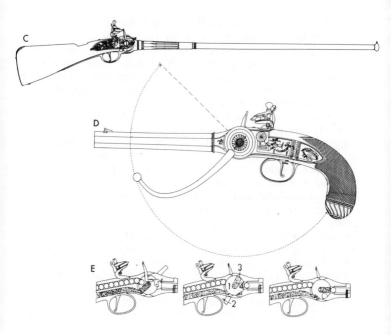

breechloading mechanism, c. 1690. The lock is inscribed BARTOLEMEO COTEL. A lever on the left of the action operates shutters which separate the chamber from magazines in the butt. These magazines, marked PALLA (ball) and POLVERE (powder), can be loaded in turn (cf. **D** below).

D A flintlock magazine pistol, also with the "Lorenzoni" action. The lock is inscribed H W MORTIMER GUNMAKER TO HIS MAJESTY LONDON. English, c. 1790.

E The "Lorenzoni" repeating system. (Left) To

load, the pistol is held muzzle downward and the breech block (**1**) is rotated back by the handle (**2**). This action also closes the pancover and pushes the cock to the half-cock position. The pan is primed from a small magazine which is not shown here. A powder chamber (**3**) and a ball recess (**4**) are gravity-fed from magazines in the butt. (Center) When the breech block is rotated forward, the ball is dropped into the fixed breech at the end of the barrel and the powder chamber is aligned with it ready to fire (right).

A.D. Perry's United States Patent of 1849.

Lorenzoni has also been given the credit for designing another repeating gun which has its tubular magazines under the barrel. When the barrel assembly is raised and rotated one quarter turn to the left, the powder magazine comes level with the fixed chamber where the movement of a cam allows a charge of powder to fall into the chamber. A further quarter-turn loads the barrel with a single ball. The barrel assembly is returned the half-turn to be locked by a catch before firing. A development of the design by a French gunmaker called Chalembron, who worked around the end of the eighteenth century at the Pondicherry arsenal in India, was made so that the action of rotating the barrel also cocked the action, primed the pan and closed the pancover.

Along with speed of loading, sportsmen demanded greater accuracy, some of which came from better methods of aiming. The seventeenth century saw optical sights for rifles described by de Lana, in his *Magister Naturae et Artis* (1684), and by Johann Zahn of Nuremberg, who in *Oculus Artificialis Teledioptricus* (1702) discussed a four-lens sight which had a plain central disk etched with a spot at its center. Telescopic sights are mentioned throughout the eighteenth century and Frederick the Great noted in his diary that he tried a rifle fitted with a telescopic sight at a *Schützenfest* in 1737. These early designs were used for target and sporting shooting, but by the American Civil War they were being used in battle. In the two world wars they were used by most armies, usually by trained snipers armed with rifles which had received the special finish that some later generations of shooters know by the horrid word "accurizing." Telescopic sights have also been fitted to some pistols, but they give insufficient increase in accuracy to be popular.

A search for more efficient firearms was accompanied by an attempt to widen the range of uses to which gunpowder might be put in war and peace. No doubt inspired by Otto von Guericke's experimental attempts to get power from pistons forced through an evacuated metal cylinder by air pressure, Christian Huygens (1629-95) tried in 1673 to create a vacuum in a cylinder by the explosion of gunpowder. In his own account of the results, Huygens echoed other men's attempts to produce some means of throwing cannon balls, "great arrows and bomb shells" from an apparatus as powerful as a cannon but much lighter. While his designs anticipated the internal-combustion engine by two centuries, he regretfully announced that "it seems impossible to design some vehicle that will move through the air, as no machine can be made which is at the same time light yet develops sufficient power." Huygens' failure to produce a near-perfect vacuum, and the difficulty of feeding fresh supplies of powder to his cylinder, presented two insuperable problems which made his engine incapable of development to the point where it would serve "every purpose to which weight is applied [and] most cases where man or animal power is needed."

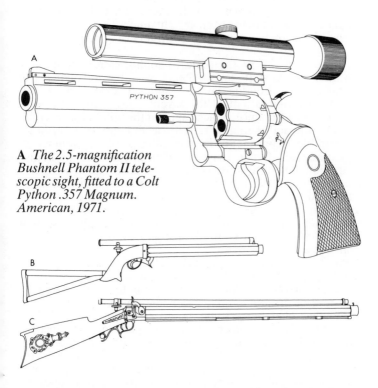

A *The 2.5-magnification Bushnell Phantom II telescopic sight, fitted to a Colt Python .357 Magnum. American, 1971.*

B *A pistol-carbine, .38-inch (9.6 mm) caliber, with a telescopic sight. It was made by W. Billinghurst of Rochester, New York, c. 1860.*

C *A heavy-barreled .45-inch (11.4 mm) rifle with telescopic sight. Made by Edwin Wesson of Hartford, Connecticut, it was used by a sniper in the American Civil War, Edwin Stanclift of the 8th Battalion of Sharpshooters, Army of the Potomac.*

Chapter 13

For centuries the ox-goads, pitchforks and flails used by most of Europe's peasantry provided ready-made weapons in times of conflict. Another rural implement, the scythe, lent itself to adaptation as a weapon if its blade was reset to follow the line of the haft instead of being fixed at right angles to it. The refitting of the blade made a long spear with a cutting edge.

At the other end of the scale of sophistication from these primitive, makeshift scythe-spears was the revolving gun invented by a London lawyer, James Puckle (1667-1724). During the second half of the seventeenth century Britain's Office of the Ordnance, which supplied the military stores used by the army and the navy, tested – as did almost every other comparable department throughout Europe – a number of repeating guns. Other designers failed to convince the British board that they were worth considering for service issue. But in the inventor of "the machine called a defence, it discharges so often and so many bullets and can be so quickly loaden as renders it next to impossible to carry a ship by boarding" the board met a new type of salesman, whose self-advertisement foreshadowed Baron Heurteloup's and even that of Samuel Colt himself.

Puckle's business acumen enabled him to float a company to sell the gun, which he marketed with the advertisement that it could fire sixty-three times in seven minutes. This extremely high rate of fire for the day was made possible by the use of pre-loaded chambers, some bored to shoot round bullets against Christian enemies, others for square ones against the barbarian Turk. The three surviving specimens, of calibers 1.2, 1.3 and 1.6 inches (30.5, 33.0 and 40.6 mm) respectively, show that the gun must have been a formidable weapon, but the only record of its going on service is in an account of an abortive expedition against the French in Saint Lucia and Saint Vincent in 1727. Like other commercial ventures he was concerned with, *Puckle's Machine* was ridiculed in a contemporary pack of playing cards.

A rare invention to Destroy the Crowd,
Of Fools at Home instead of Foes Abroad:
Fear not my Friends, this terrible Machine,
They're only wounded that have Shares therein.

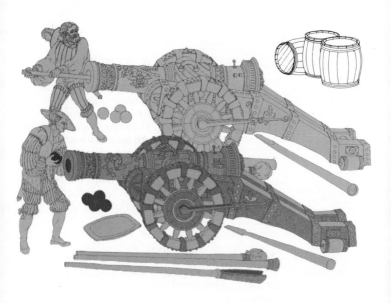

By the middle of the fourteenth century, shooting cannon was already an established science. The explosive mixture of sulfur, saltpeter and charcoal had been described in De secretis operibus artis et naturae, in 1242 or earlier, as being "productive of a flash of lightning and the noise of a thunderclap," but the first known representation of a gun to utilize the power of gunpowder dates from 1326. The simple metal tube did not change much for six centuries or so. During that period, the techniques of aiming and firing saw very little development, although ballistic theory advanced. Eventually, the tubes were rifled to give a more accurate shot, projectile and charge were loaded from the breech, sights were improved and the barrel became a complex and tough compound of tubes. Au fond the closed tubular barrel remained the basis of the gun.

Until the nineteenth century, the vast majority of guns were loaded from the muzzle. A charge of gunpowder was ladled into the barrel, followed by a wad and the round projectile. These German gunners of the first half of the sixteenth century are loading smooth-bore bronze guns ornamented, as so many were, with cast decoration which often included the coat of arms of the owner.
(See also pages 140–141 and 144.)

137

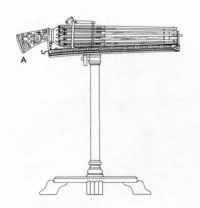

A *A twenty-barreled matchlock gun, inscribed* IL FIDEL – GIO. MARIA – BERGAMIN – F, *in the armory of the Palazzo Ducale, Venice. An inventory of 1773 records that it was the maker's gift to the Council of Ten, and was deposited in the Venetian arsenal in 1622.*

On April 16, 1746, 5.5 miles (8.9 km) east of Inverness, the Jacobite army under Prince Charles Edward Stuart (1720-88) faced the Duke of Cumberland (1721-65) at the head of George II's government forces. Charles' army of twenty-two infantry regiments, four hundred cavalry and twelve guns totaled 5,400. Cumberland had fifteen regular infantry battalions, four regiments of dragoons and sixteen guns, with a contingent of Scottish volunteers which made it up to 9,000. The government army had had three months to recover from their mauling by the Young Pretender's clansmen at Falkirk when the Jacobites had their last victory of the rising. The army that Cumberland took over from Hawley had been demoralized when the Jacobites were exultant, but Charles' empty treasury and violent dissension between the Scots and the Irish, always an inflammable mixture, had changed this by Easter. Perhaps as important a contribution to morale was the new bayonet drill practiced in Aberdeen barracks to prepare the Redcoats and their allies to defeat the targe and broadsword of the rebels.

At the time of Culloden fully-equipped Scottish soldiers carried a dirk and a pair of pistols, "a round targe on their backs, a blew bonnet on their heads, in one hand a broadsword and a musket in the other. Perhaps no nation goes better armed." When the bullet bag and powder flask, or a bandolier were added, it is difficult to imagine that the infantry were capable of marching as much as sixty miles (96.6 km) in thirty-six hours.

"The formation of artillery hath been very little improved in the last 200 years." These words from the preface to Benjamin

B *Count Maurice de Saxe's* amusette, *a breechloading flintlock gun on a two-* *wheeled carriage.* (**1**) *The* amusette *removed from its carriage.*

C *In the mid-eighteenth century, Scottish soldiers were notoriously heavily armed, and ready to fight with, in turn, musket, pistols,* *and sword and targe. After George Grant,* The New Highland Military Discipline *(London, 1757).*

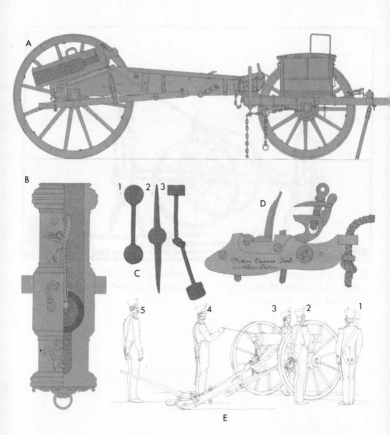

A The howitzer is a short artillery piece used to throw shells. Its angle of fire is usually higher than a normal cannon's and lower than a mortar's. Here the 7-pounder field howitzer is shown in section limbered (left), and ready to fire (right).

B This partially sectioned eighteenth-century howitzer has its shell in place. Note

how the shell sits neatly on the shoulders of the constricted chamber.

C Cannon projectiles: (**1**) Bar-shot, (**2**) Spiked shot, perhaps to carry incendiary material. (**3**) A form of chain-shot.

D A flintlock for use on cannon. It is inscribed PATTERN CANNON LOCK/MILLAR'S

pattern, English, c. 1830.

E *This field gun has a crew of five, each with his own part in the firing drill.* **1** *swabbed out the barrel;* **2***, the gun captain, aimed;* **3** *rammed home the powder, wad and ball;* **4** *pulled a lanyard to fire a flintlock, on the order of* **2***, so discharging the cannon;* **5** *helped to align the gun, using a handspike.*

F *A United States 12-inch (30 cm) coastal defense gun on a disappearing carriage. It is shown here raised, ready to fire. When fired, the recoil forces the gun backward, rolling the top carriage to the rear on the chassis rails and raising the counterweight, as the gun is lowered through the arc of an ellipse to the retracted position, where it is reloaded.*

141

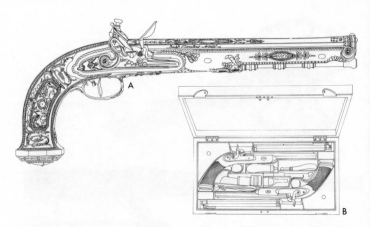

A *A French flintlock pistol,*
c. *1810, one of a pair made by*
Nicolas-Noël Boutet at the
Manufacture à Versailles,
where he was Directeur
Artiste.

B *Cased percussion dueling*
pistols with hair triggers,
1834, originally owned by the
Earl Canning (1812-62). The

fitted mahogany case contains
a powder flask, a bullet mold,
a nipple key, a patch cutter, a
mallet to start the bullet in the
barrel, a powder measure, a
linen bag of bullets, and two
bone boxes of linen patches
and spare nipples. Each pistol
has a pair of barrels, one
rifled, .455-inch (11.6 mm)

Robins' *New Principles of Gunnery* (1742) state quite
accurately the position of the science of gunnery two centuries
after Tartaglia's day. Robins, one of Britain's greatest
mathematicians, was born in Bath in 1707, the year of Vauban's
death. His researches concerned external and interior ballistics,
that is, the behavior of the ball before and after it leaves the
cannon's muzzle. Further, by using an improved version of
Cassini's ballistic pendulum he produced new theories on the
performance of the projectile at the target. His various
publications proved flaws in the hypotheses of Galileo and
Newton, discussed the flight of rockets and made the first
definite statements on the effect of air currents on the bullet's
flight. Robins' reputation as a military thinker caused the East
India Company to appoint him as the company's chief engineer
in 1749 to repair and reconstruct its forts. He died of a fever at
Fort St. David, Madras, on July 29, 1751, pen in hand, writing a
report.

Despite the wide circulation of Robins' *New Principles of*

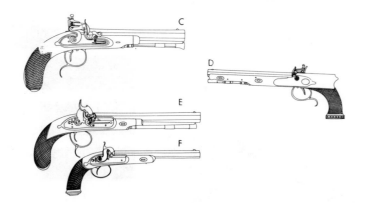

caliber, and one smooth, .47-inch (11.9 mm).

C *A dueling pistol engraved* FOWLER DUBLIN *on the octagonal barrel.*

D *Jeremiah Patrick, Liverpool, made this dueling pistol, c. 1815.*

E *A dueling pistol with pill-lock mechanism, by Charles Moore, London, c. 1822.*

F *A dueling pistol made by Isaac Riviere, London, and fitted with his enclosed lock, patented in 1825.*

Gunnery, which was translated into German by Leonhard Euler and into French by Le Roy, there were only a few small improvements in artillery around the middle of the eighteenth century. Hollow projectiles filled with explosive were already in the field, and grape shot, consisting of lead balls arranged round a central axis and netted together so that they flew in a regular pattern or firing like modern shot, were the scourge of many an infantry advance. Lighter field pieces and carriages were made and dispersed into separate brigades or batteries. The ladle was abolished for heavy siege guns which were now loaded with the ball mounted on a wooden sabot to fill the bore and reduce the windage. But credit for great reforms in artillery must go to the French general Jean Baptiste Vacquette de Gribeauval (1715-89). After service in Austria during the Seven Years' War, de Gribeauval held a command in the artillery of Prince Lichtenstein, who was an able organizer of an outstanding force. Impressed by what he had learned under the prince, although aware of weaknesses in the tactical employment of his

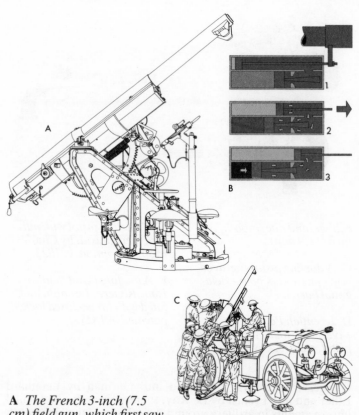

A *The French 3-inch (7.5 cm) field gun, which first saw action in China in 1900 during the Boxer rising, continued in service with the French and other armies until the Second World War. It employed the Nordenfelt breech in conjunction with a new long-recoil mechanism.*

B *The 75 recoil system. (1) The gun is linked to the rod of a piston in the upper of two cylinders set below. (2) On firing, the gun's recoil drives back the piston in the upper*

cylinder, forcing oil into the lower one to increase the air pressure by the forward movement of the floating piston. (3) The end of the recoil comes when the tapered floating piston closes a valve. The compressed air in the lower cylinder then reverses the movement to return the gun to the firing position.

C *The recoil system used on the French 75 was efficient enough to allow it to be used*

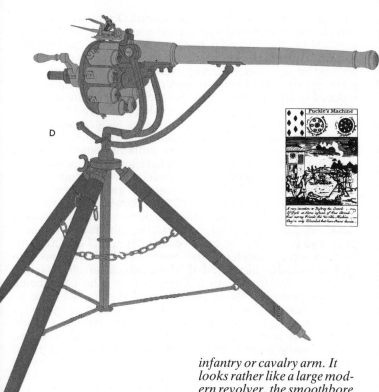

in an anti-aircraft role, from the back of a vehicle. Here, the equipment is served by United States anti-aircraft gunners near Montreuil in June, 1918.

D In November, 1717, the British Board of Ordnance witnessed a demonstration of a revolving matchlock or flintlock gun by James Puckle at their ranges at Woolwich.

The weapon was in effect light artillery rather than an infantry or cavalry arm. It looks rather like a large modern revolver, the smoothbore barrel being supported by a swivel bracket on a stout folding tripod. The barrel was served by a heavy cylinder, containing six or more chambers, which was revolved by hand. A handle at the rear enabled the gunner to screw the coned mouth of each chamber into the countersunk breech end of the barrel to form a relatively gas-tight joint. The patent drawing shows three cylinders, one of which is chambered for square bullets to be used against the Turk.

145

guns, de Gribeauval strove on his return to France to build up a complete system of staff training and assemble the best possible material for the dissimilar needs of field, siege, garrison and coastal artillery. His knowledge of the importance of mobility for field artillery caused him to banish from the gun park every piece heavier than twelve-pounders. Those he retained were reduced in length and weight. Smaller charges were used and the fit of projectiles to the bore made more accurate.

The more reactionary of his colleagues resisted successfully for a time, but in 1776 he became France's first Inspector General of Artillery and this new authority enabled him to carry out the improvements which have made him perhaps the most famous of all artillery commanders. De Gribeauval's field artillery had four-pounders as regimental guns with eight- and twelve-pounders and six-inch (15.2 cm) howitzers as a reserve. These last a modern commander would consider his divisional guns. For garrison and siege use sixteen- and twelve-pounder guns, and eight-, ten- and twelve-inch (20.3, 25.4 and 30.4 cm) mortars were considered the most useful of all arms. De Gribeauval also instructed that the wheels of all carriages should be constructed to a single pattern, the parts being interchangeable so far as possible, and for the first time he ordered horses to be harnessed in pairs instead of in file. A newly designed ammunition wagon to transport fixed ammunition also came into use. Alongside solid shot and hollow mortar bombs, canisters of sheet iron holding cast iron balls (case shot) replaced the old grape shot. De Gribeauval's most serious failure was his inability to persuade the king of the value of changes which were not to be introduced into the French service until 1791. In the same year they were adopted by the Swedes and two years later by Great Britain.

The increasing use of artillery during the later eighteenth century gave rise to yet one further military development, the *chasseur à pied* or *de cheval*, light infantry and light cavalry which were required to protect the lengthening columns of artillery. This in turn led to the splitting of infantry into two types whose functions varied but whose arms were the same, the light infantry being capable of faster movement over any given ground than the standard infantry.

Indirect consequences of this increasing use of artillery were the hastening of factory organization in the face of growing demands on craftsmen who produced the brass, wood and iron, and the need to standardize arms and equipment.

De Gribeauval's reforms bore fruit in the Wars of the Republic. His tables of construction ensured uniformity of manufacture, and the reduction in the weight of guns gave a mobility in the field which allowed artillery to be used with the greatest effect in Napoleon's new tactics. The last step in the field artillery's reorganization occurred in 1800, when a driver corps was established to put an end to the old system of horsing by civilian contractors.

While the styles of European firearms tended to draw closer together, and even as the peripheral differences found in Scotland, Scandinavia and the Iberian peninsula were disappearing, emigration led to the development of a new type of weapon across the Atlantic. Among America's German settlers who had used rifles in their home country were men with the skill to make new rifles to replace those worn out or irreparably damaged. During the eighteenth and early nineteenth centuries there evolved a long, almost elegant muzzle-loading weapon, now popularly known as the Kentucky rifle. American rifles were first made in Pennsylvania, which had a large population of German settlers. Later they were made in most of the original colonies and in Ohio, Tennessee, Kentucky and a few in Indiana. The earlier rifles, which gained a high reputation as hunting arms and saw service in the French and Indian wars, were little different from those made in Europe. Gradually their "Europeanness" gave way to typically American features. Maplewood stocks, very long octagonal barrels and patchbox covers of sheet brass, often elaborately fretted, are the means of identifying the work of the men who created the "Kentucky" rifle by the outbreak of the Revolutionary War in which it played an important part. It was used with skill in the war of 1812 without making any massive contribution to the result, although riflemen from Tennessee, Kentucky and the valley of the Ohio River helped in Jackson's victory at New Orleans in 1815.

Some pistols made during the period when the Kentucky rifle was popular bear a strong resemblance to the long arms in the details of their construction. Most were made in Pennsylvania. Like the rifles, the large-scale production of pistols, shotguns and rifles in the factories of the Eastern seaboard brought the local manufacture of pistols to a close around the middle of the nineteenth century. A few rifles, however, are still made for traditionalists who enjoy shooting them in muzzle-loading competitions.

A fowling-piece with a pivoted chamber hinged so that it could be tipped up or swung sideways for loading was made as early as the reign of Henry VIII. John Bicknell, gunmaker to King Charles II, connected the rear of a hinged chamber to a long

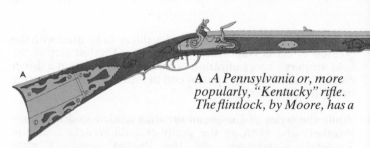

A *A Pennsylvania or, more popularly, "Kentucky" rifle. The flintlock, by Moore, has a*

trigger guard in his design of *c.* 1660. When the trigger guard is depressed the front of the chamber rises. The absence of a tight seal between the chamber and the barrel meant that gas leaks with their unpleasant effects began as soon as the action started to wear and corrode.

A more complicated design in the Museum of Artillery, Woolwich, has a chamber hinged at the rear and joined to the barrel by an interrupted screw thread. When the barrel and fore-end are twisted to disengage the thread they can be pulled forward and the chamber tilted up to load. The other interesting features which its maker, Peter Duringer of Mainz, thought would commend it to possible military purchasers are combined match and flintlock ignition and a hollowed butt to give a better grip when it was used with the long bayonet hinged to its muzzle.

For a century the pivoted breech was neglected, to be rediscovered by Guiseppi Crespi of Milan in 1770. The Austrian cavalry carbine of *c.* 1775, based on Crespi's design, was copied by the Swiss-born gunmaker Durs Egg ten years later and offered to the British Board of Ordnance who tested thirty carbines of three different barrel-lengths in 1788. The carbines were supplied complete with long socket bayonets reminiscent of the Roman *pilum*. A short socket that slipped over the muzzle was attached to a long steel rod ending in a small leaf-shaped blade. Egg fitted the trials carbines with the lock designed in 1784 by a Lewisham arms contractor, Jonathan Hennem. It looked much the same as the locks then in common use, but the moving parts and the springs were held in position on the lockplate by pegs and clips. Using a special tool a trooper could dismantle the lock quickly and easily to clean it or replace a broken part. Other screwless locks were designed by Henry Nock (1775), Sir George Bolton (1795) and Johann Christian Wilcken Kyhl, the last being adopted by the Danish army as its Model 1806.

In America, a version of the Crespi and Egg tip-up breech was patented by John Hancock Hall and William Thornton in May 1811. In 1817, Hall made a .54-inch (13.7 mm) caliber rifle for trials held by the United States Army. The success of his rifle earned him a contract to supervise its manufacture at the Harpers Ferry Armory. Modern collectors of arms know the rifle as "The U.S. rifle, Model 1819 (Hall's)." Contracts for making the rifle continued to be granted until 1835, Simeon North of Middletown, Connecticut, receiving several. It was North who made the .64-inch (16.3 mm) caliber smooth-bore Hall carbines of 1833, which were the first percussion arms made in any quantity for the United States Army. Hall himself made a single flintlock carbine at Harpers Ferry, the profits from the rest accrued to North.

The under-hammer breechloading rifle invented by Captain Frederik Wilhelm Scheel and adopted by the Norwegian army for infantry and rifle regiments from 1842 to 1848 was based on a very similar action to Crespi's of 1770, the Løbnitz.

The year of the de Gribeauval's appointment as France's Inspector General of Artillery, 1776, saw the introduction of the first military breechloader to be used in the British Army. Patrick Ferguson's rifle has captured the imagination of collectors in Britain and America, but although an interesting development it was no more than a modification of a 1704 design by Isaac de la Chaumette, a Huguenot refugee who patented it in London in 1721. De la Chaumette's design consisted of a plug with a quick-acting thread screwed vertically through the breech, the base being joined to the front of the trigger guard. A single turn of the guard lowered the plug to allow the bullet and the charge of powder to be poured into a hole on top of the breech. In practice the plug was found to jam because of powder fouling, and Ferguson's idea was to cut channels in the male threads to keep the plug free. Before the king at Windsor, and a committee of officers at Woolwich, Ferguson demonstrated the rifle with great skill. The committee of officers recommended an order for one hundred rifles with bayonets for trial. After supervising their manufacture at Birmingham, Ferguson trained a company in their use and embarked with them for America in 1777. The only known example of the government model which survives is preserved in the Morristown National Historic Park Museum in New Jersey. It has a 34-inch (86.4 cm) barrel of .68 inch (17.3 mm) caliber rifled with eight grooves. A number of other rifles were made for the East India Company, for sporting purposes and for volunteer regiments. Patrick Ferguson was Inspector General of Militia in Georgia and the Carolinas with the acting rank of lieutenant-colonel when he led a battalion of militia against the Revolutionaries. At the battle of Kings Mountain in South Carolina on October 7, 1780, he was killed with many of his men after a long and bloody battle. A monument and a cairn mark the traditional site of his grave on the hillside.

Chapter 14

Lewis Mumford has stated that the 1780s "mark the definite crystallization of the paleotechnic complex." By the middle of the century the Industrial Revolution had arrived, and the day of the small-scale craftsman working with a few assistants and feeble power resources was drawing to a close. For example, John Smeaton trebled the production of a blast furnace in 1761 by driving his air-pumps by water wheels. On January 5, 1769, James Watt patented his steam engine and in 1781 and 1782 solved the problem of producing rotary motion from its reciprocating pistons. In France, Cugnot in 1770 had already made a steam artillery carriage whose intelligent conception was not matched by its design, and it was left to William Murdock (1754-1839), one of Watt's employees, to design a successful model of a high-pressure steam locomotive in 1784. The same decade saw the creation of Cort's reverberatory furnace, Wilkinson's iron boat, Cartwright's power loom, Bramah's screw propeller, and Jouffroy's and Fitch's steamboats. The Carron Company's short guns achieved success, and a system of interchangeable-parts gun manufacture was introduced in France and Britain. Each had its effect on the technology of war.

A 24-pounder carronade for use on ships and small craft. It has an inclined carriage slide to check recoil.

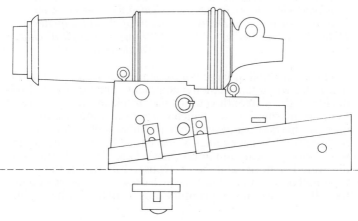

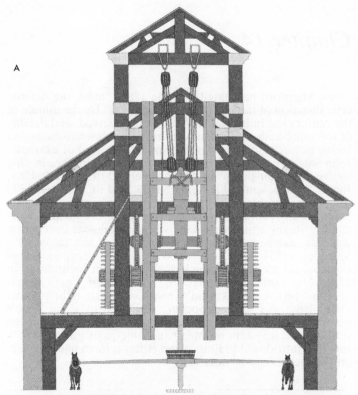

A *A vertical drill for boring out cast cannon barrels. The casting was lowered onto a drill head which was rotated by horse-power. After Denis Diderot,* Encyclopédie *(1751-65).*

B *A bronze "partridge" mortar, French, c. 1700. It fired one 4.3-inch (11 cm) shell and thirteen smaller shells of about 1.2 inches (30 mm), in a single discharge. It was described and*

The application of large boring-machines to the metalworking trades was a fairly late development. The main use of this device in the sixteenth century was to clean out the bore of cannons of bronze or iron which were at that time cast around a mandril that was withdrawn to leave them hollow. Leonardo's designs for boring engines were basically the same as the woodworkers used, and in his *Pirotechnia* (1540), Biringuccio illustrated a horizontal borer whose drill was turned by a treadmill or by water power; a winch drawing the work onto the tool. By the seventeenth century most cannon-boring engines

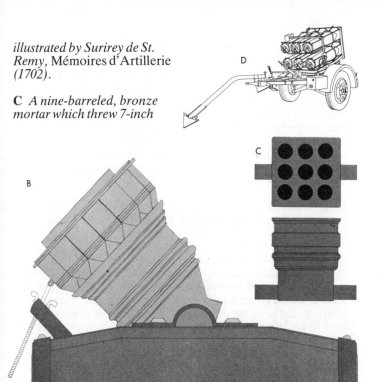

illustrated by Surirey de St. Remy, Mémoires d'Artillerie (1702).

C *A nine-barreled, bronze mortar which threw 7-inch*

(17.8 cm) shells in groups of three. This piece was used to discharge fireworks in celebration of the Peace of Aix-la-Chapelle on October 7, 1748.

D *The* Nebelwerfer 42, *a German rocket-launcher designed to fire six 11.8-inch (30 cm) rockets simultaneously. Second World War.*

worked vertically, the weight of the cannon suspended above the drill giving sufficient pressure. In 1713, improvements in the cannon drill introduced by the Swiss Jean Maritz allowed cannon-founders to cast their barrels solid and drill the bore on a horizontal drill. Maritz exhibited this engine in Spain and France and it was not long before the system was in use in Sweden and Britain.

A considerable improvement in the techniques of cannon-making was embodied in the patent granted to John Wilkinson on January 27, 1774, which described a method of boring cannon from solid castings. His drill was mounted on a heavy bench on which it could be moved forwards and backwards by a rack and pinion. The barrel was mounted in wooden sleeves and rotated by a spindle driven by steam or water power. Drills of increasing sizes were used in succession until the desired caliber was reached. The accuracy of the finished barrel was due to the independent suspension of the work and the tools. When the Carron Company was trying so desperately to bring its products up to the standards set by the Board of Ordnance, the Wilkinson system was one which its southern representatives were ordered to investigate.

Shortly before 1785, Le Blanc, a French gunmaker, began to make musket parts in quantity to standard sizes that were closely checked on gauges. In theory arms could thus be made up from a random selection of parts. Until Le Blanc's venture into the field of mass-production to supply the increasing pressure of military demand, which itself hastened factory organization, there had been little true uniformity even in screw threads, although attempts had been made to standardize calibers as early as the middle of the sixteenth century. One visitor to Le Blanc's workshops who was handed the pieces of fifty locks "put several together myself, taking pieces at hazard as they came to hand, and they fitted in the most perfect manner." The news soon crossed the Atlantic and the inventor of the cotton gin, Eli Whitney, successfully applied for a contract in 1798 to supply the United States government with 10,000 similarly standardized muskets at a cost of $13.40 each. These were to be modeled on the Charleville musket, bought from France at $5 apiece to arm the revolutionaries twenty years before. Whitney was late in delivering the arms, which did not reach the arsenals until 1809, but he was granted further federal and state contracts for some thousands of arms before his death on January 8, 1826 at the age of sixty.

In a letter to the Secretary of the Treasury, Oliver Wolcott, Whitney pressed the point that he could also produce cartridge boxes: "I have a machine for boreing wood of my own Invention which is admirably adapted to this purpose." He also offered to make swords, hangers and pistols as there was water power enough for grindstones and trip hammers near his property at Whitneyville, Connecticut, where he proposed to set up his factory. But the muskets were the key to his future success. His second application for a federal contract opens with the statement: "A good musket is a complicated engine and difficult to make–difficult of execution because the conformation of most of its parts corresponds with no regular geometric figure,...each musket, with Bayonet, consists of fifty distinct parts." By the outbreak of the war of 1812, he had overcome the problem of cutting the irregular shapes by inventing the milling machine and applying it to a broad range of purposes.

Although the arms produced at the Whitneyville factory between its opening with a staff of about sixty in 1800 and Whitney's death were accepted as a miracle of engineering technology, recent research has shown that the parts of the Whitneyville muskets in the United States national collection are not as fully interchangeable as their creator claimed. With the help of Eli Whitney and his commercial rival, Simeon North, the system of interchangeable-parts manufacture was introduced to the government factories at Springfield and Harpers Ferry after the adoption of Hall's breechloader by the federal government in 1819.

The process of mechanization meant that the basic skills no longer needed to be in the hands of the men who made the pieces of the firearms, as it was supplied by the makers of the machine tools. Even at the earliest stages, while hand-filing was still an essential part of gun-making, the fact that workmen were guided by jigs made a lower degree of skill acceptable. In theory, if the part fitted the jig to which it was being made, it would fit the parts made to an identical jig by the man at the next bench. The system was fully refined in the fourth decade of the nineteenth century when drop-forging, die-stamping and pattern-turning were in regular use in the arms factories of Europe and America.

Before the end of the eighteenth century, in the year of Frederick the Great's death, students of the history of arms and armor received their first formal instruction from the pen of Francis Grose (1730/1-91). By profession a topographical artist, Grose's enthusiasms seem to have been equally shared between a love of antiquities of all sorts and a passion for food and wine. When he inherited his father's fortune in 1769, he was thirty-eight or thirty-nine, had served as an officer in the Hampshire Militia, been Richmond Herald, a member of the Incorporated Society of Artists and a Fellow of the Society of Antiquaries of London–almost a perfect blend of experience for a man whose histories of war and arms are still much sought after despite a certain quaintness in some of their judgments. His *Treatise on Ancient Armour and Weapons* (1786) was a prelude to a better book, *Military Antiquities of the English Army*.

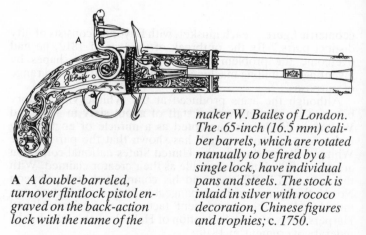

A A double-barreled, turnover flintlock pistol engraved on the back-action lock with the name of the maker W. Bailes of London. The .65-inch (16.5 mm) caliber barrels, which are rotated manually to be fired by a single lock, have individual pans and steels. The stock is inlaid in silver with rococo decoration, Chinese figures and trophies; c. 1750.

In the year that Grose published his *Treatise*, the leading London gunmaker Henry Nock devised one of the most satisfactory of all flintlock breechloaders. A reloadable cartridge which forms part of the breech is pivoted on a slide. When the slide is drawn towards the butt, the cartridge hinges upwards to a vertical position for loading. In the firing position, in line with the barrel, it is locked by a vertical peg attached to a short chain which also serves as the handle when opening the breech. An example in the Tower Armouries shows that this was an efficiently-made arm, and much less complicated to use than its appearance would suggest. However, it had little success, although it was a considerable improvement over Guiseppi Crespi's design of 1770, itself so like Bicknell's breechloader of *c.* 1660.

Henry Nock was also closely involved in the production of a volley gun offered by James Wilson to the British Board of Ordnance in 1779, when the inventor described it as "a new Invented Gun with seven barrels to fire at one time." When the version with rifled barrels was recommended for use from ship's rigging, Nock, who had made Wilson's prototypes, supervised the manufacture between 1780 and 1788 of 655 at £13 each. Perhaps inspired by the interest shown by Colonel Thomas Thornton, several of London's leading gunmakers made versions for game-shooting. The most distinctive survivor was the colonel's own, an 11.5-lb (5.2 kg) sporting encumbrance by Dupe and Company with fourteen barrels in two sets of seven placed side by side. The gun is now in the Musée d'Armes, Liège.

With the development of percussion ignition, the inventive Forsyth and Pauly designed neater seven-barreled sporting

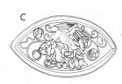

B *A silver-gilt trigger guard from a flintlock sporting gun which was made at Versailles, under Boutet, for King Charles IV of Spain, c. 1803.*

C *The butt terminal of a wheellock pistol inlaid with stag antler and mother-of-pearl. Swiss, c. 1620.*

D *The engraved steel butt-plate of a breechloading flint-lock rifle by Robert Rowland of London, 1718.*

arms, and as late as 1900 the Belgian Henri Pieper made a rolling breech rifle firing seven .22-inch (5.6 mm) cartridges from seven barrels on a single pressure of the trigger. Pieper's design was the last hand-held example of a series that began soon after the introduction of fire-arms and proceeded by way of a seven-barreled handgun mentioned in a Bastille inventory of 1453; sporting guns with several barrels drilled from a solid block; pistols with two, three or more barrels–of which the "duck's foot pistol" is perhaps the best known–through J. Lillycrap's patent of 1842, which shows a belt set with five pistol barrels that were fired simultaneously.

The appeal of the same idea to some artillerists resulted in the so-called "partridge mortar" of *c.* 1700, which had a large central bore surrounded by a ring of thirteen smaller bores firing one standard mortar shell and thirteen grenades. The vent of the parent barrel also gave fire to the smaller ones to produce an almost simultaneous discharge. Although never common or especially successful, they were used by the French in defense at Bouchain in 1702, and in attack at the siege of Lille six years later. One survives in the Museum für deutsche Geschichte, Berlin.

The psychological effect of these coveys of explosive shells must have been much the same in their day as the much more devastating clusters of rockets from the 5.9-inch (15 cm) *Nebelwerfer 41* and its 8.3-inch (21 cm) successor, respectively six- and five-barreled, that rained down on the Allied armies at Cassino and later at the defensive complex occupied by the Wehrmacht east of the Orne. There, almost three hundred of these rocket-mortars were emplaced, each capable of discharging six rounds every 90 seconds at targets up to 7,700 yards (7,041 m) away.

The military history of the eighteenth century saw few changes of more lasting consequence than the French revolutionary government's introduction of universal conscription on August 23, 1793. The country's army was increased to 700,000 men under the inspired guidance of Lazare Nicolas Marguerite Carnot (1753-1823), who achieved popular acclaim as France's "organizer of victory." Carnot, himself a mathematician, saw the value of officers trained in science, so the Ecole Polytechnique was founded in 1794 to teach gunners mathematics and military engineering. By then the factories of Paris were turning out 750 muskets a day, instructions for gathering saltpeter had been broadcast across the country, and two citizens from each district were called to the capital to learn how to cast iron and bronze, and how to make gunpowder by the latest techniques.

A side-effect of the great revolution was the establishment at Versailles of a state arms factory. Primarily it was intended to supply military weapons of all types, but, in a separate workshop, *armes de luxe* of the highest quality were made and decorated. It was founded with the title *Ateliers révolution-naires* by a decree of the National Convention dated August 22, 1793, and installed in the palace of Versailles on October 6. Its first director, who held the post of *Directeur Artiste* from the beginning until 1815, was Nicolas-Noël Boutet (1761-1833). The son and son-in-law of well-known gunmakers, Boutet has been described as the last of the great artist-gunsmiths under whose direction the Manufacture à Versailles produced more than 600,000 weapons. Of the service arms used by the French forces, the factory produced thirteen models of muskets, carbines and blunderbusses; three models of pistols; and thirteen types of swords, as well as daggers, maces, axes and lances. Enriched versions of simple arms, *armes d'honneur*, were presented to men and units for outstanding service. These were made to twelve different patterns ranging in price from sabers costing 600 francs for divisional commanders down to infantry hangers (*briquets*) at only 111.68 francs. These were cherished awards made at the order of the emperor or his minister of war, but their intrinsic value fades into utter insignificance beside the weapons ordered by Napoleon as first consul and emperor for presentation to his supporters and allies. A saber mounted in gold with rock crystal, and the finest of precious stones set among cast and chiseled compositions cost France 28,000 francs when Napoleon considered that a gift of such splendor would further his political ends. From the inception of the factory, which was staffed by local craftsmen and outsiders from as far afield as Liège, until its decline between 1815 and 1818, a flood of highly decorated luxury arms flowed from its benches. The list of recipients holds a mirror to the history of France during Boutet's unique directorship. Extravagant gifts went to Charles IV of Spain, the kings of Rome and Naples, princes, dukes, marshals of the empire and a host of other French and foreign dignitaries.

A by-product of this sumptuousness was the continuation throughout the Napoleonic Wars of a tradition of fine gunmaking in the face of urgent demands for munition arms. The state studios at Sèvres and Gobelin were required to train young men in the arts of the ceramist and the tapestryweaver. By the same inspired philosophy Boutet was ordered to instruct thirty pupils each year in the gunsmith's craft. A three-year apprenticeship included the study of design under a drawing-master employed by Boutet. The result was a flawless finish to the ornamental metalwork in steel or precious metals – three colors of gold were sometimes used with silver on a single weapon – and to the woodwork of the stocks. The quality of a deathdealing weapon *per se* was always important, but ornament took pride of place at Versailles.

Before the close of the sixteenth century, Levantine smiths combined the coil-wound gunbarrel with the ornamental features found in the patternwelded sword of the Migration period to make strong, decorative gunbarrels. These "damascus" barrels were made from a more or less alloyed mixture of iron and steel that was worked so that the varied colors of the metal formed an attractive watered pattern. The first recorded European gunsmith to experiment with this process was an Englishman, William Dupc. His work done in 1798 was followed eight years later by a patent granted to the Birmingham inventor John Jones for the manufacture of gunbarrels by wrapping a spiral band of bevel-edged metal around a mandril hammer-welding the spiral into a tube. The raw material was re-used scrap – horseshoe nails, old scythe blades and razors – smelted in a charcoal furnace. After the finished tube was polished, dipping in acid baths brought out the pattern that many lovers of rich arms found so attractive.

By 1812, barrel makers in Liège sold pairs of damascus barrels, bored after welding, for 17 Brabant florins, while pairs of ordinary barrels cost just over 5 florins. The nineteenth-century French gunmakers Bernard and Leclerc and their contemporaries produced many different surface designs, among them *Bernard, Leclerc, Paris damascus* and *Turkish*. But at the Paris and Liège exhibitions of 1900 and 1905 it was a Nessonvaux smith, E. Heuse-Lemoine, who walked off with the prizes for a selection of damascus barrels that ignored the current trend toward cast steel. Examples in the Musée d'Armes, Liège, have complex surface figuring involving the names of King Leopold II and Prince Albert. Laboratory analysis has proved that the inscriptions, like *Liège 1905* on a third, are the result of combining heterogeneous metal right through the barrel wall. Although the process demanded much technical skill, experience and pertinacity, the result invites an irreverent comparison with a souvenir candy stick inscribed through its length with the name of a seaside resort.

In the sixteenth century many firearms barrels and sword hilts were chiseled in high relief, a technique that reached its finest development in the workshops of the brothers Emanuel and Daniel Sadeler, and Caspar Spät, who succeeded them as *Eisenschneider* to the Bavarian court at Munich. Elsewhere, for example in Spain, Portugal, Scotland and Italy, the patterns derived to a large extent from vernacular folk art.

In addition to the difficult but straightforward process of carving their patterns directly onto the basic metal, arms decorators often used a combination of the techniques of damascus work and chiseling by attaching, not a thin sheet or wire of precious metal, but a substantial, partly shaped lump that could then be carved into a relief design.

The relief technique that demanded the least local skill from the gunsmith was the application of pre-cast silver, gold or bronze mounts which he could buy from a specialist and apply, in the form of sideplates and buttcaps to his own products.

The first screw-cutting lathe probably appeared in the last quarter of the fifteenth century, and one well-finished specimen in the Smithsonian Institution was made *c.* 1600 by Manuel Wetschgi, a member of a well-known Augsburg family of mechanics. Nevertheless, until Maudslay's invention, screws were costly and used as little as possible, so his screw-cutting lathe was one of the most decisive contributions to standardization. Without it, modern machinery could not be made in real quantity. Maudslay took the greatest delight in

A version of the Perkins steam gun, exhibited in England, c. 1851-61. Only the barrel (1), the valve mechanism (2) and the loading

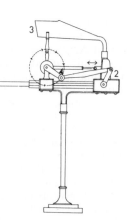

magazine (3) are shown here. Pipes connected the breech to a generator and furnace which, each hour, turned 120 gallons (c. 454 liters) of water into high-pressure steam. One turn of the handle (4) dropped a ball into the breech and released a blast of steam through the valve.

standardization, refinement and the continual reduction of the limits to which his men worked. He founded a workshop tradition which fathered a dynasty of mechanics, including Roberts, Muir, Lewis, Nasmyth the inventor of the steam hammer, and Joseph Whitworth, who did so much to improve the accuracy and destructive power of the rifle and the cannon. "It was a pleasure to see him [Maudslay] handle a tool of any kind," said one of his workmen, "but he was *quite splendid* with an eighteen-inch file."

By about 1750, shells were made with a fuse of beechwood cut into lengths according to the time needed for their passage to the target. For very short ranges, the gunner had to accept the danger of a premature explosion in the bore of the gun or of the charge failing to ignite at all. During the siege of Gibraltar (1779-83) the defenders of the North Front were faced with this kind of frustrating situation. The Spanish lines were within the range of the English guns, but the solid shot dropped harmlessly into sand instead of ricocheting until it hit some solid object, while mortar shells, dropping at a very steep angle, buried themselves in the ground before exploding.

Captain John Mercier of the 39th Foot evolved a system of "calculated" fuses based on ranges which the gunners already knew exactly. The fuses of 5.5-inch (14 cm) mortar shells fired from 24-pounders could be made to explode over the heads of the Spanish working parties. Side benefits from Mercier's "operative gun shell" were that firing it from the longer gun barrels gave greater accuracy. When combined with the shells' lighter weight this meant that less powder could be used for each shot. By the end of the siege, 129,000 of the 200,600 rounds fired were shells, yet it was twenty years before the Royal Artillery accepted Mercier's innovation as more than a makeshift, suited only to Gibraltar's peculiar siege conditions. The final acceptance of spherical case shot was due to a young artillery officer's efforts to develop it to the point at which it was recommended for adoption in 1803, and was praised by Wellington in the Peninsula and by Sir George Wood at Waterloo. It was officially given Henry Shrapnel's name in 1852, ten years after his death and more than seventy years after he had been so impressed by its service when he was a junior officer on the Rock.

Gibraltar still bears the marks of another artillery invention from a few years before the siege. A hole three feet wide by four feet deep (.9 by 1.2 m) was cut in the virgin rock, to take 50 lb (22.7 kg) of gunpowder and 1,470 stones between 1 and 1.3 lb (.45 and .57 kg) separated by a wooden, obturating tompion. The five-minute fuse ran through a copper tube into the heart of the powder. The invention, by a civilian called Healy, aroused some interest at its peacetime trials but it was never used in its proposed role against enemy landings.

Despite the British Army's experience in fortifying Gibraltar with deep underground tunnels cut in the eighteenth century, it was left to a French engineer officer, Lieutenant-Colonel M. Mouzé, to write the first comprehensive study of underground fortification, *Traité de Fortification Souterraine*, in 1804. Throughout the Napoleonic Wars British military philosophers paid scant heed to the gap in skill and experience between them and their Continental brothers. For instance, in the extensive series of sieges undertaken during the campaigns in the Peninsula there was no trained sapper or miner with Wellington's army until 1813, and even then there was a school of opinion that felt that the laboring in sap and countermine could best be done by civilian labor recruited locally.

It seems probable that trap-guns or alarm-guns, fired by pressure on a wire stretched between two posts, were in use by the early seventeenth century at the latest. The Stadtmuseum, Cologne, has an example fitted with a wheellock mechanism. By the turn of the eighteenth century they were common around game preserves, either to warn keepers of the presence of poachers or to inflict injury on intruders. Like the man-trap the barbarity of these spring-guns was eventually recognized in Britain, and an Act of 1827 outlawed them. Before then they also rendered service as a protection against another sort of thief, the "resurrection-men," grave-robbers who stole bodies

162

from graveyards to sell to the anatomists of the medical schools. "If the men intended going to a certain grave at night, late in the afternoon a woman, in deep mourning, would walk round the cemetery in which the grave was situated, and contrive to detach the wire from the guns." In the more sophisticated spring-guns, the wire which fired the lock also swung the gun on a pivot so that its load of shot or metal fragments was projected in the direction of the pull.

A century later the German army developed a .31-inch (7.92 mm) fully automatic machine gun, the *Zf. Ger. 38*, for a similar role. Its barrel was threaded as a deep bullet-shredder which fragmented the bullet to give a shotgun effect against any escaping prisoner who might trip its firing wire. Between the first wheellock trap gun and the *Zf. Ger. 38*, a variety of types were made which fired blank cartridges to frighten or to warn, or ball, harpoon or shot cartridges to kill or wound men or animals.

Leonardo da Vinci gave the credit for the invention of the first steam-gun to Archimedes, an architect who was his contemporary, and described and illustrated it under the title *architronito*. According to Leonardo, the gun threw a ball weighing about 80 lb (*c.* 36 kg) about 1,200 yards (*c.* 1,100 m), but even in the turbulent Italy of the early sixteenth century it did not arouse much interest. Little was heard of the steam-powered gun for another three centuries until, in 1797, three Philadelphians experimented with a steam-musket. In 1819, another American was granted patent protection in respect of a system for "shooting by steam." In France, General Girard built a wheeled boiler which fed steam to six musket barrels which were hopper-loaded with balls at a rate of 180 per minute. This was in 1814, ten years before Jacob Perkins of Newport, Massachusetts, began his experimental work on a steam-gun that he patented in Britain in 1824 as "an improved mode of throwing shells." Perkins' shells were in reality water-filled cylindrical rockets, their tails closed with fusible metal plugs. The shells were heated in a tube until the plug melted and the water was quickly converted to steam which drove the shell from the barrel. In 1825 Perkins had advanced far enough to persuade the Duke of Wellington to bring officers of the Board of Ordnance to witness trials. They were not impressed, but the French ordered a rifled four-pounder firing about thirty round per minute. At the Adelaide Gallery of Practical Science in London in 1832, and in Salford Mechanical Institute in 1840, a machine gun was displayed to a public whose imagination had already been captured by 1825. The cartoon

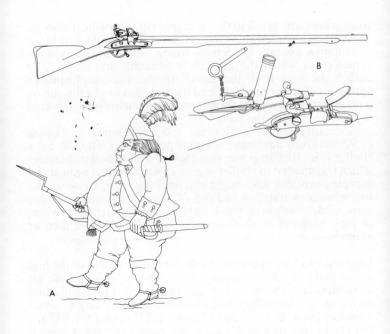

A *Captain Francis Grose, the first major arms historian to write in English, caricatured in the uniform of a captain in the Surrey Militia, the second regiment in which he served. After his own* Rules for Drawing Caricatures *(London, 1788).*

B *Henry Nock's flintlock breechloading musket. London, 1786. The "cartridge" hinges upward for loading when the slide, on which it is pivoted, is drawn back. The breech is locked, when in* firing position, by a vertical peg.

C *A German, four-barreled flintlock carbine, c. 1660, signed* FRANCISCO MAMBACH. *One barrel is loaded and fired in the usual way, and the flame of its discharge passes through internal holes to ignite charges in the other barrels, until a total of twenty-nine shots is fired.*

D *A three-barreled pistol with self-spanning wheellock mechanism. The barrels,*

164

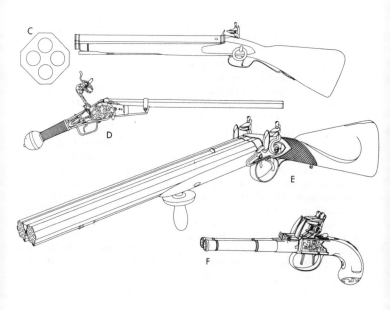

which are brazed together,
are rotated by hand and
locked in each firing position,
in turn, by a catch. German,
Nuremberg, c. 1570.

E An English volley-gun
with two sets of seven barrels,
c. 1790. Each set had its own
lock, which could be used
separately, or with the other
lock to fire a fourteen-
barreled weapon. One set is
inscribed PERDITION TO CON-
SPIRATORS, the other GLEN-
MORE FOREST 1793. The rib is
inscribed WITH THIS ALONE

I'LL DEFEND ROBRO CAMP
1795. The gun was the property
of Colonel Thomas Thornton
(1757-1823) of the 2nd West
Riding Militia, who commanded Roborough Camp,
Devon, at the time of a mutiny
in 1795. The locks are marked
DUPE & CO.

F A double-barreled flintlock
pistol, one of a pair, the box
lock engraved GRIFFIN & TOW
LONDON; c. 1775.

165

Britannia's Steam Navy was accompanied by the jingle—
> Five hundred balls, per minute, shot,
> Our foes in fight must kick the beam,
> Let Perkins only boil his pot,
> And he'll destroy them all by steam.

About the time that Perkins' invention was being most widely discussed, Viscount Palmerston was asking for trials for a steam-gun invented by General Henri Dembinski; "a very responsible man, and was reckoned one of the best officers in the Polish Insurrection in 1831 and 1832." However, not even Palmerston's commendation could rouse any interest at the Board of Ordnance, which showed an equal lack of interest in invitations to view a gun built in 1854 by Edwin Dike of Cirencester. The Perkins family exhibited their gun at the 1851 Exhibition in London and as late as 1861, when Gatling's eminently practical gun was almost ready for public demonstration, Angier Perkins shot sixty 1.5-ounce (42.5 gr) Minié balls per minute and kept his machine going for ten consecutive hours. But his military audience noticed that the skeletal apparatus with its pipes, valves, generator and furnace used 120 gallons (454.6 l) of water an hour and decided that it was not a venture in which public money should be invested.

Chapter 15

To the modern student of firearms, Howard's most surprising assertion is that mercury fulminate would not ignite gunpowder. Fortunately for the future of firearms development this statement was not accepted by the Reverend Alexander John Forsyth, a Scottish minister of religion, who was himself an enthusiastic amateur mechanic and chemist with a deep and lasting interest in shooting. Forsyth's familiarity with the flintlock's weaknesses, namely the time-lag between the pressure on the trigger and ignition, the difficulties of shooting in bad weather and its telltale puff of smoke, led him to experiment to see whether detonators could be substituted for the priming to give practically instantaneous ignition of the gunpowder in the chamber.

First he had to create a mechanism that would store the powder safely and deliver only a tiny charge to be ignited by a hammer blow near the touchhole. He succeeded in doing this in the spring of 1806 and brought to London an ingenious gunlock design with the advantage that most flintlocks could be converted to it with very little cost or difficulty.

Forsyth was encouraged to continue his experiments in the Tower of London, where he was given a small workshop and, after some problems were solved, locks were produced for a carbine and a carronade, but these failed to satisfy Colonel Thomas Blomefield when tested at Woolwich in 1807. On April 11 of the same year Forsyth patented an "advantageous method of discharging or giving fire to artillery and all other firearms, mines, chambers, cavities and places in which gunpowder or other combustible matter is, or may be put for the purposes of explosion." He must have been very well advised by his agent, for the patent successfully blocked the efforts of other inventors to patent other new and improved methods of detonating locks throughout its fourteen-year life. Once he was satisfied that he had a successful lock, the London gunmaking firm of Alexander Forsyth and Company was formed to make and sell his sporting guns and he seemed to lose interest in the subsequent experiments to improve the detonating lock. However, he continued to protect his invention with successful legal actions against a number of competitors, among them Joseph Manton, perhaps the most famous London gunmaker of all time. One interesting by-product of the case was the series of experiments that Manton's defending counsel carried out on Forsyth's locks over a period of six months. After thirty discharges the lock began to falter, the first plug lasted three firings, the second but two and the third a single firing. In sixty discharges twenty-two plugs were broken and the chamber was so enlarged that it received more of the fulminating powder than was necessary, or indeed safe, for its firing. Despite these criticisms many examples of Forsyth's firearms have survived to the present. In addition to locks made in Britain, the French gunmakers led by Prélat and Le Page patented several types of magazine locks in which a piston or firing pin and its housing were separated from the powder magazine. De l'Etrange of Versailles produced an improved lock in 1810 and in 1819 Bruneel produced yet another improvement in which the movement was made automatic by linking the hammer to a sliding magazine. This type of lock may have originated in Forsyth's workshops since a number of locks signed by his firm still exist.

During this exciting period in the history of weapons development, an outstanding contribution was made by the son of a Swiss wagon-maker. Samuel Johannes Pauly was born near Berne on April 13, 1766. By the age of thirty-two, he was an experienced sergeant-major of artillery and the author of a memorandum for the Swiss army on the use, equipment and manning of "galloper guns." This was written in the light of active service conditions in 1799 when he fought with the French and Helvetic troops under Masséna. In 1802 he designed a balloon, and two years later a single-span bridge. He then moved from Berne to Paris where he continued his ballooning ventures and came into contact with the gunmakers of St. Etienne. By 1809, he employed as a gunlock-maker in his Paris establishment Johann Nikolaus Dreyse, the Prussian who was later to design the needle gun. Dreyse left his native Sömmerda to work for Pauly who had by then adopted the French spelling of his name, Jean Samuel Pauly, embellished with the title colonel, to which he had no right.

But Pauly's pretensions cannot blur the inventive genius which appears in his first firearms patent application of September 29, 1812. In association with the Paris gunmaker François Prélat he produced the world's first center-fire, breechloading, self-obturating cartridge arm which was to be developed by others into the modern shotgun, rifle and pistol. This one step rendered possible virtually every subsequent stage in firearms development.

The reloadable cartridge was by no means a new idea, as artillery on this principle was used in the fifteenth century, but with his cartridge Pauly used the new percussion ignition compounds in a clever way that had completely escaped his contemporaries. While Forsyth, Manton and the others were

168

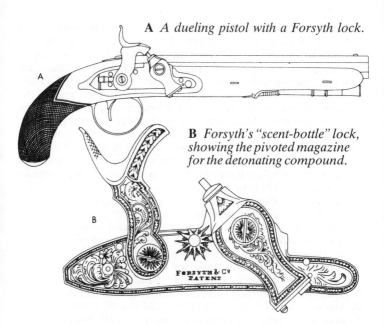

A *A dueling pistol with a Forsyth lock.*

B *Forsyth's "scent-bottle" lock, showing the pivoted magazine for the detonating compound.*

FORSYTH & Cº
PATENT

fiddling with pellets, disks, tubes, tapes and caps charged with fulminates, Pauly saw that to render the best service the "cap" should be incorporated into the cartridge. When coupled to a finely-made and ingenious breech mechanism the system impressed many men, among them officers of the czar of Russia, who tested it and saw it shot. The laudatory report of a trial by a committee led by Brillat de Savarin in July 1814 maintained that it "must be placed in the front rank of hunting arms known up to the present time," and listed its advantages over its contemporaries. It is impossible to load twice; it is easy to unload; the entirely enclosed action ensures quick certain ignition, even in mist and rain; the firer is not exposed to the very real danger due to burst barrels caused by double loading; the gun can be loaded quickly and even when walking so that one man can shoot as often and as quickly as he could if he used several guns and a loader. When Pauly fired twenty-two shots of ball in two minutes at another trial he deeply impressed the Duc de Rovigo who told his friend Napoleon, who then ordered an official trial. But it failed to convince the emperor that every condition needed to fulfill the requirements of military service had been met, despite de Rovigo's enthusiastic plea for the great potential increase in cavalry firepower which it offered.

When Paris fell to the Allies on April 5, 1814, Dreyse

returned to Prussia and Pauly lost no time in making for London. Within a few months his first British patent was granted in respect of an "Apparatus for Discharging Firearms by means of Compressed Air," designed for breechloading cannon and cartridge guns. The latter is like his 1812 Paris design, but with the substitution of a small strong syringe for the firing-pins and guides. When the cocked mechanism is released the piston sends a blast of air, heated under the compression, through a tiny hole to ignite "the charge of explosive powder of any kind or description" which is contained in a "rosette" in the rear of the cartridge. Examples survive of pistols made to this pattern, but shooters have always been a conservative company and it met with little success. The patent reveals Pauly's awareness of the importance of a good seal between the cartridge base and the chamber either by the expansion of the cartridge or by the fitting of a "small metal door or lid...to confine the cartridge, and make a more secure joint." After a third flirtation with aeronautics, which proved to be an extremely expensive interlude for his partner and benefactor, the great gunmaker Durs Egg, Pauly reverted to his compressed-air ignition. Repeated attempts to sell designs for mortars, cannon igniters and breechloading cannon to the Board of Ordnance ended in near-ignominy. His final plea for a re-examination of his cannon-lock was met with the blunt rejection that the Board "did not consider Mr. Pauly's Lock deserving further trial." Despite his ingenuity and persistence, Pauly appears to have made next to no profits from his brilliant breakthrough, which was developed by so many, lesser men.

Elsewhere in Europe locks to Forsyth's design were made by Contriner of Vienna, who was also a crossbow-maker, and Joseph Gutierrez of Seville, but by the time Gutierrez made his lock in 1820, percussion locks using loose detonating powder were beginning to go out of favor. As soon as Forsyth's patent expired in 1821, the English gunmakers William Webster and William Westley Richards patented improvements in England. Already, however, other types of detonators were beginning to appear, pills or pellets, disks or patches, tubes, tapes and caps. All were attempts to feed a measured quantity of detonating powder to the lock, and they differed only in the way the detonating powder was wrapped. The earliest was probably Joseph Manton's pill-lock, patented in 1816, and as late as 1834 Henry Shrapnel patented what may well have been the last new design.

Even after the pill-lock had been superseded it still had some supporters. For instance, in 1852 Joseph von Winiwarter of Vienna patented new detonating compositions using explosive chemicals bonded with a solution of guncotton in ether which also acted as a waterproof protection. The resulting mixture could be molded into any shape to be used either as a means of ignition or as a propellant itself, but as all these pills or pellets were so tiny as to cause difficulty in handling, some manufacturers wrapped the detonant in disks of paper or soft metal. In Joshua Shaw's patent of 1825, a cardboard disk was waterproofed by coating it with wax. During the 1842 trials held by the British Ordnance Office into methods of igniting by percussion, Westley Richards claimed that used pasteboard disks covered by tin foil were less likely, when thrown on deck, to hurt the bare feet of sailors, than were other metallic primers. Like pellets these disk primers were difficult to load by magazine and a French inventor, Leboeuf de Valdahon, patented, in September 1821, an ingenious primer in which the fulminate was packed in a continuous strip. De Valdahon used a piece of straw filled with fulminate. One end projected over the nipple and was cut off and struck at the same time by a sprung hammer. The straw was then moved forward to bring another section of priming into position for the next shot. No example of de Valdahon's design is known and it may never have been made.

It was left to the distinguished French urologist Baron Charles Louis Stanislaus Heurteloup (1793-1864) to design a gun whose primer he described as a small pipe or tube made of soft metal, or other substance which may be easily cut, containing the priming. This was fed onto the nipple by a cogwheel that turned when the cock was pulled back. Heurteloup described his gun in *Mémoire sur les Fusils de Guerre* and called it *koptipteur* from the Greek words for to cut and to strike. In 1837 and 1838 improved models were patented in France, Scotland and Belgium and the patent of 1839 showed the self-priming tube being moved by hand. The Board of Ordnance examined the gun and tried it at Woolwich and Chatham in 1837. Of the twelve guns that were made at Enfield for these trials eight are preserved in the Tower of London Armouries. Other trials took place at St. Petersburg. One rifle preserved in the Musée de l'Armée, Paris, has a lock made to Heurteloup's patent, dated 1841 and with a Russian inscription, suggesting that Heurteloup may not have been entirely unsuccessful in his attempts to sell it to the czar.

In de Valdahon's and Heurteloup's patents, the fulminate formed a continuous strip contained within a tube, and it was not until an American dentist, Doctor Edward Maynard (1813-91), patented a primer made of two narrow strips of paper enclosing small pellets of fulminate that the tape primer fulfilled its potential. That was in 1845, Maynard's primer was an immediate success both as a means of converting flintlocks to percussion and for the new designs made by the Maynard Arms Company of Washington. In due course the patent rights were bought by the United States government and used in pistol-carbines, rifle-muskets and rifles, all of the 1855 model.

In tube primers the fulminate was contained in a small tube of thin copper usually less than an inch (2.5 cm) in length. In the most popular form, invented by Joseph Manton and patented in 1818, the tube was pushed into the touchhole and the other end was held in position by a pincer-like spring against a flat pan or anvil. The hammer of English-made tube-locks struck the tube directly to detonate it, but in the Austrian army version, invented by Giuseppi Console and modified by General Augustin, the tube was struck by a firing-pin which passed through a cover. This design had two advantages; the tube could not be blown out of the touchhole, and the firer was protected by a metal plate from the fragments of the exploding tube. A handier tube primer for the shooter was recommended by Colonel Peter Hawker and patented by Westley Richards in 1831. Tubes of this type were made with a flanged mushroom-like top, the stalk was thrust into a nipple with a wide aperture and the tube was fired by the hammer hitting it on the flat top.

In adverse weather conditions of wind, sea-spray or rain it was as difficult to prime and fire a cannon as a sporting gun. Loose priming powder was replaced by tubes filled with combustible material which could be pushed into the gun-vents. As early as 1768, Muller mentions that tubes filled with quick-match primed with mealed powder and spirits of wine had been used a generation earlier. In 1778, quill tubes were used aboard HMS *Duke* in conjunction with a flintlock. As portfires and linstocks could be fatally dangerous near cannons and their ammunition, especially aboard ship, the combination of flintlock and tube was generally adopted for naval use in 1790 and for limited use by the Royal Artillery in 1820. A decade or so later, Mr. Marsh of the Royal Arsenal Surgery made a tube to take advantage of percussion ignition that was approved for the Royal Navy in 1831. By 1846, when the Artillery received a similar tube, the new *cross-headed detonating tube*, of pigeon's quill fired by a percussion cap, recommended by Colonel Charles C. Dansey, Royal Artillery, was undergoing trials to be approved by the Master-General of the Ordnance in September 1846.

Colonel Dansey also designed, in 1841, quill tubes fired by friction, but it was not for another ten years that a satisfactory

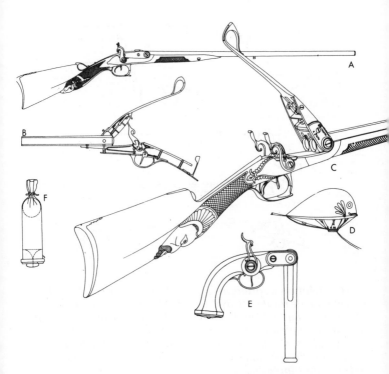

A *A sporting gun, .59-inch (15 mm) caliber. Inlaid with gold on the action is* INVENTION PAULY BREVETEE A PARIS, *and the stamp of Albert Renette (a crown over* AR). *French, c. 1813.*

B *The mechanism of a Pauly gun opened for loading. The cock is in the fired position.*

C *Another sporting gun designed by Pauly, the hammers cocked and the breech open. The gun was bought from Pauly's associate, Durs Egg, for £65 in 1824. French, c. 1813.*

D *"The Dolphin," an airship designed by Pauly and financed to the extent of several thousand pounds by the gunmaker Durs Egg.*

E *A design by Pauly for a breechloading pistol. After the patent drawing enrolled in Paris in 1812.*

F *A Pauly cartridge, formed of paper wrapped around the raised flange of a brass base which also houses the detonator pellet.*

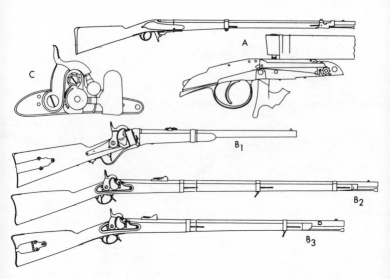

A *Heurteloup's* koptipteur *musket, made for the British Ordnance trials held at Woolwich and Chatham in 1837. The detail shows how the tube containing the fulminate was fed onto the nipple and sheared by the sharpened front edge of the cock, before the detached section was fired.*

B *Service arms fitted with Maynard's tape primer. (1) Sharps Model 1855 Carbine, .55 inch (14 mm) caliber. It was part of a British order for 6,000 carbines delivered by May 1858. They were issued to five cavalry regiments but were unpopular due to the poor gas seal at the breech. American, c 1856. (2) The American Model 1855 Rifle Musket, .58 inch (14.7 mm) caliber.*

(3) The American Model 1855 Rifle, .58 inch caliber (14.7 mm). The lock plate is stamped U.S. HARPERS FERRY and dated 1857. About 5,500 of these rifles were made.

C *An early form of Maynard's patent primer. A roll of priming charges, in paper tape protected by shellac, is fed over the nipple as the lock is cocked. As the hammer falls, the sharp edge severs the paper and explodes the priming agains the nipple.*

Maynard's system was used to convert flintlock arms. This example, dated 1855, is from a converted American Model 1842 Musket.

metal friction tube was designed by William Tozer, later Superintendent of Compositions in the Royal Laboratory, who perfected a copper friction tube that was adopted for land service on June 24, 1853. To eliminate the potential dangers to sailors' feet of metal friction bars scattered on gundecks, the Navy adopted Captain Edward M. Boxer's quill friction tube in 1856.

By 1866, when electricity was used to fire *Tubes, electric, high tension, Abel's pattern, Mark I*, the Royal Laboratory was making six different tubes for the armed forces: common tubes of quill and copper; friction tubes of quill and copper; the percussion tube; and Abel's design.

With the single exception of Maynard's tape primer, all percussion methods mentioned above had at least one serious disadvantage, and although the military authorities and sportsmen sought an effective, safe and handy primer, the percussion cap which was finally accepted and adopted almost universally was by no means perfect. A number of famous men, among them Hawker, Joseph Manton, James Purdey and Joseph Egg, claimed to have invented the percussion cap, but the English artist Joshua Shaw is generally accepted as its creator. There can be little doubt that Shaw introduced the copper cap to America as, when the American government adopted it, Congress granted him eighteen thousand dollars under an "Act for the Relief of Joshua Shaw" passed in 1847.

Maynard advertised his tape primer with a puff to the effect that "the act of priming the Cap gun is the most difficult that the soldier has to perform in battle." Soldiers and sportsmen both found that the small size of the cap made it almost impossible to handle when the loader's hands were gloved, cold, or slippery with the sweat of fear or excitement. This led to the development of Maynard's tape primer and to the increasing use of cappers; little magazines holding a number of percussion caps that could easily be fitted onto the nipple. The credit for their invention is given by Hawker to an unknown Frenchman. Once they became an accepted accessory, they were recessed into powder flask bases, and even fitted to gunlocks in a design by the Frenchmen Lancry and Charoy and incorporated with a nipple primer. Some had spring or manual feed from a metal magazine, others, the simpler sort, consisted of nothing more complex than a leather or rubber strip with keyhole slots cut to take the caps which could easily be pulled off once they were engaged on the nipple.

In setting his action below the stock, Heurteloup had avoided the danger of pieces of exploding priming tape flying into the shooter's eye. This was a relatively common accident which a number of gun designers took steps to avoid.

Some enclosed the lock in the stock, as had been done by some wheellock and flintlock makers. Others utilized an under-hammer action with the cock and nipple placed under the fore-end in front of the trigger as in Heurteloup's design. As early as 1823, the Devonian John Day was granted one of the first percussion lock patents for a very trim under-hammer lock which was soon taken up by the makers of the percussion walking-stick guns.

Chapter 16

James Puckle's invention was obsolete for almost a century before the production of the first satisfactory revolving firearm. A United States patent was granted on June 10, 1818, to Captain Artemus Wheeler of Concord, Massachusetts, for a revolving pistol with a priming magazine and perhaps also with an automatic mechanism for rotating the cylinder between shots. The patent was avoided by Elisha Haydon Collier of the same state, who took an example of Wheeler's pistol to London where he patented it in his own name in November 1818. In France, it was patented by Cornelius Coolidge, apparently a partner of Collier's, who claimed that he had improved Wheeler's design in his patent.

The nature of the improvements is unknown, but they may have included the automatic rotation that was later scrapped by Collier, a new type of priming magazine and a better means of sealing the joint between the chambers and the barrel. Puckle had made the mouth of his chamber with a cone which fitted into the countersunk breech. Surviving Collier arms use this system in reverse, with the chambers closing over a coned breech. Collier approached the British Board of Ordnance about the action which now bears his name in 1819 and 1824, but without success although a considerable quantity of pistols, rifles and guns were sold on the civilian market. They were advertised under the heading COLLIER'S PATENT FEU-DE-JOIE as being just the thing for naval officers and "gentlemen who are in the habit of shooting Deer in their own Parks." Collier claimed that he sold £100,000-worth of his revolving arms, one-tenth of which went to India. The percussion system was used on the latest of Collier's products, which may fairly be called the first of the modern revolvers.

The inventions of Collier and other designers of pistols with a single barrel and a series of revolving chambers containing the charges, made in Europe since the first half of the sixteenth century but never entirely satisfactory, were brought to the highest degree of efficiency that was possible with black powder and muzzle-loading methods by Samuel Colt (1814-62). He had barely reached his majority when he was granted patents in Britain (1835) and America (1836) in respect of a single-barreled revolver with a five-shot cylinder rotated and locked in proper alignment for firing when the hammer was drawn back to the full cock position. His patents covered the method of indexing and locking the cylinder, the way that each percussion nipple was isolated from its neighbors and other details of an efficient mechanism. Colt had first tried to patent his ideas three years before, when he laid a crude wooden model on William P. Elliott's desk in the United States Patent Office in Washington, but he had not then worked out the details sufficiently carefully for a successful patent application. He also showed these wooden models of his pistol in 1831 to Anson Chase, a gunmaker in Hartford, Connecticut, who later made his first experimental rifle.

In 1834 a Baltimore man, John Pearson, began to make sample firearms to Colt's patent. With these refined models Colt began the sales campaign which quickly led to the establishment of the Patent Arms Manufacturing Company at Paterson, New Jersey, in March 1836. This was within a fortnight of the grant of the American patent, which protected Colt's design until it expired in 1857. For a couple of years, while he sold his pistols and rifles to private individuals, the United States government showed little interest, but in 1838 fifty Paterson eight-shot rifles were issued to the troops fighting the Seminole Indian War and some five-shot revolvers were issued to the Texas Navy. These two small official orders plus a few others were not enough to keep Colt in business. The Paterson factory was closed and the company liquidated in the closing months of 1842 and the first of 1843. But the seeds of interest sown by these minor sales and by judiciously placed presentation arms which he had already started to distribute were beginning to germinate. By 1847, Colt had enlisted the skills and experience of the factory run by Eli Whitney, Jr., son of the early exponent of the theory of interchangeable parts for firearms. The considerable havoc wrought by Colt's arms in Florida and Texas, where the revolver's rate of fire surprised Indian warriors who were used to having a lull in firing after each volley in which to press home an attack, gave small bodies of soldiers a new advantage in combats where they were outnumbered. The word soon got around the military camps, and helped by the pressures put on the army by the country's expansion westward and the Mexican War (1845-48), Colt was again able to set up on his own account in Hartford in 1848. From that date on, there was no holding the dynamic young inventor.

Colt formed a collection of weapons that is now the oldest in the United States. With the strange, to American eyes, group of firearms from Japan and the Ottoman empire he acquired a number of swords and daggers which were to be the foundation of a museum. Some were bought, others were gifts. A set of

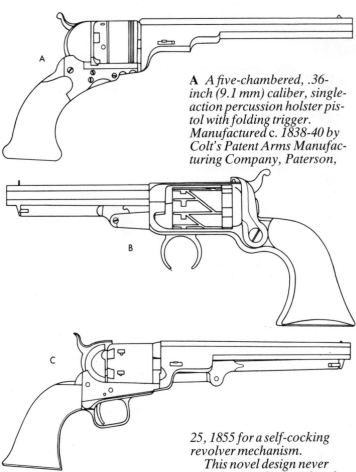

A A five-chambered, .36-inch (9.1 mm) caliber, single-action percussion holster pistol with folding trigger. Manufactured c. 1838-40 by Colt's Patent Arms Manufacturing Company, Paterson, New Jersey. Approximately 1,000 of this model, the No. 5 Paterson Colt, were made. About twenty-five percent were sold cased with their accessories.

B Elisha K. Root's patent number 13,999 of December 25, 1855 for a self-cocking revolver mechanism.

This novel design never went into production, but the use of the grooved cylinder to increase the rate of fire was revived forty years later by Colonel G. V. Fosbery, VC (c. 1834-1907).

C The Model 1851 Navy or Belt Revolver, .36-inch (9.1 mm) caliber.

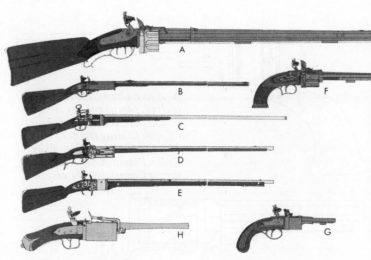

A A German, flintlock revolving rifle to the design patented by Elisha Collier, inscribed BERLIN, *1824. The* lock has set-triggers and a magazine which primes each of the five chambers in turn.

B A three-chambered, flintlock revolving gun, the stock inlaid with silver. French, c. 1670.

C A four-chambered revolving gun. The flintlock has a priming magazine signed ROVIRA, and the breech tang is signed PERA CARBUNELL EN BARCELONA. Spanish, 1702.

D A four-chambered, flintlock revolving gun. German, 1732.

E A four-chambered revolving gun, the lock signed

DULACHS, the side-plate IASINTO IAVMANDREV M(e) F(ecit) MANRESA 1739.

F A five-chambered, .44-inch (11.2 mm) caliber, flintlock revolving pistol marked E H COLLIER, 14 PATENT. English (London) c. 1820.

G A five-chambered flintlock revolver, .42-inch (10.7 mm) caliber; the lockplate inscribed E.H. COLLIER PATENT NO. 23. This is the first model of Collier's pistol with internal cock and the primer operated by a ratchet.

H A six-chambered pistol, .5-inch (12.7 mm) caliber, with a single-action snaphance lock. The barrel and cylinder are brass. English (London ?) c. 1680.

The Revolver

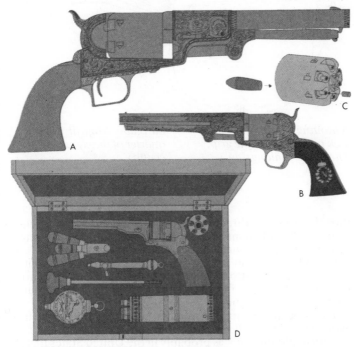

Modern students define a revolver as a firearm in which a cluster of barrels, or a cylinder with a series of chambers, revolves round an axis, bringing each barrel or chamber in turn into alignment with the firing mechanism and, in the case of the latter type, the barrel.

A Colt's Second Model Dragoon Pistol, .44-inch (11.2 mm) caliber, engraved with foliate scrollwork. About 2,500 were made, c. 1850-51.

B Colt's Old Model Navy or Belt Pistol, Model 1851, .36-inch (9.1 mm) caliber. One of a pair made and cased in London for the emperor Napoleon III (1808-73).

C A percussion revolver cylinder, loaded by cartridge from the front and ignited by a copper percussion cap fitted over the nipple at the rear.

D Colt Pocket Model Paterson Pistol, cased with accessories in use c. 1839-41. (See also pp. 184–185, 188.)

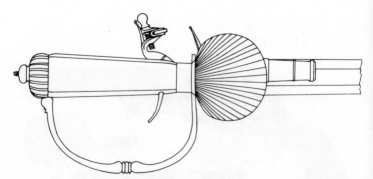

A hunting sword with a flint-lock pistol fitted to the grip. The barrel is alongside *the blade. English, second quarter of the eighteenth century.*

three firearms and three swords of the Prussian army was sent to Colt in acknowledgment of his gift to the family of the king of Prussia. Japanese guns and swords were brought back by Commodore Perry in 1855. After Colt's death, his wife added a series of mint Hartford Colt revolving pistols and longarms, thus almost completing the set of Colt models made during Samuel Colt's lifetime.

The collection includes a number of knives. They come from Morocco, Turkey, the Caucasus and Malaya, but none from America, although it was probably in the United States that the knife achieved its greatest notoriety as a fighting weapon rather than as a useful implement which might, on occasion, be used in a brawl or a formal duel.

In 1837, George Elgin was granted a U.S. patent for a "new and useful instrument called the Pistol-Knife or Pistol-Cutlass." Elgin's invention, which combined "the pistol and the Bowie knife, or the pistol and cutlass," was by no means new, and unworthy of patent protection, but Robert B. Lawton, the inventor of another weapon combining blade and pistol, claimed that Elgin's design infringed his own patent application. This was for a sword whose straight blade was surrounded by the six barrels of a pepperbox revolver. Both patents were granted, Lawton's design to pass promptly into oblivion, Elgin's to achieve limited adoption by the U.S. Navy which bought 150. These were made by Cyrus Bullard Allen of

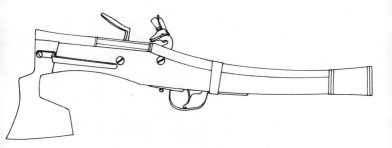

A battle-axe with a flintlock pistol, the stock inlaid with *stag antler. German, mid-eighteenth century.*

Springfield, Massachusetts, for issue to the South Seas Exploring Expedition. The expedition's commanding officer, Captain Thomas ap Catesby Jones, wrote in 1838 of the "unquestionable superiority of the weapon over any other for arming Boats crews and exploring parties for penetrating into the interior of Islands inhabited by savages."

Elgin and his competitors were not the first to offer combined arms. Two or more weapons were occasionally combined since as early as the fifteenth century, when the hafts of some maces served as the barrels of primitive pistols. Among the relics of Henry VIII's personal armory are two-hand maces, their heads enclosing short barrels that were fired individually with a hand-held match. These, and almost all the other sixteenth-century weapons in which various firearms mechanisms were combined with swords, daggers, crossbows, boar spears, axes and lances, were oddities made by individual gunsmiths to amuse themselves or their patrons. They appeared during the tremendously fast spread of the manufacture and use of firearms throughout Europe in the sixteenth century. In the seventeenth and eighteenth centuries, there was a fashion for hunting swords with one or two short flintlock pistols fitted to the hilt. These were revived again in Britain and elsewhere in the nineteenth century, when attempts were made to incorporate pistols into hilts of military swords and the heads of lances, but in every case the fixed bayonet was accepted as a better combination.

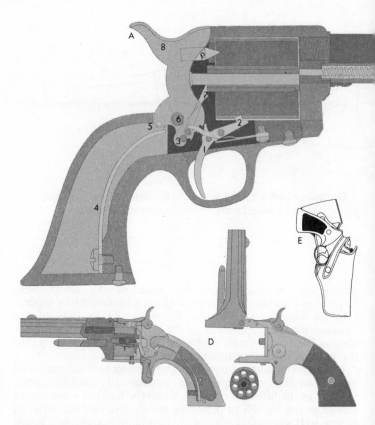

A *Section view of the Colt
revolver. (1) Trigger and
screw. (2) Bolt and screw. (3)
Hammer cam. (4) Main
spring. (5) Hammer roll and
rivet. (6) Hammer screw. (7)
Hand and hand spring. (8)
Hammer. (9) Firing pin and
rivet. (10) Ejector rod and
spring.*

B *The Schofield-Smith &
Wesson.*

C *The Schofield-Smith &*

*Wesson, section view showing
the joint screw (1) which con-
nects the frame to the barrel,
(2) extractor, (3) extractor
spring, (4) cylinder catch, (5)
barrel catch, (6) hammer, (7)
main spring, (8) strain screw,
(9) trigger and trigger pin,
(10) trigger spring.*

D *Smith & Wesson also made
revolvers whose barrels tipped upward to allow the removal of the cylinders for
loading. This example is the*

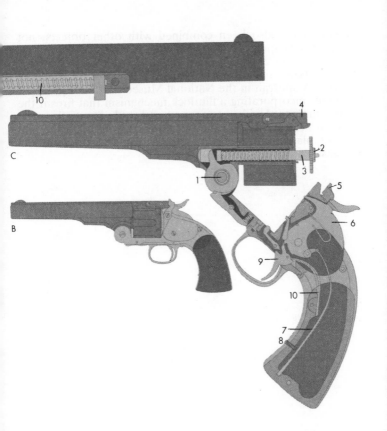

Model 1, seven-shot, single-action revolver in .22-inch (5.6 mm) rim-fire caliber.

E *A modern holster for Smith & Wesson revolvers. (see also page 188).*

In 1875, the United States Ordnance Office approved the publication of Rules for the Inspection of Army Revolvers and Gatling Guns, *which gave detailed accounts of the two commonest service*

revolvers, the "Colt's Revolver, Calibre .45" (**A**) *and the "Schofield-Smith & Wesson Revolver, Calibre .45"* (**B**). *These arms illustrate two divergent views of revolver design. The Colt has a solid frame, its cylinder being loaded through a "gate," while the Schofield-Smith & Wesson breaks open to load and unload. Both types were chambered to take the same 230-grain bullet and 28-grain powder charge.*

Pistols have also been combined with other objects, not themselves weapons. The gun-shields of Henry VIII and the brandistock have been described above. Men also carried whips, walking sticks and even umbrellas that concealed swords or guns. A sporran in the National Museum of Antiquities of Scotland, incorporating a flintlock mechanism that fires if the clasp is tampered with, presages a belt-buckle reputedly made between 1933 and 1945, with four pistol-barrels hidden behind a cover plate decorated with the emblems of the National Socialist Party.

Chapter 17

In the wake of experiments carried out by Benjamin Franklin (1706-90) and Luigi Galvani (1737-98), Alessandro Volta (1745-1827) discovered that priceless phenomenon, the electric current. European scientists were immensely excited by the publication of his findings in 1800, and by the subsequent public demonstrations of his electric battery, the first source of continuous current. Immediately, there was a scramble to find commercial uses for the new marvel, and as might be expected not all were peaceful.

In contrast to the attempts by Huygens to use the energy of exploding gunpowder to operate an engine for peaceful purposes, Volta's battery inspired more than one designer to use electrical energy to ignite explosive compounds. This method was first attempted in Prague within a decade or so of the first appearance of the battery. By 1845, the British Ordnance Select Committee had discussed Thomas Beningfield's design. Its details remain a mystery, as he neither patented it nor explained the mechanism, even to support his claim that it might shoot between a thousand and twelve hundred rounds a minute. Even the Duke of Wellington, who then had the honor of being Constable of the Tower of London, was impressed when he saw a Beningfield model in action, but the inventor's secrecy made official support impossible. The nearest explanation to account for its propulsive system is a

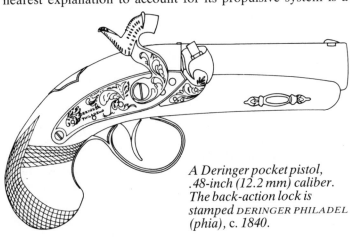

A Deringer pocket pistol, .48-inch (12.2 mm) caliber. The back-action lock is stamped DERINGER PHILADEL *(phia), c. 1840.*

A A .38-caliber (9.6 mm), needle-fire revolver by F. Dreyse of Sömmerda. In 1852, G.L.L. Kufahl patented the design in Britain.

B The twenty-shot, double-barreled revolver made by the Liège firm of Henrion, Dassy and Heuschen, 1911-28.

C Swedish officer's revolver, model 1887, .3 inch (7.5 mm) caliber, made by Nagant of Liège. The lock is a variation of that made during the 1870s

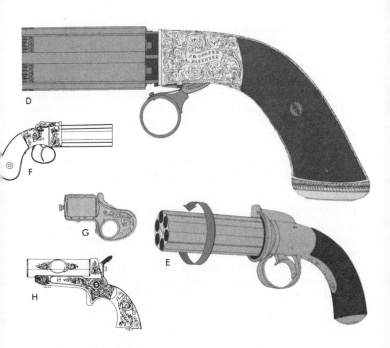

by Galand in Paris. (**1**)
Trigger. (**2**) Main spring. (**3**)
Frame. (**4**) Hammer. (**5**)
Hand, or cylinder pawl. (**6**)
Ejector-rod spring housing.

D A six-barreled, self-
cocking percussion pepperbox pistol inscribed J R
COOPER PATENT. The system,
which uses an under-hammer
cock and has its nipples in line
with the barrels, is known
after its alleged inventor,
Mariette. He was a Liège
gunmaker, who is reputed to
have produced
pistols to this design in 1837.

E Percussion pepperbox
pistol with a bar hammer and

a nipple shield. The first
mechanism of this type was
patented in America in 1837
by Ethan Allen, who subsequently patented improve-
ments in 1845.

F Allen's pepperbox pistol
with a double mechanism,
patented in 1837.

G A seven-barrelled, self-
cocking pepperbox pistol for
.22-caliber (5.6 mm) rim-fire
bullets, patented in 1865 by
James Reid of Catskill, New
York, and called MY FRIEND.

H A four-barrelled Deringer
for rim-fire bullets, patented
by Christian Sharps in 1859.

189

newspaper report referring to "gases exploded by galvanic electricity."

The next step was a French invention, patented in 1866 by Le Baron and Delmas, who used a special cartridge fitted with a device like the sparking plug of an internal-combustion engine to ignite its charge. The power was supplied by a battery and an induction coil housed in the butt. A British patent, granted to the Liège gunmaker Henri Pieper in 1883, shows a lighter, simpler version of a system which never received public acceptance.

On a grander scale, an electric charge has been used to ignite the propellant of a number of military rockets for many years past.

In 1883, Lovell's Improved Brunswick Rifle came into service in the British Army. The Brunswick had a pair of opposed spiral grooves cut in the barrel. These received the raised band which was cast onto the "belted" ball. The pattern, based on developments for the armies of Brunswick and Hanover, was part of an uninterrupted search for the perfect combination of barrel and bullet which has continued to the present day and which will be with us for years to come.

Ignition methods were also constantly under review. To some inventors working in the field of firearms, it seemed that the best place for the percussion cap was buried inside the charge of gunpowder which it was to ignite. In 1828, Johann Nikolaus Dreyse placed a fulminate primer in the base of the bullet. A long firing-pin, the "needle" that gave the name "needle gun," *Zündnadelgewehr* in German, passed through the powder charge to ignite the primer. This early design was modified by a number of gunmakers, including its originator, until 1841, when the Prussian military authorities tested a breechloading bolt-action version which they eventually introduced into service in 1848. The needle gun was a prime instrument in Prussia's defeats of Denmark in 1864 and of Austria in 1866. In the words of *Chambers Journal*, the introduction of the needle gun caused "one universal cry from every civilized nation for the arming of their troops in like manner."

Seven years after Dreyse placed the igniter in the middle of the load, a French inventor, Casimir Lefaucheux, patented a paper cartridge for a breakaction breechloading gun which he had designed three years before. A percussion cap was set at right angles in the thin brass base. Above the cap was a small pin which projected through the breech when the chamber was loaded. A blow from the flat-nosed cock drove in the pin and

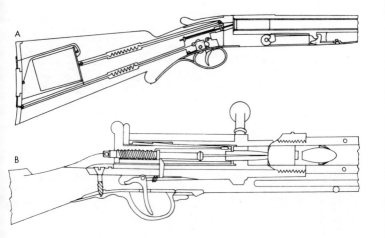

A *In Henri Pieper's gun, the gunpowder charge was ignited by an electric charge supplied by "a battery or accumulator or otherwise." Pressure on the trigger completed the circuit and fired the charge. After the patent drawing filed in London in 1883.*

B *Johann Nikolaus Dreyse's bolt-action "needle gun" in which the firing-pin (the needle) drove through the powder in the cartridge to strike the fulminate primer at the base of the bullet. Dreyse's breech, adopted by Prussia in 1848, carried her to victory against Denmark in 1864 and Austria in 1866.*

detonated the cap. This new "pin-fire" mechanism was an immediate success, especially after another Frenchman, C.H. Houillier, improved the cartridge in 1850. It was used in sporting and military longarms, and in a revolving pistol patented by Eugène Gabriel Lefaucheux in 1854 which may lay claim to being the most common type of pistol made in Europe in the second half of the nineteenth century. Thousands of Lefaucheux pistols were among the arms supplied by the workshops of St. Etienne and Liège to both sides in the American Civil War, in which the Union Army alone gave official recognition to nineteen different types of single-shot pistols and revolvers. Although single-shot pistols survived in a few countries as a service arm until *c.* 1885, they were largely superseded for civilian use except for target shooting and as a pocket-weapon for self-defense.

191

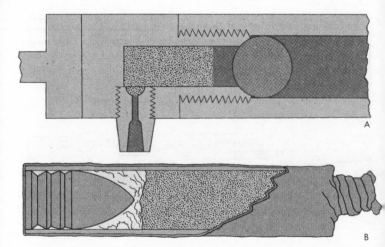

A rifle utilizing Heurteloup's primer in conjunction with a new form of breech achieved some acceptance in the French and Belgian armies. The breech proposed by Captain Gustave Delvigne in 1828, and formally accepted by the French army in 1842, had its chamber of a smaller diameter than the rest of the barrel. When the ball, which was a loose fit in the bore, rested on the shoulders of the chambers, two or three sharp blows with the rammer expanded it into the grooves of the rifling. When the French authorities eventually agreed that the round ball was obsolete, and acceded to Delvigne's own suggestion that a cylindro-conoidal bullet was better, Pontcharra, Thouvenin, Minié and Tamisier experimented with other methods of achieving the required close fit between bullet and rifling. Colonel Thouvenin's breech with a pillar (*tige*) that served as an anvil against which the bullet was expanded was further improved when Captain Claude-Etienne Minié of the Chasseurs d'Orléans designed a solid cylindro-conoidal bullet at the base of which was a single deep groove (*cannelure*), which helped the expansion of the bullet and held a quantity of lubricant that eased the bullet's path and reduced fouling. When the 1851 rifled musket was adopted by the British services, which were to use it through the horrors of the Crimean War (1854-56), it employed a further modification of Minié's design incorporating an iron cup that was forced into the base of the bullet by the explosion of the charge, in order to expand the softer lead into the groove. The American designer, James Burton, later proved that the cup was unnecessary if the cavity at the base of the cartridge was properly shaped.

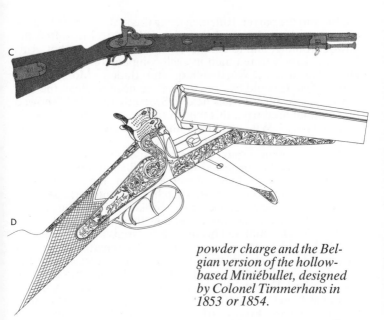

A *General Baron Augustin improved on Delvigne's system by reaming out the neck of the chamber to make a seat for the round bullet. Both designs left some clearance between the bullet and the powder to allow faster ignition than was possible if the powder was compacted. Austrian, 1841.*

B *A card-and-paper cartridge containing the powder charge and the Belgian version of the hollow-based Minié bullet, designed by Colonel Timmerhans in 1853 or 1854.*

C *A percussion service rifle with 14-groove barrel inscribed OBERNDORF, the lock-plate engraved KONIGL. WURT. FABRIC. Made in the Württemberg Arsenal, c.1840.*

D *The pin-fire mechanism invented by Casimir Lefaucheux in 1835. The cock drove a metal "pin" against the percussion cap to explode it and ignite the gunpowder charge.*

Wild, an engineer in the service of Zurich, invented his system of rifling during the period of the international arms exchanges. As has already been noted, Captain Delvigne developed a breech in 1828 in which the powder did not quite fill the constricted chamber, and so was not compacted when the rammer was used to distort the ball. Wild adopted another type of rammer with a shoulder which prevented its being pushed too far into the barrel. Riflemen using this system carried a flask of water, which was used to moisten the barrel to soften the powder fouling, and to ease its removal by the next shot. This arm was issued to ten men in each company of the armies of Hesse-Darmstadt, Württemberg and Baden. More than a hundred shots could be fired before the need to clean the rifle arose. The results of trials held in Switzerland in 1842 showed that a bullet fired from this type of rifle was still effective at six hundred paces. Wild had successfully combined ease of loading with increased range and accuracy.

When Captain Pontcharra was experimenting with Delvigne's design he suggested that the ball should be set in the hollowed end of a cylindrical wooden sabot, the lower end of which was wrapped in a greased patch. But Pontcharra's system failed when the sabot stuck, or was broken in ramming and the ball was distorted – as was sometimes the case.

While Wild completed his models for trials in 1841, Russian and Belgian experts were carrying out comparative tests at Liège. These proved that the Delvigne rifle, using the cylindro-conoidal bullet, was much better for military use than the standard French rifle using Colonel Thierry's cylindro-spherical bullet, or the Brunswick's two-grooved barrel with the belted ball. French trials of Delvigne's new bullet, in competition with that of Pontcharra, confirmed the former's superiority. Despite the known faults of the resulting compromise Delvigne-Pontcharra system, it was adopted for use in the French, Belgian and Austrian armies. It was known as the "chambered" rifle, and was issued to ten French battalions in 1840.

A modified form was also introduced into the Austrian army in 1841. This was the *Consolegewehr*, a percussion lock rifle designed by General Baron Augustin. This version did not employ the wooden sabot, but it did have the shoulder of the chamber reamed to give the ball a neatly fitting seat. In place of a touchhole, its barrel had a horizontal cylinder pierced with a vent, the cylinder resting in a pan similar to that of a flintlock. A spring lid with a hole in the top, through which a plug passed, closed around the cylinder. The plug rested on the primer, which consisted of fulminate of mercury wrapped in a tube of thin brass sheet. For safety in handling, a fine brass wire was pinched into one end. This served also to fasten it to the cartridge.

Around 1830, organic chemistry began to lay claim to being a distinct branch of science. Within half a century, the new scientists had found ways of wreaking undreamt-of destruction for civil and military purposes. In 1846, the Italian chemist Sobrero first nitrated glycerin to make nitroglycerin, a substance which Alfred Bernhard Nobel was to use as a blasting explosive in 1863 under the name of "Nobel's blasting oil." In 1866, this great Swedish chemist invented dynamite, which like his later blasting gelatin of 1875, removed the need to use capricious nitroglycerin except for jobs for which it was especially suited, or as the base for more stable explosives.

After experiments made by Théophile Jules Pelouze in 1838, Christian Friedrich Schönbein produced a new and practical explosive whose power far exceeded that of gunpowder. His process of nitrating cotton with a mixture of nitric and sulfuric acids to produce guncotton was capable of practical application by the end of the American Civil War. Twenty-one years after the war, Vieille had so tamed the power of nitrated cellulose that it could be used as a propellant in cartridges, while high explosives produced the shattering effect that artillerists had sought for explosive shells since the sixteenth century. The treatment of nitrated cellulose with a mixture of alcohol and ether gave Vieille a smokeless powder, known as "Poudre B" after General Boulanger, used in the French Lebel rifle cartridge in 1886.

Nobel's genius united the progress made with cotton-and-glycerin-based explosives when he invented a smokeless powder called "Ballistite" which he patented in 1888. Nobel, who admitted to working only intermittently, is the greatest name in the history of explosives. In Great Britain alone, he held 122 patents. The most important was probably the one he took out in 1864 for a detonator which used the detonation of a small charge of gunpowder, or one of the fulminates, to release the highly concentrated power of the so-called high explosives. Many demolition charges later used in warfare employ a fulminate detonator pushed into a guncotton primer. It in turn is set into a hole in the secondary charge, which actually destroys the target, or ignites by sympathetic explosion an unexploded shell or bomb.

During the course of an ironic address to the House of Lords, delivered on March 19, 1850, Lord Brougham and Vaux marveled that English manufacturers were such fools as to subscribe their money to provide accommodation for their foreign competitors to come to England and undersell them in their own market. In this speech, his lordship, himself a notable collector of ancient armor and arms, expressed the typically obscurantist opposition to the proposed Great Exhibition, planned to be held in London in 1851. Its patron, Prince Albert,

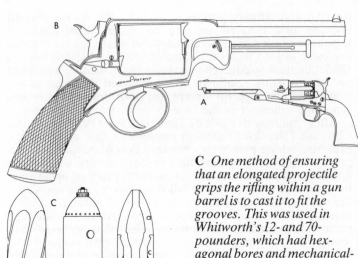

A Colt's Model 1860 Army or Holster revolver in .44 caliber with 8-inch (20.3 cm) barrel and hinged loading lever.

B Beaumont-Adams 40-bore revolver, no. 40614, made under license in Birmingham, England, c. 1862. The barrel is engraved with the retailer's name and address WILLIAM GREEN, 138 NEW BOND STREET, LONDON.

C One method of ensuring that an elongated projectile grips the rifling within a gun barrel is to cast it to fit the grooves. This was used in Whitworth's 12- and 70-pounders, which had hexagonal bores and mechanically fitting projectiles (1). Another technique, attributed to Treuille de Beaulieu and subsequently used at Woolwich, was to set a number of studs in the projectile (2). The studs engage the rifling as the shell is loaded into the barrel, and remain engaged on firing so that a rotary motion is imparted to the shell as it passes up the bore. In the Hotchkiss projectile (3), the parts a and b were of iron, and were held apart by a ring of lead c. The gas pressure on b forced the lead outward into the rifling.

felt very differently. He saw the exhibition as bringing "a living picture of the development at which mankind had arrived, and a new starting point from which all nations will be able to direct future exertions." In the field of arms development, these were prophetic phrases, for the exhibitors included the young American, Samuel Colt, who had been developing his patent revolving pistol for fifteen years, and who already dominated a market which inspired patent applications had made almost his

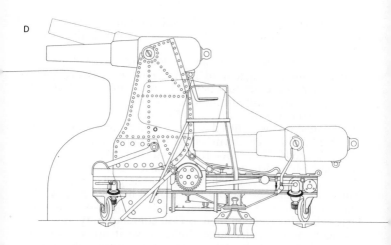

D *Alexander Moncrieff's design for a disappearing artillery carriage, 1868.*

It had three advantages: It gave the gun-crew protection from direct fire by enabling it to raise the gun to shoot over a solid parapet from a lower position which was convenient for loading. It stored the force of the recoil so that it could be used to raise the gun back from the loading to the firing position. The interposing of a moving fulcrum between the gun and its platform lessened the strain on the latter and allowed it to be of lighter construction.

In the Mark II carriage for the 7-inch (17.8 cm), or 7-ton, rifled muzzle-loading gun, shown here, the recoil pushes the gun on its curved elevators back and downward to the loading position, the energy of the recoil being used to raise a heavy, cast-iron counterbalance weight, which can be used to return it to the firing position. Later "disappearing" carriages employed hydropneumatic or hydraulic recoil buffers.

own. Colt's main English competitor was Robert Adams, who patented his revolver action in the year of the Great Exhibition, where he, too, showed his wares. The 1851 Adams revolver, with a solid frame and self-cocking action, had no rammer, but using special wadded bullets it could be loaded and fired five times in two minutes. Two years later, a rammer designed by Rigby was fitted to the second Adams model. Both types were made by the London firm of Deane, Adams and Deane, and sold to officers who were setting sail to take part in the Crimean War.

In connection with the Crimean War and the development of arms, it is interesting to note that three hundred British patents for firearms were granted between 1617 and 1852. Twice that number were granted in the next six years.

During the war, the Board of Ordnance became interested in an Adams revolver fitted with a double-action mechanism which could be cocked with either the thumb or the trigger, an idea patented by Frederick Beaumont. In 1856, orders for both 38- and 54-bore Beaumont-Adams pistols went to the London Armoury Company, which Adams had helped to found and in whose Bermondsey factory he installed his own patent rifling machines. Despite claims that the Beaumont-Adams was a faster-shooting weapon than its Colt contemporary, that it was stronger, and that its larger bullet gave it greater stopping power, it never achieved the universal success of Colt's models.

The first arms produced at Colt's new factory at Hartford had been .44 (11.1 mm) holster pistols, improved versions of the Walker model made at Whitneyville. Between 1848 and 1860, about twenty thousand were produced in a variety of styles. A year after the appearance of the First Model Dragoon, Colt produced the Wells Fargo, a .31 (7.9 mm) caliber pocket model, which was to become a best seller. When it went out of production in 1873, a third of a million had been made. The pocket model introduced in 1849, the year that Colt's patent protection was extended until 1856, was made both at Hartford and in London, where Colt had set up another factory.

One of the most successful Colt designs was the 1851 Navy Model. It was .36 (9.1 mm) caliber, between the Pocket Model of 1848 and the Dragoon, with the former's balance and characteristics. Like the Wells Fargo model, it remained in production until 1873. Many pirated copies were made by Confederate gunsmiths during the Civil War, and in Belgium and other European states by men who saw the sales potential of this model.

A quaint group of "guns" made around the middle of the nineteenth century are really rather closer to the catapult, in that they derive their power from stressed fibers, in this case elastic rubber. An English patent of 1849 was granted to Richard Edwards Hodges, who exhibited his wares alongside those of Krupp, Colt and Adams at the Great Exhibition. Hodges could hardly be considered a competitor, for his exhibit was a syringe-type airgun, reminiscent of the sixteenth-century designs except that the piston was forced up the cylinder by a "previously extended India-rubber spring." Another Hodge line was an elastic-rubber catapult on a gun-shaped stock.

A contemporary rival of Colt and Adams produced a revolver which had marginal advantages in certain circumstances when one man faced a mob: for example in a prison, where fear of the spread of small shot could be as effective as a single bullet. In October, 1856, a French-born doctor, Jean Alexandre François le Mat, was granted a patent for a two-barreled pistol with a nine-chamber .42 (10.7 mm) caliber cylinder revolving upon a central barrel of .63 (16 mm) caliber. The nose of the hammer was movable so that it could be made to fire the central "grapeshot" barrel or one of the chambers when it was aligned with the normal barrel. In partnership with Pierre Beauregard, who was to achieve the rank of general in the Confederate army, and later in partnership with Charles Girard, le Mat made about two and a half thousand pistols at New Orleans and Paris for the Confederate forces. In 1864, another thousand were made in Birmingham, England. British manufacture, however, was stopped when the Civil War ended in 1865, the year when le Mat's pistol was again made in France in pin-fire and center-fire models. These were used widely in France's penal colonies. The combination of rifle- and shot-barrels continues in the *drilling* sporting arms used in areas where the game is likely to vary from partridges to deer.

A year after le Mat's patent, Lieutenant-Colonel Durrell Greene patented one of the first breechloaders with a bolt-action, as we now understand the term. The bolt was used to seat the hollow-based Minié bullet in the chamber, then was withdrawn, and a paper cartridge containing the powder charge and another bullet in its base was rammed home. In theory, the second bullet acted as a gas-check when the charge was fired, and was then pushed forward for the next shot. Greene's breechloader was an oddity in other ways, for it had an under-hammer action, and an oval-bored barrel instead of the more usual form in which spiral grooves were cut to induce a stabilizing spin to the bullet.

The problem of getting lead bullets and iron shells to grip the rifling of cannon and small arms without stripping, or without inducing pressures too high for the strength of the barrels, was re-examined by one of Britain's greatest engineers in the years following the Crimean War. Joseph Whitworth (1803-87) was in the forefront of the movement to standardize measures, gauges and threads. The skills which enabled him to measure with unrivaled accuracy served in the production of fine target rifles in the 1860s. All his rifles have the common distinguishing feature of a hexagonal bore.

The efficiency of many types of firearms was the prime contribution to the success of the wars of colonial expansion in which Europe's great powers were engaged in the middle of the nineteenth century. The British Army had its first issue of the new Minié rifle in February 1852, when twenty regiments in the south of England and the Channel Islands each received twenty-five stands of the Pattern 1851 for use by infantry. Twenty-three thousand more were ordered from six gunmakers at about twenty-three shillings and six pence each. By the end of the year, Minié's bullet had proved its worth in the Kaffir War, when, "at a range of from twelve to thirteen hundred yards small bodies of Kaffirs could be dispersed."

The Great Exhibition at London's Crystal Palace in 1851 may well have been a singular victory for the advocates of freedom of enterprise, invention and of access to all the world's markets, but it was also the scene of Krupp's first ominous attempts to enter the international arms market. Eight years before, Alfred Krupp had produced the first mild-steel musket barrel. At the 1844 Berlin Exhibition, he won the Gold Medal for a display which included breastplates and cast steel barrels. His first cannon barrel of cast steel, a three-pounder, was made in 1847, but remained untested for two years while bureaucracy blanched at its cost, and generals remained unconvinced that the weights of the bronze and iron guns then in service were becoming excessive.

Krupp's display at the Crystal Palace included one of the new steel guns mounted on mahogany and framed by a Prussian war tent. For all the sensation it caused, the gun remained unsaleable, a fate it shared with the excellent twelve-pounder Krupp showed at Paris in 1855. It was modeled on the current French bronze gun, but was 200 lb (90.8 kg) lighter. Napoleon III, arms collector, connoisseur of artillery and coauthor with Colonel Favé of a standard work on the history of artillery, liked the Krupp gun enough to grant its maker the honor of Knight of the Legion of Honor. The exhibition committee added its Gold Medal, and the Crédit Mobilier tried to get Krupp to move his factory to France.

Nobody wished to buy Krupp's guns until a small order arrived in 1857 from the Viceroy of Egypt, and another in 1859 from Prussia. Two years later, Krupp's huge trip-hammer "Fritz" went into action. The following year, a Berlin newspaper coined for Krupp the title "Cannon King." On the threshold of the new age of competitive arming, Krupp sold

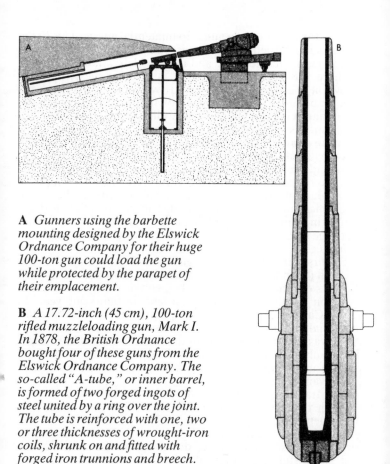

A *Gunners using the barbette mounting designed by the Elswick Ordnance Company for their huge 100-ton gun could load the gun while protected by the parapet of their emplacement.*

B *A 17.72-inch (45 cm), 100-ton rifled muzzleloading gun, Mark I. In 1878, the British Ordnance bought four of these guns from the Elswick Ordnance Company. The so-called "A-tube," or inner barrel, is formed of two forged ingots of steel united by a ring over the joint. The tube is reinforced with one, two or three thicknesses of wrought-iron coils, shrunk on and fitted with forged iron trunnions and breech.*

guns to Argentina, Austria, Belgium, Britain, Egypt, Holland, Spain, Sweden, Switzerland and Russia.

Napoleon III staged another exhibition on the Champs de Mars in 1867, and again Krupp went all out to promote his products. His fifty-ton cannon which could fire a 1,000-lb (453.6 kg) shell dominated the pleasure grounds, at an enormous cost to his company. As usual, he won the best prizes, and as usual, nobody was interested in buying his gun, which Krupp gave to his friend, King William of Prussia. These were not particularly good years for Alfred Krupp, as he came rather badly out of comparative tests with Vickets and Armstrong. This was in 1868, but brilliant public relations, which included gifts of smartly turned-out "gala guns" to influential guests at his Essen home, soon turned apparent disappointment into success as Krupp guns became more and more widely known.

There was nothing particularly new about the Krupp gun shown at the Champs de Mars. It was based largely on the experimental designs and models of an Italian artillery officer, Lieutenant-General Giovanni Cavalli, who set out to improve his country's emplaced ordnance about 1830. He had three points in mind: economy of space, simplicity in serving the gun and the use of a minimum number of men in each gun crew. To these ends, he created a breechloading arm, thus satisfying the first two requirements; and by controlling its recoil, he reduced the amount of space needed to load, aim and fire it. His breech mechanism utilized a sliding wedge in combination with an obturating cup that resembled a larger version of Pauly's early cartridge cases, or the later "Broadwell" ring used in American ordnance.

The first gun to Cavalli's design was made in Peidmont. It was 3.5-inch (90 mm) caliber, with a cast iron barrel that withstood the tests of March 1832, June 1833, and of 1835, but which, as cast iron guns so often did, burst later in that same year. In 1837, Cavalli explained his requirements to the Swedish industrialist, Baron Martin von Wahrendorff, whose factory at Aker was then making some of the finest iron guns in Europe. The resulting gun was so well received that others to the same pattern and of the same 3.5-inch caliber were for made for Italy, France and Prussia.

The Italian association with Åkers Styckebruk continued through the development of Cavalli's rifled gun, which was manufactured in 1845 and tested in 1846, the year that Christian Friedrich Schönbein invented guncotton. Cavalli was recognized as a master of ordnance design and as the creator of the first successful rifled breechloading cannon. Using his own design of rifling machine, Cavalli had two spiral grooves cut in the tubes, in the same fashion as in the Brunswick rifle. His elongated projectile was fitted with quarter-inch (6.4 mm) projecting lugs that engaged the spiral, so avoiding some of the problems of jamming that plagued Whitworth's hexagonal bores, both in his rifled muskets and his cannon.

As well as his cannon designs and his rifling machine, Cavalli also published his specification for a two-horse galloper gun, *artigleria cacciatori*, in 1837; a metal-testing machine in 1847; and a telescopic sight for artillery. After his breech designs, his greatest single contribution to the gunner's craft was his carefully calculated emplacement carriage, which limited recoil so accurately that military engineers were able to reduce the size of casemates, and so minimize the danger to gunners from high-angle fire.

In the field, smoothbore cannon were effective up to a thousand or twelve hundred yards (*c.* 900 to 1,100 m), a sufficient range to give a distinct superiority over smoothbore muskets. When the rifled musket came into general service in most of the armies of the Western world, artillery also had to progress if it was to retain its advantages in battle. Soon after the end of the Crimean War, French field artillery was rifled on Treuille de Beaulieu's system, in time to show its worth in 1859 at Magenta and Solferino. While the French faced the Austrians in the confident knowledge that their own guns had far greater range and accuracy, the rest of Europe experimented. In a very short time, artillery regained its dominance, with the early Armstrong guns used by Britain's Royal Artillery, by the Broadwell and Krupp designs used in Prussia, and by other countries which copied the French plan. The fine ores used in Scandinavian gun foundries persuaded the northern kingdoms of Denmark, Sweden and Norway to continue to use cast iron for field ordnance, while Prussia already had steel smoothbores in service, and Armstrong's coil system was giving Britain good guns which were economic to produce.

Sir William Armstrong was the first to have any success in making guns out of wrought iron coils shrunk over one another in such a way that the inner tube was in a state of compression, and the out in tension. Accurate calculation ensured that each coil gave the maximum resistance to the pressures built up in the barrel when the gunpowder exploded behind the shell. Some of the earliest Armstrong guns weighed over twenty tons and fired a 600-lb (*c.* 270 kg) projectile with acceptable velocity. Towards the end of the nineteenth century, guns were made with coils of wire or steel ribbon wound around the central tube.

Chapter 18

In 1844, Dr. Richard Jordan Gatling moved from North Carolina, where he was born in 1818, through several cities in Missouri, Ohio and Indiana, seeking wider markets for his agricultural inventions. But it is for his firearms designs that Gatling is remembered. The first years of the Civil War saw the creation of his prototype rapid-fire gun, intended for use in the defense of special objectives. Like most arms inventions, it was a combination of earlier principles. Gatling combined the hand-cranked revolver mechanism of Ager's "Coffee Mill" gun with the multi-barrel principle which Ezra Ripley had based on the pepperbox firearms of the percussion era. The Gatling Gun, demonstrated at Indianapolis in 1862, used paper cartridges that soon gave way to copper rim-fire cartridges fired from six musket-caliber barrels. In November of that year, the inventor was granted United States Patent 36,836.

After numerous modifications, the gun was chambered for one-inch (25.4 mm) ammunition to give it the range that was needed to fight off direct fire from artillery. In 1866, the United States Army ordered one hundred guns, fifty in the one-inch caliber, and the remainder to fire the half-inch (12.7 mm) round which resulted from Colonel S.V. Benét's experiments at the Frankford Arsenal. Colt's Patent Fire Arms Manufacturing Company made the guns at Hartford for delivery in 1867, including among them some of the new ten-barrel version. This

The .45-inch (11.4 mm) caliber Gatling gun, mounted on a wheeled carriage for field use.

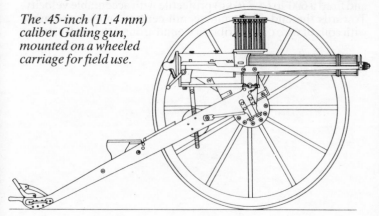

Magazine Arms

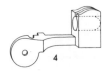

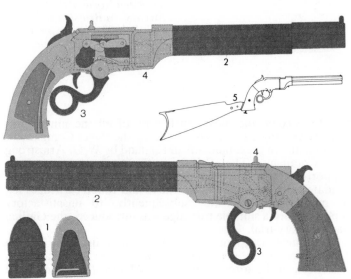

In 1847, Walter Hunt of New York patented his "Rocket Ball" self-contained cartridge in England. Two years later, he designed and patented his "Volitional Repeater", a gun with a tubular magazine, in the United States.

In 1854, the Smith and Wesson Company was formed to make a rifle, based on Hunt's design, at Norwich, Connecticut. The company also manufactured a tubular-magazine pistol (shown here), named the "Volcanic" after the Volcanic Repeating Arms Company, the succes-sor to Smith and Wesson. Eight to ten loaded bullets (1) were fed into the tubular magazine (2) through an opening revealed when the end of the barrel was swung to the side. Moving the lever (3) down and forward and then returning it to the first position loaded the chamber with a bullet from the carrier block (4). The lever was operated by the second finger of the shooting hand. Some models of the Volcanic pistol were fitted with shoulder stocks (5). (See also pp. 208-209 and 211.)

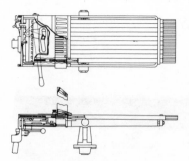

A ten-barreled, .45-inch (11.4 mm) caliber Nordenfelt Machine Gun, invented and financed respectively by Helge Palmcrantz and Thorsten Nordenfelt, both Swedes. At British trials held in July 1882, the gun fired 3,000 rounds in 3 minutes 3 seconds.

was to become the most satisfactory of all the nineteenth-century Gatlings. It was also made by the Paget Company of Vienna, and in great numbers in England by W.G. Armstrong and Company. The British authorities saddened their supporters by testing this extremely efficient gun with the outdated Boxer ammunition, whose thin-rolled cartridges led to many stoppages and, subsequently, to unsatisfactory reports. Once a suitable cartridge was introduced, the Gatling passed every trial.

The official acceptance of Gatling's rapid-fire gun, and the 1866 orders from the United States Army, did not pass unnoticed in the foreign press. The *Montreal Gazette*, dated January 10, 1867, recorded that "the American Government is now having made at Hartford, Connecticut, one hundred battery guns of a new invention. Fifty of them will have a one-inch bore. ... This terrible weapon...can be discharged at the rate of 200 shots per minute."

Within twenty years, Gatling's "labor-saving device for warfare" was in action in the Franco-Prussian War, had been mounted on camel saddles in Egypt, and had seen service in Cuba, Russia and West Africa, in the Russo-Turkish War, in the Zulu War and almost everywhere else where men who could afford it were in combat.

A point to be noted in connection with the Gatlings made in the arsenals of Russia is that they carried the name of General Gorloff. This was not intended to give the false impression that Gorloff was the inventor, but was in keeping with the rule in the czar's service that the official who superintended the construction of a gun had to have his name engraved on it. Gorloff, when a colonel, spent most of 1868 and 1869 in Hartford ensuring that the Colt work force kept to the closest possible engineering limits.

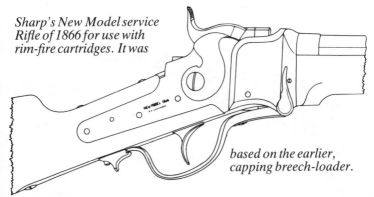

Sharp's New Model service Rifle of 1866 for use with rim-fire cartridges. It was based on the earlier, capping breech-loader.

The reliability of the Gatling was quite phenomenal. During three days of tests in October 1873, one hundred thousand rounds were fired from an 1865 model, using James G. Accles' gravity-feed drum magazine. Just as important as its reliability was its accuracy. At Hartford in 1869, all one hundred and ten shots hit a 10-foot (3.1 m) square target at a range of 500 yards (*c.* 457 m). At Karlsruhe in the same year, one hundred riflemen armed with the needle gun hit a target 6 feet (1.8 m) high by 72 feet (21.9 m) long 196 times out of 721 shots in one minute. In the same time, at a similar target, a half-inch Gatling had 216 hits out of 246 shots.

As the Gatling reached its peak of efficiency, and as it played a major part in Britain's colonial wars, where it was used in military and naval actions, so it was approaching obsolescence. In an attempt to fight off the growing threats from the Gardner, Hotchkiss and Nordenfelt, Gatling challenged all comers to a shooting match at 500 yards (*c.* 457 m) and 1,000 yards (*c.* 914 m), the winner to be the one whose gun registered the most hits in some given time, say one minute. The loser was to pay a wager to a selected charity.

Even as Gatling's challenge was published in the *Army and Navy Journal* of August 1881, Hiram Maxim was in Europe and on the brink of making the discoveries that were to dominate future generations of machine-gun designers. Nevertheless, Gatling saw his gun evolve from a relatively crude weapon using loose powder and percussion ignition to the sophisticated version firing primed metallic cartridges with its propellant changed from black to smokeless powder. Before he died in 1903, Gatling saw the handcrank supplemented by an electric motor, and even saw an experimental version which used gas bled through a vent to turn the barrels and fire the next round.

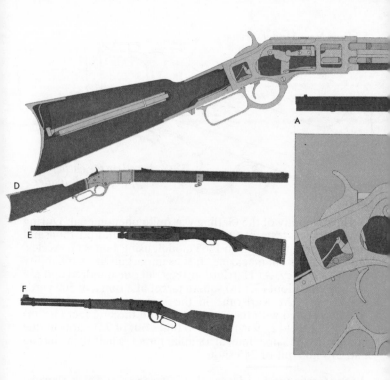

When Oliver F. Winchester took over its assets in 1857, the Volcanic Repeating Arms Company was renamed the New Haven Arms Company. It continued to make Volcanic pistols until about 1865. From 1862 to 1866, the new company also made the Henry rifle, based on the Volcanic action. In the latter year, with the introduction of an improved model of the rifle, the firm became the Winchester Arms Company.

A The Winchester '73 was a modification of the Model 1866, with a strengthened mechanism to take the .44-caliber (11.2 mm) Winchester center-fire cartridge, the first of its type developed by the company. Sporting versions of the rifle were made in a variety of barrel lengths. Advertisements of the day claimed the rifle could fire two shots a second without loss of aim.

The '73 and its successor the '76 were both part of one of the greatest marketing devices in firearms history. During pre-sale testing, barrels, which showed up especially well, were set up as ONE OF ONE THOUSAND, fitted

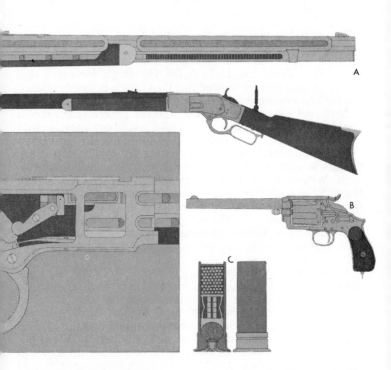

with set-triggers, and given a special finish. Only 124 guns, out of the 720,610 Model '73 Winchesters made, reached the required standard, and even fewer of the less marvellous rifles, marked ONE OF ONE HUNDRED, were made. But the company reaped great publicity from the scheme.

B Hugo Borchardt, who later returned to Germany where he designed his famous automatic pistols, worked for Winchester for a number of years, during which time he designed this single-action revolver with side-lever extractor.

C The Double A target load 12-gauge cartridge.

D The Winchester Model 1866 was essentially a Henry with improvements made by Nelson King. It was a good rifle, but a more powerful cartridge than it could shoot safely was needed. This led to the most famous of all Winchesters, the '73.

E The Model 1200 Field Magnum slide-action shotgun is used today for wildfowling.

F The Winchester Model 94 lever-action carbine, 1972.

Towards the close of the Second World War, ordnance experts in the United States sought a higher firing rate than was possible with a reciprocating action. Studies made by the Small Arms Branch of the U.S. Army Ordnance Research and Development Service showed that the Gatling principle offered the highest potential for a modern aircraft machine gun. With an external electric or hydraulic power source, each round could be fired independently, and misfires did not interfere with the cyclic rates as duds were ejected automatically. In 1945, a Gatling ten-barrel .45/70 was bought from the New York dealers in arms and other military objects, Francis Bannerman Sons. When fitted with an electric motor it gave a cyclic rate of fire of 5,800 rounds per minute for fifty rounds. Ten years later, the U.S. Army and Air Force ordered the production of the *M.61 mm Vulcan Aircraft Gun*. Two 1.2-inch (30 mm) Vulcan guns, each three times more powerful than the .8-inch (20 mm), were also made for trial purposes, but were not standardized for service use.

In its first form, the Vulcan gun fires up to 7,200 shots per minute from six barrels. It is 72 inches (1.8 m) long, and weighs 255 lb (*c.* 116 kg). Its ammunition is the standard electrically-primed .8-inch (20 mm) M53A1 armor-piercing incendiary, M56A1 high-explosive incendiary and the M55A1 ball, fired with a muzzle velocity of 3,380 feet (1,030 m) per second. A modified, three-barrel version firing up to 3,000 rounds per minute was developed for use from helicopters, and a model made by General Electric has been redesigned to fire percussion-primed ammunition of the NATO .30-inch (7.62 mm) caliber. It has probably reached the highest point of development possible in a machine gun, and is certainly not the anachronism one might think in the day of the aircraft missile. Apart from the problems of target range, adverse weather conditions, evasive action on the part of the target, and the use of electronic countermeasures which confront a pilot using missiles, he may often find himself with no more than a fraction of a second of time-on-target. The almost continuous stream of shells from these latter-day Gatlings, "Puff the Magic Dragon" in the military slang of the mid-1960s, gives the gunner the greatest possible chance of a hit, even when target saturation is impossible.

In 1871, a 1.5-inch (37 mm) revolving cannon resembling Gatling's gun was designed by Benjamin Berkeley Hotchkiss of Watertown, Connecticut. It used five barrels firing explosive shells. The gun was made for the British Royal Navy at the Armstrong factory at Elswick.

The Hotchkiss company continued after its founder's death

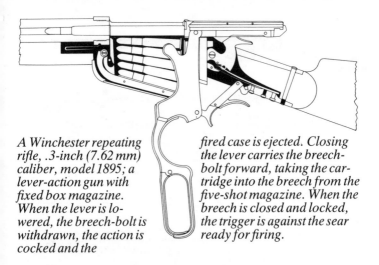

A Winchester repeating rifle, .3-inch (7.62 mm) caliber, model 1895; a lever-action gun with fixed box magazine. When the lever is lowered, the breech-bolt is withdrawn, the action is cocked and the fired case is ejected. Closing the lever carries the breech-bolt forward, taking the cartridge into the breech from the five-shot magazine. When the breech is closed and locked, the trigger is against the sear ready for firing.

in 1885, one of its finest products being a light air-cooled, single-barrel .31-inch (8 mm) machine gun. This new gas-operated weapon employed the reciprocating piston system, the ammunition being fed from 30-round metal strips. Although it had shortcomings, the Hotchkiss remained in use by some units of the British and Indian armies as a cavalry weapon until the late 1930s.

The years between 1870 and the end of the century saw many more machine-gun types of varying success. In 1874 another American, William Gardner of Toledo, Ohio, invented yet one more hand-cranked gun. As it aroused more interest in Britain than in America, Gardner moved to England, where he lived until his death. In his last years he went on to design a five-barrel gun for sea service and light single- and double-barrel guns for land use. The cartridge fired from Gardner guns against the Sudanese at El Teb and Tamaai in 1884-85 and the Matabele in 1893 was intended also for the Gatling and the Nordenfelt machine gun designed by Helge Palmcrantz, a Swedish engineer. It was a solid-drawn brass case charged with 85 grains (5.5 gr) of powder and firing a 480-grain (31.1 gr) .45-inch (11.4 mm) lead bullet.

Thorsten Nordenfelt was a Swedish banker who financed the development of Palmcrantz's 1873 design. About fifteen years later another financier, Sir Basil Zaharoff, recommended an association that resulted in the Maxim-Nordenfelt Gun and Ammunition Company Limited of London, which was to enjoy considerable success despite long-running legal disputes.

The French army's interest in the first Gatling guns was

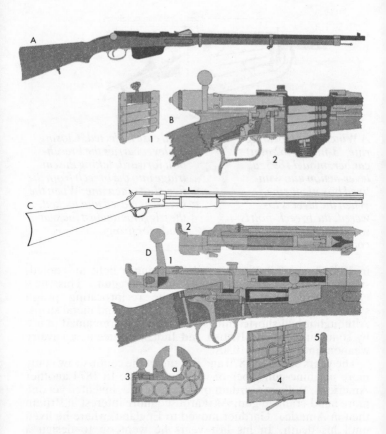

A *The .43-inch (11 mm) straight-pull bolt-action Mannlicher rifle was adopted by the Austrian army in 1885.*

B *The Italian Vetterli-Vitali Model 1871-87 bolt-action rifle with box-magazine, .41-inch (10.4 mm) caliber. (1) Cartridge clip. (2) Mechanism.*

C *The Colt New Lightning Magazine Rifle with slide action, 1884. Cartridges*

were loaded into the breech from the tubular magazine as the shooter "pumped" the action back and forward.

D *In 1889, the Danish Army adopted the .32-inch (8 mm) Krag-Jørgensen bolt-action magazine rifle. (1) Bolt. (2) Mechanism. (3) The magazine, shown from the front, was fed through a loading gate at a. (4) Cartridge clip. (5) Cartridge.*

212

certainly increased by the news that the weapon was under consideration for the army of her arch enemy, Prussia. However, the manufacture of the Montigny *mitrailleuse* at the Meudon arsenal was already in progress, and Montigny's gun was not to be replaced by the more efficient Gatling. The *mitrailleuse* was originally invented in 1851 by a Belgian, Captain Fafchamps, who offered his invention to the Belgian engineer and manufacturer, Joseph Montigny. It had thirty-seven rifled barrels set in a wrought iron tube. An iron plate with thirty-seven matching holes was used for loading, all thirty-seven shots being fired by a single turn of a hand-crank. In one minute, a skilled team could get off twelve bursts, or about 444 rounds. In 1867, the weapon was adopted for the French service, where it lasted for one year as France's secret weapon before repeated failures and an inability to appreciate the need to use it among infantry rather than in batteries, proved that it was quite unsuitable for modern warfare. Nevertheless, its name has been preserved by the French to describe a machine gun, whatever its design.

In the American Civil War, the first war in which breech-loading and repeating weapons were used in any numbers, the United States tested many of the fifty-odd breechloading mechanisms which were patented before 1865. Some were effective, others were as dangerous to the firer as to his target and were used only because of the acute shortage of weapons. More than thirty varieties were used in military service, and their impact was enough to drive the muzzle-loader from the battlefields of North America by the end of the Civil War.

As breechloading firearms came into more regular use, national governments demanded cheap ways to convert their vast stocks of muzzle-loaders and so avoid the costs of total reequipment. Two Americans, Erskine S. Allin, Master Armorer at Springfield, and Jacob Snider of New York, prepared competing designs, using a trap-door breech hinged respectively at the front and on the left. With minor improvements Allin's breech was accepted in 1865 by the United States Army, and the conversions remained the standard rifle until the adoption of the Krag in 1892, although the latter was intended only as a stopgap until a new breechloader could be developed.

The Allin conversion was no competition for a rifle that was already available five years before, when a design by B. Tyler Henry, superintendent of the New Haven Arms Company, was offered for sale as the "Henry Rifle." Its tubular magazine held fifteen of Henry's newly developed .44 (11.2 mm) rim-fire cartridges. All fifteen could be brought in turn to the chamber by a toggle-link lever action and fired in ten seconds. Improvements introduced in 1866 by another superintendent, Nelson King, improved the rifle, and a new model was launched as the Model 1866, the first of the renamed Winchester Repeating Arms Company's outstanding line of underlever repeating arms that were made for many different cartridges from .22 (5.6 mm) short to the .45-90. The Winchester has been given the credit, or blame, for subduing the American Indian, all but exterminating the buffalo, and reducing the big game of the American West to insignificant numbers.

In the year of Allin's success, Britain adopted Snider's design and used it to convert the 1853 Enfield rifled musket. From 1867, when it was used with Boxer's center-fire .577 (14.7 mm) cartridge, it was a fairly effective arm until its replacement in 1871 by the .45 (11.4 mm) Martini-Henry. Snider's simple hinged breech-flap, housing a firing-pin to transmit the blow of the cock to the center-fire cartridge, is little different in principle from the breech of Henry VIII's breechloading fowling-pieces. The Snider first saw action with the British Army at Arogee, in Napier's Abyssinian campaign of 1867-68, when 10,000 rounds were fired.

The most satisfactory newly-designed single-shot breech-loader was the creation of Christian Sharps of Philadelphia. It was made in carbine and musket calibers at the Hartford factory of the Sharps Rifle Manufacturing Company. John Brown's raiders, who attacked Harpers Ferry in 1859, carried rifles with the simple but strong action patented by Sharps in 1848. The trigger-guard served as a lever to move the breechblock vertically in a mortice cut in the action frame. In the earlier models, the block was shaped so as to shave off the rear of the paper or linen cartridge that the action used with separate primers. These were either Maynard's tape or Sharps' own disk design. An American clergyman named Beecher expressed the opinion that one of Sharps' carbines carried more moral weight than a hundred Bibles, so giving the weapon the nickname "Beecher's Bible."

During the Civil War, the Union government bought 9,141 rifles and 80,512 carbines of the Sharps models designated as 1859 and 1863. The rifles, fitted with sword bayonets, were the weapons issued to Hiram Berdan's Sharpshooters, some of whom were armed with Colt revolving rifles. At the end of the war, the Sharps action was modified to use the new metallic cartridge. Before it went out of production, it was accepted as an excellent rifle for amateur and professional hunters. It was also the rifle with which the American team won the first

International Rifle Shooting Match on the Creedmoor Ranges, Long Island, in 1877.

One of the qualifications for entrance to Berdan's Sharpshooters, according to *Harper's Weekly*, was the ability to shoot a 5-inch (12.7 cm) group at 200 yards (183 m). This was well within the accuracy of the heavy-barreled snipers' rifles which were used by both sides, but as some weighed from 25 to 30 lb (11.3 to 13.6 kg), they were too heavy to carry into an assault and so saw service from entrenched positions only. Apart from these rifles with their fitted bullets, the most accurate weapon used in the Civil War was the English Whitworth. Modern muzzle-loading enthusiasts have shot 3-inch (7.6 cm) groups at 200 yards (183 m), and groups of less than 11 inches (*c.* 28 cm) at 500 yards (457 m) with their Whitworths.

The outstanding repeating rifle of the Civil War was invented by the Quaker Christopher M. Spencer (1833-1922) and patented by him on March 6, 1860. A tubular magazine in the butt held seven rim-fire cartridges that were fed in turn into the chamber by a spring when the breech was lowered by depressing the trigger guard. The same movement extracted the empty cartridge case. In all, the Union government bought 77,181 Spencer carbines for the cavalry in addition to 12,471 rifles. They were frequently praised in battlefield reports as more than a match for muzzle-loaders.

The cavalry and many of the officers of North and South carried revolvers as their personal arms. Colt's .31-, .36- and .44-inch (7.9, 9.1 and 11.2 mm) caliber models were the most popular in the North, where the government bought over 160,000 pistols. Next in popularity were the Remington Army .44 (11.2 mm) and the Navy .36 (9.1 mm) revolvers, of which more than 130,000 were sold to the Union government. Altogether, the Union side bought 64,385,400 cartridges for the nineteen types of pistols which were used in its armies, presenting the quartermasters with an awesome logistic problem.

Most of the cavalry on both sides carried swords as well as their pistols and the occasional knife, for the days of Black and Bowie were only a few years past. The knives were American in character and origin, but the swords were much the same as those used by men carrying out similar duties in Europe and exchanged among the various governments from 1835 to 1846.

Lances were rare in America, but an account of the 6th Pennsylvania Cavalry (Rush's Lancers) tells us that, before the lance was found to be an impossible weapon in the broken, wooded country of northern Virginia, they carried a 9-foot (2.7

m) shaft of Norway fir, with an 11-inch (*c*. 28 cm) steel point. In France at this time, lancers were armed with lances just over 7 feet (2.1 m) long. When their lances were taken out of service, Rush's Lancers had only a dozen carbines per troop, issued for scouting and picket duties. In conformity with military practice elsewhere, they were eventually armed with carbines and sabers.

Bayonet exercises were made a little more realistic when man could face man at practice with little danger of either of them receiving a wound. Many varieties of blunt-tip bayonets evolved. Some bayonet-drill instructors used the simple expedient of tying the scabbard to the musket, but the damage from a jab from a metal chape was enough to lead to the manufacture of devices such as the American John G. Ernst's "Improved Bayonet Guard" of 1862, which consisted of a rubber ball attached to the end of the scabbard like a foil-button, and a fastening to ensure that the scabbard was not pulled off accidentally, to leave one man facing his opponent's naked steel.

There seems to have been little real appreciation of the true role of artillery in battle on either side at the beginning of the Civil War. While their European contemporaries were soon to learn that artillery should be used in mass to make its maximum effect, American generals still tended to disperse their guns in penny numbers, a battery to each infantry brigade. The weakness of this system was finally exposed at Malvern Hill, when a concentration of sixty guns crushed each Confederate battery as it was brought into action, almost like tin ducks on a shooting range. These brigade batteries did not consist of a single gun type, but mixed four 12-pounder guns with two 24-pounder howitzers, or four 6-pounder guns with two 12-pounders, or smoothbores with rifles. In all this, the Confederate artillery was less well supplied than the Union. A four-gun battery using three different calibers of ammunition was not unknown in the South, and even these guns may have come from different sources; from Southern foundries, from capture on the battlefield, or from abroad on ships which ran the Union blockade.

The Northern quartermasters had a slightly less difficult task in supplying ammunition, for their gunners were usually more uniformly equipped. The 3-inch (7.6 cm) rifle and the 10-pounder Parrott were supported by the 20-pounder Parrott and the very popular 12-pounder Napoleon. The Napoleon was an efficient gun-howitzer, officially designated as the Model 1857. It was served by five or six men who could get off two

The Machine Gun

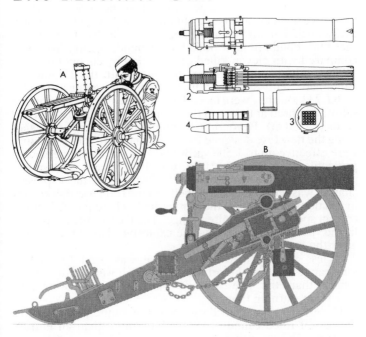

A *A Battery Sergeant Major of the Royal Artillery, c. 1884, fires a three-barreled, .45-inch (11.4 mm) Nordenfelt machine gun by moving a lever on the right of the action backward and forward.*

B *The* mitrailleuse, *invented in 1851 by Captain T.H.J. Fafchamps and developed by Joseph Montigny, could fire a volley of twenty-five shots in under a second. An iron plate, drilled with twenty-five holes, each loaded with a cartridge, loaded the twenty-five barrels which were in a wrought-iron tube.*

*To load, the gunners dropped the plate into guides and rotated the loading lever to force the plate forward and the cartridges into the chambers. The same action cocked the mechanism. By rotating the firing handle on the right, the gun could be fired rapidly or slowly, at will. (***1***) The 1870 de Reffye model, from above. (***2***) From the side, sectioned, before firing. (***3***) The muzzle. (***4***) The .51-inch (13 mm) Chassepot cartridge used. (***5***) The 1870 model on a wheeled "trail mounting."* (See also pp. 220-221 and 228.)

217

aimed shots per minute, shells or solid shot, or four rounds of canister. Parrott guns were not satisfactory, however often they may have been used in battle. In the action before Fort Fisher, every single Parrott gun in the fleet burst. The five that burst in the first bombardment killed or wounded forty-five men compared with eleven killed or wounded by enemy fire.

The antipersonnel canister shot used with the 12-pounder contained twenty-seven cast-iron balls each weighing just under .5 lb (.23 kg). They were loaded in a tin case nailed to a wooden sabot, and fired at troops in the open at ranges up to about 350 yards (*c.* 320 m). Beyond that, shrapnel or spherical case shot using the new fuse designed by the Belgian, Captain Bormann, were effective up to 1,500 yards (1,371 m) as an antipersonnel projectile. The Bormann fuse, usually a discoid white-metal plug containing a train of powder leading to the explosive charge, was screwed into the shell. As the train was marked off in fractions of a second, the gunner had only to pierce it at the correct spot for the required range. The flash of the propellant lit the fuse at that point and the explosive charge was ignited after the measured time.

A less sophisticated wooden fuse was used for heavy, long-range shells and mortar bombs which were in the air for longer than the five seconds which was the Bormann's maximum burning time.

The greatest single artillery innovation in the Civil War was the use of rifled cannon as something more than an untried novelty. The Austrian artillery, always preeminent in its *matériel* and the way in which its excellent guns were handled in battle, had rifled guns as early as 1859. In field batteries, the greater range and accuracy of the rifled cannon gave it distinct advantages over the smoothbore. For siege purposes, rifled cannon with cylindro-conoidal projectiles virtually put an end to large masonry fortifications. Some excellent new breech-loading guns from the British factories of Armstrong and Whitworth found their way to America, but they made little difference to the outcome of the war; for they were few, and ammunition for them was scarce.

Siege batteries used by both sides were even more mixed than the field batteries. In addition to the guns used to batter fortifications, howitzers were employed in the ricochet fire which Vauban had advocated two centuries before, and mortars lobbed explosive shells into defenses which could not be reached by direct fire.

At the beginning of the war, some of the forts built in the days before rifled ordnance came into the field had been considered invulnerable to cannon fire. At the mouth of the Savannah on Cockspur Island, a fort was built between 1829 and 1847 and named after the Polish hero of the American Revolution, Count Casimir Pulaski. The original plans for the massive building were made by a graduate of France's Ecole Polytechnique, General Simon Bernard, who envisaged a two-story structure mounting three tiers of guns. By the end of 1860, twenty-five million bricks had been laid, and an immense quantity of lead, timber, iron and lime had been bought at a total cost of a million dollars; yet the initial complement of the fort amounted to one ordnance sergeant and one caretaker, who watched over 20 guns out of a proposed total of 146. The fort was to make a secondary contribution to America's military history. All but one of the many engineering officers who served on Cockspur became generals in the armies of one side or the other in the Civil War. They included Robert E. Lee, later the general in chief of the Confederate forces.

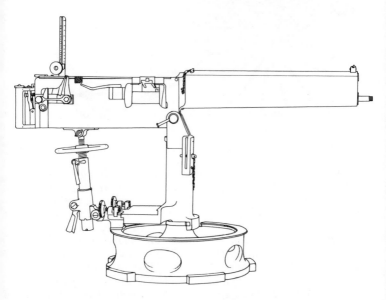

The Maxim machine gun, Model 1895, .303-inch (7.7 mm) caliber. Maxim guns *were first used by Britain's colonial forces in the Matabele War of 1893-94.*

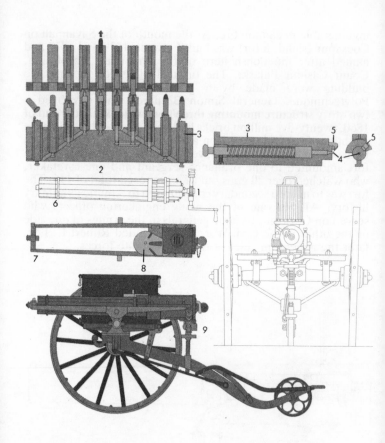

Gatling patented the first, successful, manually operated, rapid-fire gun in 1862. By 1865, he had improved the action so that two hundred rounds per minute could be fired. Turning the handle (**1**) at the rear rotated the barrels and operated the bolts in the sequence illustrated (**2**). The breech bolt (**3**), one for each barrel, carried the firing pin (**4**) and the extractor (**5**). The construction of the barrel- and breech-group and the trunnioned frame is shown at (**6**) and (**7**). The feed hopper (**8**) has a base for the Broadwell drum magazine.
The Model 1871 Long Gatling Gun (**9**) is shown here on a U.S. Navy landing carriage. The Broadwell drum magazine held four hundred .5 inch (12.7 mm) rounds, and its use allowed some 4,000 rounds

to be fired in ten minutes.
(**10**) *L.F. Bruce's gravity-fed loading mechanism, patented on September 20, 1881 and used with Gatling and other machine guns.*
(**11**) *Canister shot cartridge for the 1-inch (25.4 mm) Gatling Model 1865.*
(**12**) *The Gatling Gun Model 1895 on an armor-plated field carriage. Note the circular shield which revolved*

with the barrels.
(**13**) *Gatling's Model 1874 was made with "musket length" barrels and, as the shorter and lighter Camel Gun, weighing 135 lb (61 kg), with 18 inch (45 cm) barrels.*
(**14**) *The Model 1893 "Bulldog" Gatling with the positive-feed magazine designed by James G. Accles.*

On a cold April day in 1862, the eggnog parties were over and the Union batteries opened up on Fort Pulaski, which was by then defended by five companies totaling 385 officers and men. They had forty-eight guns, only a few of which could be brought to bear on the massed batteries on Tybee Beach. Within two days, two 84-pounder James rifled guns, and one 64-pounder, shooting from just under a mile (1.6 km) away, reduced the fort's brickwork to so much rubble. The fort, of which a United States Chief of Engineers had said "you might as well bombard the Rocky Mountains," fell to gunfire within two days. Another senior soldier, General Hunter, reported to his political masters in Washington that "no works of stone or brick can resist the impact of rifled artillery of heavy caliber."

Since 1933, apart from a few years during the Second World War, Fort Pulaski has been looked after by the National Parks Service of the Department of the Interior. It remains an exceptional monument to nineteenth-century military engineering philosophy.

The siege pieces used against Fort Pulaski were heavy, but the most massive guns of the war were the coastal artillery used from fixed batteries where the weight of the guns did not matter, for there was no need to move them. They were intended to defend coastal installations and roadsteads against the incursions of enemy warships and gunrunners. Their projectiles were huge, with one gun having a caliber of twenty inches (c. 51 cm), and they were very slow to load. This low rate of fire, coupled to the speed of the new steamships which were then coming into service (**HMS** *Warrior*, Britain's first monitor, was launched in 1860), meant that the guns had to be accurate. The fifteen-inch (38.1 cm) Columbiad needed seven men to load and fire it once in seventy seconds. Gun-laying was an equally long process, as a 90° traverse took two minutes and twenty seconds. Only a good gun crew could get off more than a single shot while a steamship was in range. Against ships, shot was sometimes brought to red heat in a special furnace before being loaded, adding the danger of fire to the smashing effect of solid iron projectiles.

Military engineers learned their lessons from the abrupt collapse of Fort Pulaski. By 1868, massive shields of chilled cast iron were designed and made by Gruson of Magdeburg. The blocks were made to key together and form a complete unit without backing or bolts. Defenses built to Gruson's designs at the St. Marie battery near Antwerp, and the two turrets guarding Spezia harbor, each mounting two 119-ton Krupp guns, could withstand a few rounds from heavy guns, but "hard" armor would break up under prolonged attack. British coastal forts differed fundamentally from those of most other nations as their construction depended on "soft" armor of wrought iron plates, either a single thickness or in a concrete or timber sandwich. Although it was made to withstand fire longer than Gruson's, it had its own disadvantages. The bolts holding the sandwich together could be driven loose, exactly as the rivets used in the construction of the American M3 tank, the General Grant, would fly round the interior like so many bullets when it was struck solidly by antitank shells.

By the end of the nineteenth century, the arguments as to which system of armor was best still raged, but it had become a matter more for the naval architects than for the soldiers, although artillerymen still sought the perfect projectile which would enable them to ignore the rule of thumb that governed fire against steel-faced targets: the thickness of wrought iron pierced by a projectile was then about one caliber for every 1,000 feet (*c.* 305 m) per second of striking velocity. They had learned that there was little point in using an explosive shell against armor unless the head was deep in the plate before exploding. The "shaped" charge, so effective against armor in the Second World War, was still a generation away as an element of a projectile's killing power, although its principle appears to have been understood since the petard of the seventeenthcentury siege.

Small arms development proceeded at a great pace in America. While British troops armed with the antiquated 1853 Enfield rifle faced a rising of fierce but ill-armed Maoris in April 1860, Horace Smith and Daniel Wesson were already patenting a rim-fire cartridge of much the same design as that used today. Based on the Flobert design of 1849, the cartridge was little more than a round lead ball stuck in the open end of a percussion cap whose fulminate was housed in the raised rim, which also served to stop the cartridge falling through the cylinder and as a hold for the extractor. The cap was extended to accommodate a charge of powder, and so improved on the range of Flobert's pattern.

Smith and Wesson had used their cartridge in their own design of small revolvers for two years before the date of their patent, adding a rim to the base of the copper case. Patents granted to G.W. Morse between 1856 and 1858 covered most of the features found in modern rifle cartridges, although the propellant was still black powder.

Chapter 19

By April 1865, the American Civil War had been won with the aid of revolving pistols and repeating carbines, breechloading cannon and a massive 13-inch (33 cm) mortar, the Dictator, so heavy at 17,120 lb (7,765 kg) that it had to be maneuvered into position on railroad tracks. Artillery observers had telegraphed orders from balloons to gunners on the ground. Nevertheless, the sword still retained a place in the doctrines of some soldiers. On June 3, 1865, the *Illustrated London News* reported the swordsmanship of noncommissioned officers of the Royal Horse Guards. At an "Assault of Arms" before the Prince of Wales, Corporal Dean severed a handkerchief and several coils of ribbon with a swinging cut. Corporal-Major Waite halved an apple held on a comrade's outstretched palm, and cut through a sheet of notepaper standing on its bottom edge. To show that this sort of airy trick was not all his sword could do, Waite went on to sever a bar of lead, and, "with a downward cut, one of Wilkinson's trustworthy blades cleft a breastplate to the depth of about six inches."

While Waite and Dean were showing their paces, a large Paris crowd was being entertained by "marvelous exhibitions of skill, strength and courage," given by the German *Turn-Verein* in the Bois de Boulogne. In the interval, the German choir in Paris sang a selection of songs during which, one newspaper observed wryly, "Was ist des Deutschen Vaterland" evoked considerable national enthusiasm. The next year, following Prussia's easy annexation of a number of German states, Napoleon III met Bismarck, but peace could only be preserved for a few years in the face of Prussia's desire to unite the German states in a nation which would have a voice in Europe's affairs.

A year later, von Dreyse's needle gun finally proved itself during the Seven Weeks' War between Austria and Prussia. Two armies, each of more than 200,000 men, faced each other at Königgrätz (Sadowa). The Austrians strove to come to bayonet distance. The Prussians laid down a devastating fire which dissolved the Austrian threat. The war was over. Prussia acquired five million new citizens and twenty-five thousand square miles (64,750 km^2) of territory.

The brilliance of the Prussian chief of staff, Count Helmuth von Moltke, and the ineptitude of Austria's commander in chief, Ludwig von Bënedek, were at least as important contributions to the victory as the needle gun. But throughout Europe, it seems to have been accepted that it was easier to rearm then to reeducate the military establishments. Breechloaders using paper cartridges appeared all over the Continent. The British experimented at Enfield with von Dreyse's needle gun. The French developed their Chassepot which could outshoot it for range and rate of fire and which, with the caliber reduced from .66 inches (16.8 mm) to .43 inches (10.9 mm), allowed the French rifleman to carry ninety rounds to seventy-five in Prussian pouches. Sweden used the Hagström, Italy the Carcano, and Prussia the Carte that was to serve her so well.

Just as the authorities differed on the rifle actions that would best suit their armies, so too did they disagree on the caliber, best sights, types of rifling, muzzle velocities and stock shapes. The selection of a bayonet was just as widely disputed, and the variety in use throughout the world can be guessed at from the fact that Britain alone used a score or so of different methods of attachment, with blade shapes that varied from the 30-inch (c. 76 cm) pilum-like socket bayonet of Egg's breechloading carbine of c. 1782 to the 13.8-inch (35.1 cm) knife used on Wilkinson's double-barreled Vivian carbine of 1835-36.

Not only Prussia profited from the short war into which Austria was baited in 1866. Many of the cannon used by both sides at the Battle of Königgrätz (Sadowa) were made by Alfred Krupp, whose firm was soon to earn the uncomplimentary title "The Merchants of Death."

At the time of the Franco-Prussian war, as a contribution to the war treasury, Alfred Krupp offered Prussia $750,000-worth of guns on the day that he heard of France's mobilization. The offer was not accepted, but it was Krupp's heavy mortars and breechloaders, all made of steel, that crushed the French forts at Metz and Sedan and opened the way to Paris.

A number of other offers and suggestions put forward by Krupp received no support, but when Léon Gambetta (1838-82) made his escape by balloon from a besieged Paris in 1870 to join the government at Tours, any admiration which Krupp may have felt for the French statesman's courage was soon drowned in the fierce burst of activity that went into the production of the first anti-aircraft gun. The arrival outside Paris of the Krupp high-angle anti-balloon gun may have been a partial deterrent to others who might have thought of following Gambetta's example.

The invention of the center-fire metallic cartridge by Colonel E.M. Boxer in 1866 brought in its wake a mass of arms inventions which had not previously been possible. Modern magazine rifles, automatic pistols and machine guns are all dependent on fixed ammunition which combines all its elements–the primer, propellant and bullet–in a single case that is stable, waterproof and strong enough to endure the rigors of magazine loading. When fixed ammunition first appeared on the military scene, almost every firearm in service anywhere in the world used either separately loaded powder and ball, or semi-fixed ammunition in which the charges were packed in cloth, paper or thin metal.

One definition of an automatic weapon states that the process of feeding, firing and ejecting should be carried out by the mechanism of the weapon, after a primary manual, electrical or pneumatic cocking, as long as the trigger is held to the rear and there is still ammunition in the belt, feed-strip or magazine. In the closely related semiautomatic or self-loading arms, the mechanism performs the same functions, but only one shot is fired each time the trigger is pressed, and the trigger must be released between shots.

The goal of the earlier designers of rapid-fire arms, from Puckle to Requa, Ager and Gatling, had been a weapon that would meet the semiautomatic definition just given. However, the first automatic weapon was not designed until an American engineer became intrigued by failures that had dogged the attempts of many gun designers throughout Europe.

Hiram Stevens Maxim was in Europe to attend the Paris electrical exhibition of 1881. A friend told him that the way to get rich was to "invent something that will enable these Europeans to cut each others' throats with greater facility." Maxim saw that the Montigny was inefficient and that the Gatling, for all its ingenuity, was much too heavy in relation to its firepower. His own experience when shooting a Springfield .45-70-405, which bruised him sorely, suggested that recoil might be harnessed to the process of loading. In a workshop in Hatton Garden, London, Maxim began work on the designs which led to his patenting between 1883 and 1885 almost every process by which automatic fire could be produced. These processes are usually described by the method by which the energy developed by the exploding gunpowder charge produces the operating cycle, either (i) the backward thrust of the recoiling mass–recoil activation, or (ii) the pressure generated by progressively burning powder in the barrel–gas operation.

Maxim decided that the most logical principle was the short

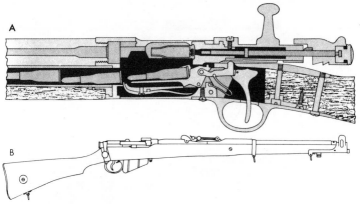

A *The Lebel Modèle 1886, .32-inch (8 mm) caliber rifle. The first small-bore, smoke-less-powder rifle issued to any army, it combined the bolt-* *action of the 1874 Gras with the Kropatschek tubular magazine.*
B *The Short magazine Lee-Enfield .303 rifle.*

recoil system, in which the barrel and breechblock move backwards together for a fraction of an inch until the residual pressure in the chamber is low enough to allow the bolt to be opened without danger of rupturing the cartridge case, with consequent malfunctioning. At this point, the barrel stops, the block continuing to the rear with its hooked lugs extracting and ejecting the spent case before being returned under the action of a spiral spring. As it returns, the firing mechanism is cocked, the next cartridge is rammed into the chamber and the barrel is forced forward into the firing position. So long as there are cartridges in the ammunition belt, a loading system first used in Baily's gun of 1874, and the trigger is pressed, the gun will continue to fire.

This was the weapon described in the London press in 1884, a few months before Omdurman fell to the Mahdi. A typical report stated: "Hiram Maxim, the well-known American electrician in Hatton Garden (London) has made an automatic machine-gun with a single barrel, using the standard calibre .45 rifle cartridge, that will load and fire itself by energy derived from recoil at a rate of over 600 rounds a minute."

Between 1900 and Maxim's death in New York on November 24, 1916, his gun had been adopted by every major power, although some were to discard it in favor of other systems. Had it been necessary his name would have been even further immortalized by Hilaire Belloc's lines: "Whatever happens, we have got / The Maxim gun and they have not."

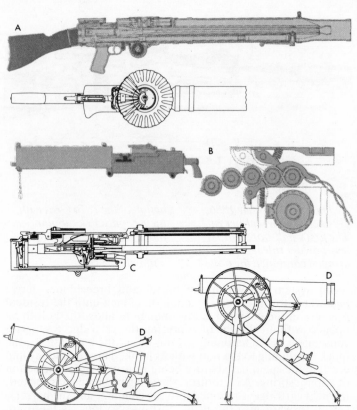

A *The 1915 model of the air-cooled, gas-operated automatic machine gun invented by Isaac M. Lewis, and first demonstrated in 1911.*

B *The Browning short-recoil-operated, water-cooled machine gun, Model 1917. The belt-fed gun was demonstrated by John Moses Browning, its inventor, on February 27, 1917, when it fired 20,000 rounds without failure at a cyclic rate of*

600 rounds per minute.

C *and* **D** *German Maxim recoil-operated, water-cooled machine gun Model 1908, with sledge mounting for use with or without wheels. The belt-fed gun is shown in the high and low firing positions made possible by this form of carriage. The basic weapon remained the principal German machine gun throughout the First World War.*

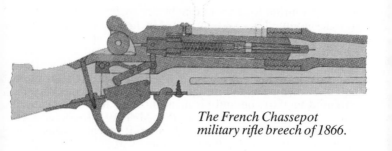

*The French Chassepot
military rifle breech of 1866.*

In the long recoil system, which Maxim also considered, the barrel and breechblock are driven back rather more than the length of the cartridge. A return spring drives the barrel back to the firing position, while an extractor on the face of the breechblock withdraws and ejects the spent case. As the breechblock is returned, the action is cocked and a round carried into the chamber.

The simplest gas-operated mechanism is the plain blow-back action in which the barrel remains stationary, and the inertia of the bolt delays the recoil against a return spring until the bullet has left the barrel. The action then follows the sequence of the recoil system. Because of the complete absence of mechanical complications, the system lends itself to mass production. It was used in the Bergmann M.34, the Schmeisser M.38 and in the British Sten machine carbine, which was made to fire the quantities of .35-inch (9 mm) rimless ammunition taken in Africa in the early years of the Second World War. Millions of crude little Stens and their slightly more sophisticated successors have been made. The design has undergone many improvements, but it still remains a less complex weapon to manufacture in quantity than those which challenged le Blanc and Whitney one hundred and fifty years before.

More complicated systems based on the same principle were the retarded blowback used in the Schwarzlose, the delayed blowback of the early Thompson and the Scotti, and the retarded primer ignition patented by Reinhold Becker for the .79-inch (20 mm) cannon he later made for installation in Germany's huge Gotha bomber.

In the second half of the twentieth century, the commonest and most satisfactory gas-operated mechanism is still that which taps the barrel to allow the expanding gases to actuate a piston or a lever.

Soon after he became interested in automatic arms in 1889, John M. Browning (1855-1926) modified his Winchester lever-action rifle to semi-automatic fire by fitting an improved muzzle-mounted gas system to it. His first new design for an automatic weapon was offered to the Colt's Patent Fire Arms Manufacturing Company in 1890, and appeared as a perfect arm by 1895, when it was known as Colt's "Potato Digger" from the vertical rotation of the gas lever arm under the gun. From one of Browning's later designs for a short-recoil mechanism, patented in 1901, he and his assistants developed the United States M 1917 water-cooled, the M 1919 air-cooled and eventually the Browning Mark II aircraft machine guns. The last of these was used in the vast majority of fighting aircraft in the services of the Allied powers during the Second World War.

After the First World War, machine-gun designers concentrated on reducing the weight of guns and increasing the rate of fire. To some extent, these ambitions were incompatible, as the higher the cyclic rate, the quicker the barrel overheated. The heat could be dissipated only by heavy fins on the barrel, by encasing it in a heavy and clumsy water-jacket, or by equipping the gunners with several barrels that could be changed as they heated to a dangerously high temperature.

The Czech magazine-fed Z-B 26 was the first successful gun with a barrel that could be changed quickly. In 1935, it was adopted for the British forces at the "Bren," after the town of Brno in Czechoslovakia and the Enfield factory in England. In Germany, the belt-fed MG 34 was preferred, and continued in use throughout the Second World War, when some were replaced by the MG 42. Both these German arms were intended for use from a bipod as a light infantry weapon, or from a heavy tripod in the role the Vickers filled in the British forces. The Bren was kept as the light machine gun, issued generally on a scale of three to an infantry platoon, an arrangement that lasted throughout the war. The Vickers, or Vickers-Maxim, was made in rifle- and 1.5-inch (37 mm) calibers between 1900 and 1914, when the German High Command had 50,000 on order. During the Second World War, the water-cooled Vickers was used from British armored carriers, and in static roles from a heavy tripod.

Many of the machine guns used by the combatants in the Second World War were capable of being fired from flexible mountings in a ground-to-ground, ground-to-air or air-combat capacity. Many had special tripods for use in defensive positions, firing on fixed lines with the gun set up and aimed in daylight, perhaps to enfilade a suspected enemy approach, and fired at random intervals, or when a sound was heard.

For use against targets as fast-moving as aircraft or motor

gunboats, machine guns were often mounted in groups. These multiple mountings could be either flexible or fixed, as in the wings of a fighter aircraft. For example, some Spitfires carried four .303 (7.7 mm) Brownings in each wing. The two-gun and four-gun turrets favored by the Royal Air Force for the defense of heavy bombers during the Second World War were also used on fast naval boats. Hydraulic power assisted the gunner in laying all four together through a single sighting system. On larger ships, multiple mountings were used with four guns firing 1.5-inch (37 mm) shells. When Maxim first created these at the request of the British government, the shells cost six shillings and six pence, and the guns fired at more than 150 rounds per minute. On hearing the price per round and the rate of fire, King Christian IX of Denmark is recorded as saying that the Maxim shell-gun "would bankrupt my kingdom in about two hours." A representative of China remarked that it fired "altogether too fast for China." In Africa, it was given the onomatopoeic name "pom-pom" by natives trying to describe the sound of its rapid firing.

Percussion ignition and the integral cartridge were two of the three elements needed before a completely successful machine gun could be developed. The third was a propellant which did not envelop the gun and its crew in a blue pall which not only obscured their target but made their own position obvious. In 1886, Paul Vieille made the first satisfactory smokeless powder. Two years later, ballistite, one of the earliest nitroglycerin smokeless powders, was patented by Alfred Nobel. In 1891, the British Army adopted cordite, which is a mixture of nitroglycerin, acetone and guncotton, for the .303 (7.7 mm) cartridge. These new propellants had another advantage. As they were slower-burning, the rate at which their energy was released in a long gun barrel gave greater thrust with lower internal pressures. As gunners adopted the new charges, the clumsy, bottle-shaped cannons of Rodman and Dahlgren soon gave way to longer, more slender artillery, whose weight depended upon the barrel length rather than the thickness of the breech. Shells could be thrown farther from a gun of the same weight once the new smokeless powder was available.

About the time that Nobel and others were experimenting with smokeless powders, the German General Wille and Colonel Langlois, a Frenchman, were developing an improved gun carriage with vastly superior recoil mechanisms than existing types possessed. The new mechanisms enabled the barrel to move backwards in a trough against coiled springs which took up the shock of recoil on firing and returned the

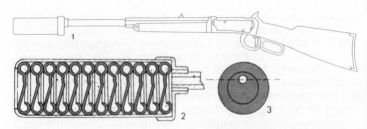

Hiram Maxim's diaphragm silencer for firearms, patented 1908. The passages were intended to make the gases whirl around. Later, Maxim made a simpler silencer which merely reduced the velocity of the gases. (1) The silencer fitted to a Winchester rifle. (2) A section. (3) Muzzle view.

barrel to its original position without the wheels of the carriage being moved far from their pre-discharge position. Elimination of the need to run the gun back after each shot permitted an increase in the rate of fire of medium guns to about twenty rounds a minute, loaded and fired by a crew who were partly protected by the gun shield that the new carriage design made possible.

Some of the mechanisms adopted for machine guns also suggested themselves for faster firing pistols. The first important self-loading, that is, semiautomatic pistol, was made by Ludwig Loewe in Berlin from the designs prepared by Hugo Borchardt in 1893. Georg Luger developed Borchardt's toggle-action recoil operated weapon, the first to use a box magazine that could be loaded before being slipped into the grip of the Luger pistol, which was manufactured from 1898 to 1942.

In the United States, John Browning continued his successful run of inventions with a blow-back action pistol chambered for the .32 (8.1 mm) cartridge. Colt produced the pistol in .38 (9.7 mm) caliber in 1900. Six years later, in 1906, after tests using .30, .38 and .45 (7.6, 9.7 and 11.4 mm) weapons on live cattle and human cadavers, the United States Department of Ordnance invited manufacturers to offer new designs for a service pistol. It was specified that the arm was to be of .45 (11.4 mm) caliber, and semiautomatic, John Browning's response was a .45 version of his .38 (9.7 mm) automatic, which competed successfully against Savage, Luger, Mauser, Mannlicher, Bergmann, Roth and Glisenti pistols. Nine hundred and fifty-eight shots were fired through the Browning with two malfunctions and one misfire. The action jammed twenty-seven times. The design was modified in the light of these

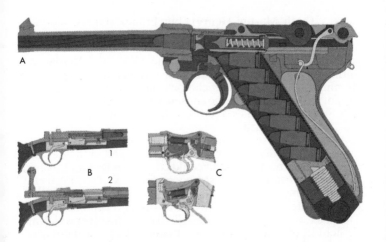

A *A Luger self-loading military pistol, improved model of 1906, for the .35-inch (9 mm) Parabellum cartridge. The recoil-operated mechanism, developed by Georg Luger (1848-1922) from a design by Hugo Borchardt, consists of a toggle-joint breech opening vertically as the barrel recoils.*

B *The 1867 prototype breech from which Peter Paul Mauser's successful .43-inch (11 mm), single-shot military rifle was developed four years*

later. (1) The breech, loaded with a metal cartridge, closed and ready to fire. (2) The breech cleared preparatory to reloading.

C *The breech mechanism developed by Friedrich von Martini, an Austrian lace manufacturer, from the American Peabody action. Lowering the trigger guard opened the breech, ejected the fired cartridge case and recocked the firing-pin.*

experiments, and the result was the automatic pistol, caliber .45 Model 1911 A 1. Browning and his pistol received a promise of immortality in Hanns Johst's play *Schlageter* (Act 1, Scene 1): "Wenn ich Kultur höre…entsichere ich meine Browning." The aphorism was later paraphrased by Hermann Goering.

The variety of opinion on the best personal weapons with which to arm soldiers is reflected in the types of mechanism employed by the leading military powers around 1880. Falling-block mechanisms were in use in Bavaria (Werder) and in Britain and

233

Turkey (both Martini-Henry), but France (Gras), Germany (Mauser) and Switzerland and Italy (both Vetterli's repeater) all preferred the sliding bolt. Russia and the United States adopted breechblocks hinged at the front, the Berdan and Springfield respectively. Another American weapon, the Remington, with its breechblock hinged at the rear and supported by a cam, was the chosen weapon of Denmark, Spain and Sweden. Austria's Werndl rifle employed a breechblock that rotated outwards.

Alongside these attempts to equip the military with ever more potent arms, the gun trade was engaged in the design of efficient firearms that a man could conceal in his hand. Among the neatest and the most successful was the "Protector" revolver which was patented in Britain in 1882, and in the United States in 1883. The inventor was a Frenchman, Jacques Turbiaux, whose pistol was described as "A revolver which may be held in the hand with no part exposed except the barrel." This "squeezer" pistol, fired by clenching the fist, enjoyed some popularity during the dozen or so years following its invention. But as with all trochal magazine firearms of its type, there was a continual threat to the firer from the loaded chamber that often pointed back towards him.

Other easily concealed pistols of the period include the so-called "Apache" pistol. Made by the Belgian gunmaker L. Dolne, it was a tiny .28-inch (7 mm) six-chambered pin-fire weapon, whose butt was formed by a vicious-looking knuckle-duster, and which had a folding dagger blade of the type patented by Waters a century before. This association of pistol and knuckle-duster had been exploited earlier by William and John Rigby of Dublin, and by James Reid of Catskill, New York, whose "My Friend" was patented a few days after the United States abolished slavery in December 1865. It was a short pepperbox revolver with a flat, pierced butt, through which the user could slip his little finger when gripping it in order to deliver a punch or a pounding blow.

A version of the Webley Mark II. 455/476 revolver was fitted with a claw-like spike on its butt to extend its possible uses as a weapon in the hand-to-hand fighting in First World War trenches for which a variety of close-combat arms were developed. Among these were many trench-knives, clubs, and a detachable bayonet-cum-dagger for revolvers, Captain A. Pritchard's patent of November 29, 1917.

The evolution of war was affected by two events which took place in 1878. Almost simultaneously, Hughes and Lüdtge invented the microphone, which revolutionized covert communication, and Ferdinand Ritter von Mannlicher designed a turning-bolt repeating rifle which, although never entirely successful, gave its inventor a certain reputation. In 1884, he introduced his first straight-pull design, accepted by the Austrian army as the Model 1885 .4-inch (11 mm) service rifle, fitted with the Mannlicher magazine. Before he died, Mannlicher had designed more than a hundred and fifty models of automatic and repeating arms that were used in many armies, and also by sportsmen who favored such rifles as the Mannlicher-Schronauer series. Of Mannlicher's self-loading pistols only the Model 1900 was made in any quantity.

A year after the Austrian army took Mannlicher rifles into service, France became the first nation to adopt a small-bore, smokeless-powder rifle, when the .32-inch (8 mm) Modèle 1886 was issued to the army. A committee which was set up in 1884 to produce a rifle for the rimmed cartridge designed by Captain Desaleux and the chemist Vieille, was chaired by Lieutenant-Colonel Nicolas Lebel (1838-91), whose name was given to the new rifle. It was a bolt-action rifle based on the 1874 Gras, with an eight-shot version of Kropatschek's tubular magazine. The Lebel was improved in 1893 and again in 1897. It saw service with the French army throughout both the First and Second World Wars.

By 1914, almost every major power had adopted one or other version of the bolt-action for its service rifles, the Lee-Enfield, Mauser and Springfield variations dominating the field.

As early as 1896, Danish naval and coastguard units were issued with the Madsen, a recoil-operated semiautomatic rifle, but the examining committees of most countries decided against the semiautomatic, with its high rate of cartridge use, for another generation. By the outbreak of the Second World War, self-loading rifles were on limited issue to some United States and Russian units. Within four years, the appearance on the battlefield of the German MP 43 assault rifle forced the other combatant nations to review their needs for weapons with the same qualities. Self-loading military rifles are now common.

The weaknesses of French artillery, sadly obvious during the war with Prussia (1870-71), were corrected in 1897, when the excellent *canon de 75 de campagne à tir rapide* was introduced. During trials in 1894, the prototype fired thirty-one shots in a minute, a record number. This was even faster than the twelve-pounder Whitworth, which in 1865 had put four shells into the air before the first had reached the target. The breech mechanism had a great deal to do with the increase in speed, but in the end the rate of fire depended on some means of absorbing the recoil.

Since the earliest days of gunpowder artillery, a variety of ways to reduce recoil had been tried: friction beds, inclined beds, rubber buffers, and carriages whose trail telescoped against a shoe that dug into the earth on recoil. In 1894, as the enemies of Captain Dreyfus were accusing him of transmitting to the Germans the secrets of the *frein hydropneumatique* used with the Baquet gun of 1890, a design for the new 75 was offered to France's Minister of War, General Mercier.

The key to the success of this excellent gun, which first saw action in China in 1900, and then gave tremendous service in the First World War, was its long recoil mechanism. Its German rival, the Krupp 3-inch (7.7 cm) Model 1897 NA, was much slower to shoot, as it did not have the 75's stability in firing. After the first shot had settled the trail spade in the earth, the layer and firer of the four-man crew who served the 75 could remain seated on the gun carriage. With the new recoil system, the 75's designers used the Nordenfelt breech and a nickel steel barrel, capable of firing six thousand rounds before it had to be returned to a depot for re-sleeving. Its brass-cased fixed ammunition was made in shrapnel and explosive rounds. The shrapnel cartridge weighed 20.3 lb (9.2 kg) and scattered 302 hardened lead balls that were lethal up to 20 yards or so, and dangerous up to 175 yards (160 m). The shell's trajectory was flat, rising to only 9.8 yards (9 m) at a range of 3,280 yards (3,000 m). The explosive shell weighed 11.7 lb (5.3 kg), the cartridge 16 lb (7.3 kg). The 75 was taken up by the United States Army on its arrival in France in 1917, and the Singer Manufacturing Company accepted an order for 2,500 in the following March. At the outbreak of the Second World War, the United States had 4,236 of this mode. A consignment consisting of one thousand guns from this stock, en route to France in the *Pasteur*, was diverted by order of General de Gaulle and brought to a British port in 1940 after the fall of France. They were manned by French troops against Field Marshal Rommel's tanks at Bir Hakeim, but the new armor and improved tank guns were soon to put an end to the 75's success in an antitank role.

Chapter 20

In 1905, while the Russian and Japanese armies were reviving the hand grenade and discovering the discomforts of primitive chemical warfare, detonating fuses containing explosives of high brisance wrapped in flexible waterproof cable were being used in Europe and America. An even surer method is the electrical detonator in which two copper wires are sealed into the mouth of the detonator tube with bitumen and sulfur. The bare ends of the wire rest in a layer of loose detonating compound, which is ignited when the long leading wires are connected to a low-tension circuit. The way that this system allows a series of charges to be fired almost simultaneously makes it the nearest to the perfect system so far devised for explosive ambushes and booby traps. Histories of guerrilla actions are full of the destruction of bridges, trains and armored columns by small groups of brave men and fanatics ramming home the plunger of a generator at exactly the right moment to cause the maximum effect—something that was impossible before the electric detonator was invented.

The last decade of the nineteenth century saw the beginning of the development of the armored car. Chariots with their sides

The British Mark V heavy tank, the first which could be driven by one man. Its 150 h.p. Ricardo engine, was coupled to the Wilson epicyclic steering units. Four hundred Mark Vs were built.

Each weighed 29 tons and was capable of 4 mph (6.4 km/h), needing a crew of eight to drive it and fire the two six-pounders and the four Hotchkiss machine guns.

strengthened to protect the driver and the warrior who rode alongside had been known for almost four thousand years. It was not until the internal-combustion engine appeared on the scene and an efficient, small steam engine had been designed that experiments in the United States produced the *Motor Scout* and the *War Car*. The former was the brainchild of F.R. Simms, who fitted a 1.5-hp de Dion Bouton quadricycle with a bulletproof shield and a machine gun. It was demonstrated in June 1899, three years before the *War Car* that Simms designed for Vickers, Sons and Maxim Limited showed its paces at London's Crystal Palace. Neither achieved the success needed to carry it into the service of any nation.

Simms' new weapon system appears to have been based to some extent on the ideas of another American, E.J. Pennington, who produced sketches for an armored car in 1896. But sketches were all he did produce, and it was left to Simms to design a vehicle with an open, boat-shaped hull of .2-inch (6 mm) plate with rams fore and aft, and an armament of two Maxim guns and an automatic one-pounder. A 16-hp four-cylinder Daimler engine drove its four steel-tired wheels through a four-speed gearbox, to give the 5.5-ton car a top speed of 9 mph (14.5 km/h) on a good surface. After the advent of the *War Car*, Britain's contribution to the development of the armored car went quietly to sleep for more than a decade. Later in the year, when Simms was trying to sell his design, French trials produced a touring-car chassis with a Hotchkiss machine gun mounted in an armored cabin behind the driver. From 1903 to 1906, the French Army held trials of a fully-armored car, and the Austro-Daimler company built a similar vehicle. Both had machine guns mounted in traversing turrets. A German anti-balloon car of 1906 was equipped with a 2-inch (50 mm) gun. Although an Italian Fiat truck chassis of 1912 had a fully-armored body, no great effort was put into armored car design until 1914, when necessity forced several powers to concentrate on this field of development in the opening stages of the war.

The British Admiralty decided that the offensive mobility of the armored car made it eminently suitable for certain duties the Naval Brigade were performing around the port of Antwerp. The war was still mobile, and roads could be used if the vehicle was armored against small-arms fire. To fill the gap in their equipment, the Admiralty bought a hundred cars and chassis to which were fitted open-topped bodies with a machine gun in the well shooting over the side armor. The first to be made ready, two cars and three trucks, were given mild steel plate armor in the *Forges et Chantiers de France*, Dunkirk. The

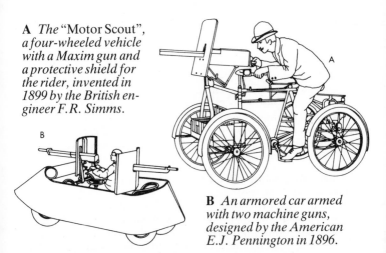

A *The "Motor Scout", a four-wheeled vehicle with a Maxim gun and a protective shield for the rider, invented in 1899 by the British engineer F.R. Simms.*

B *An armored car armed with two machine guns, designed by the American E.J. Pennington in 1896.*

strucks were the first modern armored personnel carriers, as each could carry a dozen men into action. The Belgians and the French were engaged on the same sort of preparations. For them, the available cars were the Renault, Peugeot and Minerva, while their British counterparts were the Rolls-Royce, Talbot and Wolseley.

However, the onset of trench warfare very quickly rendered the armored car as obsolete for service on the Western Front as Henry VIII's "Prawns." It was only in the Middle East and Russia that there was much use for them. The Russian army had almost five hundred armored cars at the end of the First World War, some based on the Austin chassis, and a number on the Garford truck chassis from the United States. The strength of

C *Britain's first successful armored cars were built on the chassis of Rolls-Royce touring cars.*

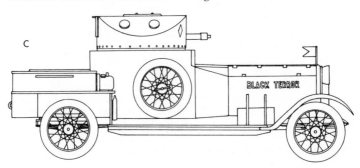

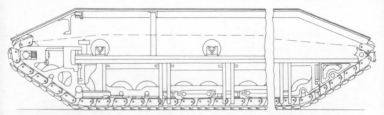

The tracked fighting vehicle proposed in 1912 by the Australian engineer L. E. de Mole. This was one of the earliest practical designs offered to the British War Office. It was not taken up.

the Garford car allowed the Russians to mount a 3-inch (7.6 cm) gun on a 1917 version.

Germany saw little future for the armored car, although she did build a small number of cars of a much heavier weight than her foreign contemporaries. The solid-tire Daimler and Büssing cars, weighing between nine and ten tons, had four-wheel drive. A third, the Ehrhadt of 1915, could be steered on all four wheels. The tactical use of these new vehicles received little serious thought, once the leaders of the massive armies which faced each other in Europe realized that it would only be on the rarest of occasions that they could be gainfully employed.

By December 1914, three fully-armored Rolls-Royce cars had been built with machine guns in turrets which could traverse through 360°. At first, the armament on these, and on similar bodies mounted on other types of chassis, was a single Maxim gun. When the Naval Brigades felt that something heavier and tougher was needed, the Seabrook truck chassis seemed the likeliest to fill the Navy's needs, and by February 1915 the Admiralty Air Department had produced a vehicle armed with a three-pounder gun and four Maxims. Crews were protected by a third of an inch (8 mm) of steel, heavy enough to cause frequent breakages of axles and springs.

After a few sorties around Ypres in 1915, the cars of the Royal Naval Air Service were transferred to the Middle East, where they were handed over to the army for use against the Senussi in the Western Desert, and in Palestine, Iraq and South Russia. The crews of the makeshift armored cars which bolstered the depleted garrisons in India in 1915 found themselves armed with .45 (11.4 mm) Maxims supplied with ammunition made in 1897. One unit was issued with a hopper-fed, hand-cranked Gatling. The vehicles were replaced towards the end of the First World War by Jeffrey Quad cars from the United States, some of which soldiered on until 1924.

The French Renault FT 17 light tank, built at the instigation of General Estienne to give close support to infantry. Almost 3,000 of these 6-ton, two-man vehicles were made, in a number of types armed with weapons ranging from machine guns to 75s. Some, with a few improvements, survived to fight in North Africa in 1942. Turrets from others were built into German pillboxes on the Channel Islands during their occupation.

The story of the Krupp dynasty has already been interwoven in the story of arms. It emerges in full flood during the years of the First World War, which may be looked upon almost as much as a contest in production between Krupp and the Vickers-Armstrong group as it was a struggle between the men who faced each other across the churned-up wastes of Flanders.

One of Gustav Krupp von Bohlen's products earned him the honorary degree of Doctor of Philosophy, bestowed on him by a grateful University of Bonn. The Schlieffen Plan, to swing a German army through Belgium and northern France and outflank the French defenses, was blocked by forts at Liège which were thought to be impregnable. Krupp had "Big Bertha" waiting in the wings. The steel fortresses were very soon disposed of by this mobile howitzer, which dropped seventeen-inch (43.2 cm) shells weighing almost a ton on their targets from as far off as nine miles (14.5 km).

Soon after dawn on March 23, 1918, a shell weighing 200 lb (90.7 kg) or so smashed down on the center of Paris. It came from another of Krupp's great guns with a family name. "Long Max" weighed 180 tons, and when the terror attacks began, was a part of Ludendorff's last attempt to break the Allies. Under the command of an admiral, for "Long Max" was based on a naval gun which had shelled Dunkirk from more than twenty miles' (*c.* 32 km) distance, this new giant had a crew of sixty, who could fire once every fifteen minutes. When "Long Max" was withdrawn on August 9, 1918, seven barrels had been worn out, and 452 shells had been fired into the heart of the French capital. On the last Good Friday of the war, eighty-eight people died in a church that was hit by one of its shells. Even this masterpiece of the art of the cannon-maker was no more than the application of meticulous engineering methods to known ballistic principles. It cannot be said to have had any effect on the outcome of the war, or even on its length.

The power of the emplaced machine gun in defense, barbed wire and the cloying mud of no man's land together made all too formidable an obstacle to offensive action within a relatively few months of the outbreak of the First World War. More and more, artillery was used by the high commands of both sides in an attempt to break the deadlock. What was really needed, however, was a means to destroy enemy machine-gun emplacements, and to flatten the wire.

In the first months of the war, wheeled armored cars had been tried with some success, but their limitations in the new active service conditions in northern Europe became immediately obvious. Tracked vehicles were proposed as the answer to the problem as early as October 1914, when Lieutenant-Colonel E.D. Swinton suggested that some form of caterpillar tracks on an armored car would probably be the attack's answer to the machine gun behind sandbagged emplacements. Swinton was backed by the commander of the British Expeditionary Force, and the combined efforts of the Admiralty and the War Office got a prototype landship onto the Thetford Heath testing grounds by the following September. The first tank, "Little Willie," was one of the ends towards which military engineers had striven for centuries: a vehicle of sufficient power to carry over obstacles, which were otherwise nearly impassable, its crew, armor plate for its protection and guns with enough fire power to destroy its targets.

American experiments had produced a steam-powered caterpillar tractor, but there was no real military future for the armored fighting vehicle until the invention of an efficient internal-combustion engine that was capable of producing the necessarily high power-to-weight ratio. An Australian inventor, L.E. de Mole, submitted designs for an endless track vehicle in 1912, but they were not given the attention they deserved, and "Little Willie" was based largely on the design of Lieutenant W.G. Wilson of the Royal Naval Air Service and of William Tritton of William Foster and Company, the makers of the "Centipede" tracked load-tower and the prototype tanks. A

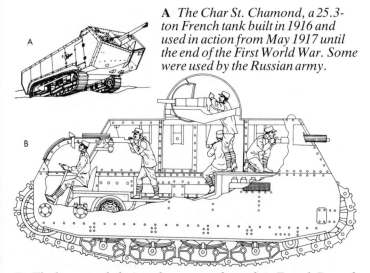

A *The Char St. Chamond, a 25.3-ton French tank built in 1916 and used in action from May 1917 until the end of the First World War. Some were used by the Russian army.*

B *The heavy tank designed by the Fiat company and designated the Fiat 2000. Two pilot models, all that were made, and six French Renault FTs formed the first Italian tank unit in December 1918.*

105-hp Daimler sleeve-valve engine pushed its 28-ton mass along at little more than marching speed. Four months later, the second generation tank, "Big Willie," which was variously known as "Mother," "Wilson" or "H.M. Land Ship Centipede," was seen in trials, which resulted in orders for one hundred and fifty Mark I heavy fighting tanks. Sponsons on each side of the hull carried six-pounder quick-firing Hotchkiss guns, and four Hotchkiss machine guns could be mounted if needed on the so-called male tanks: or one Hotchkiss machine gun and four Vickers light machine guns on the female tanks.

September 15, 1916, was the date when Mark I tanks first went into action. With minor modifications, these first models evolved into Mark II and Mark III. The first Mark IVs of 1915, built to Wilson's designs, were in the field in August 1917 to take part in the battles of Massines, Ypres and Cambrai.

German K-type machine-gun ammunition could pierce the armor of the Mark Is. Because of this, two tanks of this model fell into German hands "alive" at Bullecourt in April 1917. It was not long, therefore, before British tank crews were facing captured tanks as well as the A7V, Germany's first effective entrant in this field. The first tank-versus-tank battle was fought on April 26, 1918, at Villers Bretonneux.

The losses sustained by female tanks when faced with heavier armament led to the development of the hermaphrodite tank whose single six-pounder allowed it to answer the new challenge. Other developments led to the Mark V model, larger and heavier than its forebears. It could carry twenty infantrymen across a ten-foot (3.1 m) trench in safety if in considerable discomfort, for the fumes and carbon monoxide which affected the crews were even worse for infantrymen who were not used to conditions inside a tank. The Mark V, incidentally, was the first tank that could be driven by a single man. Drivers of the earlier models were aided by two gearsmen, who controlled the secondary gearboxes by means of instructions conveyed to them by hand-signals. In the Mark V, an epicyclic unit replaced the secondary gearboxes.

Further service requirements led to variations up to a Mark IX Duck, which could be floated with "camels" attached to its sides, to supply carriers, and to towing and bridging tanks. There was even an "Allied" tank intended for use by the United States Army. Seven of these "Allied" tanks were built by the end of 1918.

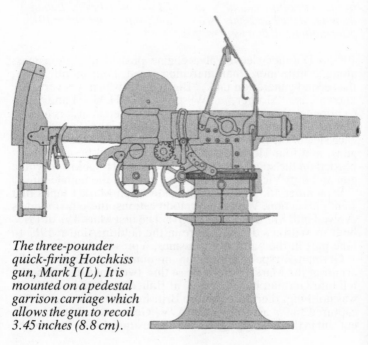

The three-pounder quick-firing Hotchkiss gun, Mark I (L). It is mounted on a pedestal garrison carriage which allows the gun to recoil 3.45 inches (8.8 cm).

In addition to heavy tanks, France and Britain manufactured light, more maneuverable machines to fight as raiders in conjunction with cavalry, filling to some extent the role of the armored car, but capable of cross-country performance. The theory was that these "Whippets" and their French equivalents, the CA 1 (M 16) Schneider, and the Char St. Chamond, would silence the machine guns and flatten the barbed wire to create a gap through which the cavalry could pour to fan out across the enemy communication trenches. But the difficulty of communicating between tank commander and horsemen prevented any real cooperation between the separate arms. Semaphore, siren and carrier pigeon are hardly suitable for the heat of a mobile action. This lack of communication and the rarity of opportunities to use medium or light tanks saw them finish the war as weapons whose promise was not to be fulfilled before the arrival of the cruiser tanks of the Second World War.

The gun-carrying sponsons were a compromise, for it had originally been intended to fit a turret to "Little Willie," but the additional weight would have made the assembly unstable. The Hotchkiss guns on the Mark I model were originally the long-barreled naval pattern with a traverse of about 100°, but

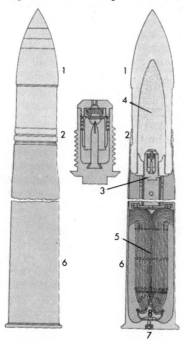

The cartridge used in the six-pounder quick-firing Hotchkiss gun. (1) Steel shell. (2) Driving band. (3) Mark IV fuse, which was screwed into the base of the shell. (4) Lyddite bursting charge. (5) Cordite. (6) Brass case. (7) Percussion cap. (8) Primer.

these soon gave way to a shorter gun firing chain or case shot against infantry, high-explosive shells against dug-in troops, and solid shot when employed in its tank-killer role. The water-cooled Vickers first used in the female tanks had serious cooling problems which led to their replacement with Lewis guns. These proved in turn to have an unsatisfactorily restricted traverse, and were dropped in favor of the air-cooled Hotchkiss in a ball-mounting.

In action, tank crews wore leather, and, later, rubber and steel helmets as protection against the splash of penetrating shots and the inevitable knocks they received as they lurched across uneven ground. Men whose duties required them to look out through the slits wore masks of steel, slotted like Eskimo sun-goggles, from which short curtains of mail hung to protect the lower half of their faces. Some United States units were issued with a neck and face guard formed of many thicknesses of Japanese silk. This was known as the American Helmet Model No. 13.

At the end of the "War to end all Wars," Britain and Germany had superheavy tanks under construction. "The Flying Elephant," which was designed by W. Tritton and built in 1916 by William Foster of Lincoln, had armor 2 inches (5.1 cm) thick on its flanks and 3 inches (7.6 cm) thick on the front. It weighed one hundred tons. Its armament consisted of one six-pounder gun mounted in front, and six machine guns. It was powered by two Daimler 120-hp engines with a common crankcase that made it, in effect, a V-type twelve-cylinder sleeve-valve engine. The engine drove two outer tracks, each 24 inches (61 cm) wide, and two additional 21-inch (53.3 cm) inner tracks at the rear. The inner tracks had a ten-inch (25.4 cm) ground clearance and were intended to prevent "bellying," one of the greatest hazards suffered by the contemporaries of the "Flying Elephant" in the mud of Flanders. The Tank Committee reconsidered its decision to authorize the construction of a supertank in January, 1917, when it affirmed that the "Flying Elephant" would be much too costly and should be scrapped without any trials.

Germany's *K-Wagen* was even heavier. It weighed 148 tons, and was driven at 5 mph (8 km/h) by means of two Daimler 650-hp engines. It resembled a submarine in several respects, as naval experience was drawn on for the design of its communication system and control equipment. Two were almost completed in the Riebe Kugellager factory at Berlin-Weissensee when the war ended.

Chapter 21

In 1929, André Maginot, France's vastly experienced Minister of War, pressed for the construction of a bulwark behind which his country would be secure from the potential threat of a revitalized Germany, or which would at least give her time to mobilize in the event of hostilities. With the support of Marshal Pétain, the hero of Verdun, and General Weygand, he persuaded the politicians to pass the immense defense budget that the project demanded. Completed, the Maginot Line was a chain of bombproof citadels stretching for 200 miles (322 km) from Montmédy near the Belgian frontier to Belfort, close to Switzerland. These citadels were sunk to between 160 and 200 feet (c. 49 and 61 m) below ground level, and were connected by electric railroads to each other and to their supply bases, which were often far to the rear. On the surface, there was little to be seen except for barbed wire, tank traps and gun turrets. The artillery was fired electrically by remote control. Every mile of the Maginot Line is believed to have cost the equivalent of five million dollars.

When war came, the German army took Belgium and Holland in a few days. The outflanked garrisons of the Maginot Line, totaling some three hundred thousand men, had hardly a chance to fire a shot before hearing on the radio that an armistice had been signed. Even if the line had not been so comprehensively outflanked and breached at the weak Malmédy-Sedan sector, it is unlikely to have served France as Maginot and Pétan intended. The ingenuity of its camouflage was more than nullified by the information Germany gleaned from the labor force that built it: about half was drawn from Poland, Czechoslovakia and from Germany herself. The electrical system was installed by Siemens, a German firm.

The years between the two world wars were a frustrating period for the men who thought most deeply about the use of armored fighting vehicles. In Britain, Fuller and Liddell Hart, and in France, de Gaulle and others, could do little to correct the misconceptions that were held by their own high commands about the role and employment of the tank. But in Germany, their writings inspired a tactical design that used armor in the attacks which rent asunder all Polish and, later, Allied resistance in the first years of the Second World War. The spearheads of the *Blitzkrieg* were armored units equipped with

A characteristic redoubt on the Maginot Line, France's massive but ineffectual defensive chain of fortifications which stretched from Montmédy to Belfort.

the tanks designated *Panzerkampfwagen III* and *IV*. Both models were medium cruiser tanks, well-armed, maneuverable, and carrying enough armor to give confidence to the crews in the face of weak antitank weapons. The Pzkw IV, which was introduced in 1937, showed considerable improvement on the earlier model. By the time that it reached the North African front to take its part in the rescue of the Italian armies, it had been fitted with a 3-inch (7.5 cm) gun of higher velocity than previously used, and its better armor included additional protection along its flanks.

Apart from being a training course for the men and the tactics which were to carry Germany through the first years of the Second World War, the Spanish Civil War had been a perfect opportunity to test the new weapons which had been under development in Germany, as well as in Sweden, Switzerland and the Netherlands, in each of which countries Krupp had commercial interests. By 1920, Krupp and the Swedish Aktiebolaget Bofors, in which Krupp held six million of the total nineteen million shares, had a 3-inch (7.5 cm) mountain gun under development.

The German troops who went to support General Franco's army took with them the 7.5-cm mountain gun, and the Krupp-designed weapon that was to become the scourge of the Allied armies in the Second World War, the almost incredibly versatile 3.5-inch (8.8 cm) gun. It has been described as "without question the single most famous artillery piece used in World War II," when it served in both antitank and anti-aircraft roles. Within two years, Krupp produced another monster in the tradition of the huge 1867 50-ton gun, of "Big Bertha" and of "Long Max." This was "Fat Gustav," on which work began in the spring of 1937 after Krupp's ballistic experts had considered an enquiry from the German army ordnance office as to what weight and velocity of shell would be needed to smash the Maginot forts.

Although they were not to reach the peak of their development until the 1930s, trench mortars were introduced into the German army as a result of lessons learned by German observers of the Russo-Japanese war. As early as October 1914, Sir John French was calling for "some special form of artillery" which British troops could use in the close-range fighting of the trenches. Initially, iron water-pipes were used as crude bomb-projectors, but by the spring of 1915, 3.7-inch (9.4 cm) caliber mortars were being specially made in France, and the Twining pattern was in production at Woolwich, twenty of these being sent to France in January 1915. Their users found themselves facing the same dangers as had worried the Council of Maryland two hundred years before, as eight out of the first eleven burst within ten days. Some were subsequently modified to be fired by a rifle mechanism.

In the nineteenth and twentieth centuries, many alarm-guns of a very simple design were made. A metal clamp sliding on a vertical peg held a blank cartridge a couple of feet above a fixed firing pin. When an intruder touched a thin wire, a retaining pin was withdrawn, the clamp dropped, and the cartridge fired. In 1915, the alarm-gun inspired F.W.C. Stokes, later Sir Wilfred Stokes, KBE, to make a mortar on the same principle, except that the rod was replaced by a muzzle-loading barrel, and the blank cartridge in its holder became a shell with its own cartridge fitted in the base. Stokes intended his gun to be made in great numbers, describing it as "little more than a piece of coarse gas-piping, sitting dog-fashion on its hind quarters and propped up in front by a pair of legs corresponding to the canine front equivalent." Shells would pour from it onto the German lines in an attempt to break the trench-war deadlock.

As in the 3-inch (7.6 cm) mortar that Britain used as a battalion weapon in the Second World War, Stokes' mortar could have its range adjusted to fine limits by elevating screws and by adding extra charges, ignited by the initial blast, to the tail of the bomb.

Between the two world wars, the spigot mortar was joined by a number of smaller types with simple lever-controlled striker actions, in which the bomb did not just "bounce" back out, but was fired when the layer was ready. They were used at platoon level with high-explosive, smoke and signal bombs, which the British 2-inch (50 mm) weapon could fire between 100 and 500 yards (91 and 457 m). The 2-inch (50 mm) Japanese version, *Tuisho 10*, could fire up to 175 yards (160 m). The 3-lb (1.4 kg) projectiles from the American 2.4-inch (60 mm) mortar carried to between 1,600 and 2,000 yards (*c.* 1,460 and 1,830 m).

The United States Chemical Warfare Service developed a 4.2-inch (10.7 cm) "goon gun" mortar to throw gas shells. It was never used in a chemical role, but fired 24-lb (10.9 kg) smoke and high-explosive shells up to a range of 6,000 yards (5,480 m). A good crew could put half-a-dozen shells in the air in the minute or so that the first took to reach its target. Its maximum calculated rate of fire was twenty rounds per minute.

The Russian 12-inch (30.5 cm) mortar, the biggest used in the Second World War, was something of a freak, as most Red Army mortars were between 2 inches (50 mm) and 4.7 inches (12 cm) in caliber.

In the Second World War, the infantry also demanded a light

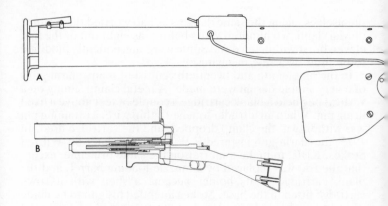

A An American 2.36-inch
(60 mm) antitank rocket launcher (Bazooka) and its 3.5-lb
(1.6 kg) hollow-charge
projectile.
B An experimental antitank
grenade projector under development by the Italian
Ministry of War in 1943.
C The German 3.5-inch (8.8
cm) rocket launcher and its
7-lb (3.2 kg) projectile.

D The trench mortar
patented by F.W.C. Stokes in
1915.
E A Spanish infantryman of
c. 1935 with a medium mortar
slung across his back.
F The Carl-Gustaf M2
multi-purpose free-flight
rocket launcher, made by the
Swedish Förenade Fabriks-
verken.

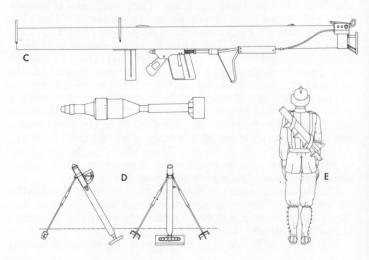

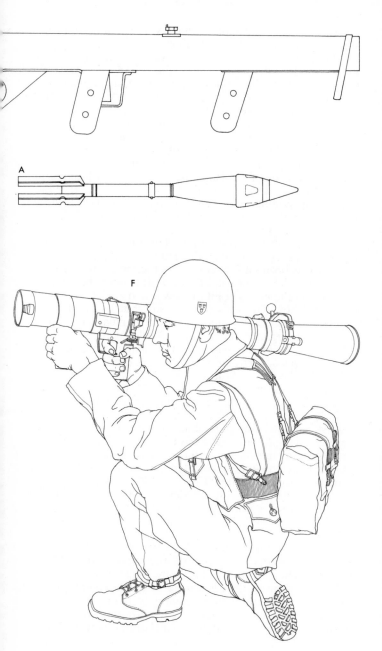

A

F

portable antitank weapon which would shoot a projectile similar to a mortar bomb against such targets as tanks and blockhouses. Britain's first answer was the unhandy, inaccurate Projector Infantry Anti-Tank, the PIAT. Firing a 2.5-lb (1.1 kg) bomb with a hollow-charge head, its maximum range was 115 yards (105 m) against armor. Against stationary targets, as in a house-clearing role, it could be used up to 350 yards (320 m). The 1943 training manual claimed that the PIAT could penetrate any known enemy tank armor and a considerable thickness of concrete.

Preliminary tests were carried out in 1943 in Italy on a grenade launcher fired from the shoulder and looking like a stubby little shotgun. A blank cartridge was discharge into an expansion chamber and thence to the mortar barrel, throwing the 30-oz (850 g) bomb 80 yards (73.2 m) on a flat trajectory or 250 yards (229 m) on high-angle fire.

German antitank philosophy led to a family of rocket launchers which were given the generic term *Panzerfaust*. The earliest was brought into service in the latter months of 1942. Unlike the 34.5-lb (15.6 kg) PIAT it could easily be used by one man. From the user's point of view it had a frighteningly short range of about 30 yards (*c*. 27.4 m), but its 3.5-lb (1.6 kg) hollow-charge bomb could penetrate 5 inches (12.7 cm) of armor. Throughout the Second World War, its range and killing power were increased, and in the hands of a determined soldier it was an extremely valuable weapon.

In 1943, the United States M1 rocket launcher (the *Bazooka*) first saw service in Tunisia. When the British Army took it up, they called it the 3.5-inch rocket launcher. It was an effective tank destroyer up to 100 yards (*c*. 91 m). Small rockets, used against balloons and Zeppelins from Sopwith Baby fighters, were used again in the Second World War in air-to-air, air-to-ground and anti-aircraft roles. Britain massed 3-inch (7.6 cm) explosive rockets in so-called Z-batteries. A later version, Type K, carried to 20,000 feet (6,100 m) a parachute from which a small bomb was suspended by 1,000 feet (305 m) of wire cable. The theory was that an aircraft flying to the wire would draw the bomb towards it. The bomb's TNT charge was fired on contact.

But it was Germany's scientists who created the most terrifying rockets fired before the advent of the atomic warhead. The *c*. 46-foot (14 m) long V-2 (*Vergeltungswaffe 2*), the result of more than a decade of development work, first crashed on Paris and then on London on September 8, 1944. In the next ten weeks, V-2 rockets, each carrying 1,654 lb (750 kg) of amatol explosive, landed on England at twenty each day.

A *The Baron, a British flail tank based on the Matilda chassis. In this attempt to defeat antitank mines by mechanical means, rotating chains terminating in ball weights beat the ground in front of the Baron as it advanced. Mines buried not more than 4 inches (10 cm) deep were exploded and a path 10-feet (3.2 m) wide was cleared.*

B *The 3-inch (7.5 cm) field gun captured in quantity from the Soviet army and re-chambered by Germany to take more powerful ammunition. The range of its 14-lb (6.35 kg) shell was about 15,000 yards (c. 14,000 m).*

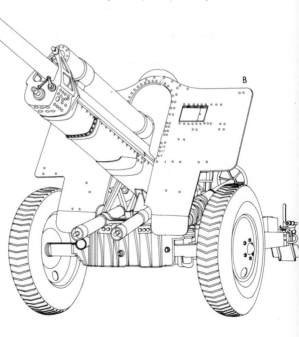

255

Soon after the outbreak of the Second World War, Swedish designers began work on a new weapon system, a gun which fired a heavy explosive shell but did not recoil. It was a stride ahead of the old-fashioned rocket launcher which used a propellant contained within the projectile, for the recoilless rifle propellant is housed in the weapon itself. A plastic disk at the base of the cartridge case ruptures at a precalculated pressure, making recoilless action possible if this simplified equation is satisfied: rearward exhausting gas weight × gas velocity = (projectile weight + forward exhausting weight) × muzzle velocity. The recoilless rifle first appeared as a .8-inch (20 mm) antitank gun which the Swedish army adopted in 1942 after two years of design and development. Within a few years, a 4.1-inch (10.5 cm) field gun and a 4.1-inch (10.5 cm) salvo weapon were also produced.

At the time of writing, the most successful recoilless weapon is a Swedish design, the 3.3-inch (8.4 cm) RCL Carl-Gustaf M2, used by at least fifteen national armies as an antitank gun firing fixed rounds, and in other direct-fire roles formerly carried out by light artillery. It is designed as a platoon weapon, being short, light and compact enough for one man to aim and fire from any position from which he could use a rifle. Its accurate spin-stabilized shells have approximately the destructive power of projectiles from a recoiling weapon weighing more than thirteen times the Carl-Gustaf's 38 lb (17.2 kg). The latest weapon based on the principle is so cheap that the light "gun" element can be discarded like an empty tin can after it has fired its single projectile.